Cashews
and Lentils,
Apples and
Oats

From the Basics to the Fine Points
of Natural Foods Cooking
with 233 Superlative Recipes

Diana Dalsass

Contemporary Books, Inc.
Chicago

Library of Congress Cataloging in Publication Data

Dalsass, Diana.
    Cashews and lentils, apples and oats.

    Includes index.
    1. Vegetarian cookery.   I. Title.
TX837.D18   1981   641.5′636   81-472
ISBN 0-8092-5935-4   AACR2
ISBN 0-8092-5934-6 (pbk.)

Published by Contemporary Books, Inc.
180 North Michigan Avenue, Chicago, Illinois 60601
Manufactured in the United States of America
Library of Congress Catalog Card Number: 81-472
International Standard Book Number: 0-8092-5935-4 (cloth)
                                 0-8092-5934-6 (paper)

Published simultaneously in Canada by
Beaverbooks, Ltd.
150 Lesmill Road
Don Mills, Ontario M3B 2T5
Canada

To my husband, MARIO,
criticizer, praiser, and most of all
enthusiastic taster of all the dishes in this book.

Contents

Introduction

When you are out shopping, do you ever pick up a box of nutritious brown rice and then put it back on the shelf because you don't quite know how to use it? Or do you glance at the bags of dried beans, knowing that they constitute an economical source of protein, but pass them by, again because you are not sure of how to cook them?

If so, help is at hand. This book is designed to guide you through the world of natural foods . . . from nuts to beans, from eggplants to cracked wheat. If you are accustomed to preparing dinners of beef or chicken plus a vegetable and salad, this book will open up whole new vistas of cooking. Presented are delicious meatless casseroles, hearty bean stews, and golden loaves of bread—all healthful and economical, exciting additions to your existing culinary repertoire.

Yes, this is a vegetarian cookbook. But even if you are new to meatless meal preparation, don't be daunted. In this book, I start with the basic ingredients and work each chapter around one of them. In the soy flour chapter, for example, you will learn how best to use soy flour, why it is good for you, what it tastes like, how it affects the texture of baked goods, and so on. Then, whenever you encounter a recipe calling for soy flour, you'll know what to expect.

Becoming involved in the rich and wonderful world of natural foods was truly a great personal adventure for me. It took months and months of experimentation with these ingredients to reach my present level of expertise in using them. Growing up, like most of you, I had never tasted millet, soy grits, lentil loaves, or chick-pea dips. But when I did begin to explore the intriguing world of these foods, I had an enormous amount of fun and a great deal of gustatory satisfaction in compiling the recipes in this book.

Your adventure with natural foods, if you follow along with me, can be equally rewarding. And you'll also enjoy the satisfaction of knowing that you are preparing budget-right, nutritious recipes that are especially helpful in keeping pace with today's inflationary times.

Even if you are already including meatless meals in your daily menus (or if you are a longtime practicing vegetarian), this book nevertheless offers you a diversified collection of great recipes. If you want to prepare a fabulous Rice-Stuffed Pumpkin to serve guests, if you need recipes to make use of your bumper crop of zucchini, if you want to get away from convenience foods with healthful banana cakes, homemade soups, and wholesome sandwich spreads, or if you just want some exciting new recipes for everyday eating, *Cashews and Lentils, Apples and Oats* will show you the way.

Beyond the introductions to each chapter and recipe, I would like to add a few more general comments that you should also find helpful:

Preparation Times

Please don't be put off by the number of minutes or hours indicated as necessary to prepare many of the dishes in this book.

A good deal of the time is not actual kitchen work; rather it is waiting time: waiting for breads to rise, beans to simmer, stews to cook, and so forth. Very few recipes require more than an hour of real work on your part, and the majority take far less.

If most of your day is spent around your home, it's very easy to work your activities around the preparation of bread or soup. But if your schedule isn't so flexible, choose the recipes with shorter preparation times and reserve the longer ones for relaxed weekends. Alternatively, begin making a dish the night before you plan to eat it. Most casseroles, for example, can be assembled beforehand and then baked just before dinner.

Everyone has his or her own pace in the kitchen. The range of dishes in this book is sufficiently broad to meet all types of cooking schedules.

Costs

During the months when I was most actively testing out recipes for this book, my food budget plummeted. Although some ingredients, like cashew nuts, are quite expensive, the cost of making a good meal based on beans, grains, or dairy products is considerably lower than that of interesting dishes made from lamb, beef, or fish.

Calories

If you are new to eating beans and grains as a main course and have a tendency toward extra poundage, be rather careful. A cup of cooked beans contains about 230 calories, a cup of cooked brown rice approximately 200, and two ounces of most cheeses 200 also. This is equivalent to the calories in a serving of fish or chicken and rather less than in a serving of beef. A cup of rice or beans and an ounce of cheese, combined in a casserole with an assortment of herbs and less caloric vegetables, should suffice as a serving for dinner, particularly if you are also eating a salad, soup, or dessert with the meal. There is often a tendency to suppose that because one is "giving up" meat that one may then pile up a plate with a great mound of beans and rice. This, alas, is not the case.

Combining Foods

Frances Moore Lappe's *Diet for a Small Planet* is an excellent introduction to combining vegetarian foods in a manner that will result in healthful eating. While animal foods (meats, poultry, seafood, and dairy products) contain complete, balanced protein, many vegetables lack one or more of the four essential amino acids that our bodies cannot manufacture. However, other vegetable foods contain a surfeit of these amino acids. By combining two such foods, a complete, high quality protein results. For example, beans and corn have a long history of being eaten together. Latin Americans fill tortillas or tamales with black beans, and American Indians traditionally mixed corn and limas in succotash. Beans are deficient in the sulfur-containing amino acids, while plentiful in isoleucine and lysine. Like the matching part of a jigsaw puzzle, corn supplies extra sulfur-containing amino acids, while at the same time is lacking in isoleucine and lysine.

Throughout this book, each chapter will instruct you how to combine the foods under discussion with others in order to make a complete protein. One easy rule to remember, however, is that brewer's yeast and dairy products—milk, yogurt, eggs, and cheese—are ideal means of completing the protein in most vegetable foods. For those not adhering to a strict vegetarian diet, meats, poultry, and seafoods also act in this manner. Thus, a casserole of beans, rice, or corn is made far more nutritious by including in it some shredded Cheddar cheese or ground beef.

Nutritional Sources

Unless otherwise stated, all my nutritional figures come from the *Handbook of the Nutritional Contents of Food, Number 8* prepared by the U.S. Department of Agriculture. For copies, write to the Government Printing Office, Superintendent of Documents, Washington, D.C. 20402 (cost is $4.00). This book lists the vitamin and mineral values of more than 2,500 different foods in various forms (raw, boiled, baked, with and without skins, etc.), and is a valuable source book for anyone interested in foods or nutrition.

Natural Foods

Using the subtitle *From the Basics to the Fine Points of Natural Foods Cooking*, I feel called upon to present a definition of "natural." Unfortunately, the word has been so misused, particularly in advertising, that it no longer has a precise meaning. A common assumption is that natural foods are necessarily healthful. But this is by no means always the case. Sea salt is natural; yet too much salt can elevate blood pressure, a factor in the precipitation of heart disorders. Butter and heavy cream are natural products but contain saturated fats which we should consume in limited quantities.

My definition of a "natural" food as used throughout this book is food that has been tampered with as little as possible. By this I mean whole grains, fresh fruits and vegetables, nuts, seeds, and other such nutritious foods. Thus, I avoid frozen TV dinners, ready-made cakes and cake mixes, packaged puddings, sugar-sweetened cereals, and similar items. However, I do on occasion use a product such as canned tomatoes. Winter tomatoes are pale, pulpy, and flavorless, really quite useless in a recipe; so then I resort to the can. But come summer, I shun the canned product like the plague.

What I have tried to do in this book is reach a level of cooking as close to unrefined as I am able within the limits of practicality. I find soaking dried beans an easy task, baking my own bread a rewarding feat, and making homemade soups a simple matter of combining ingredients in a pot. The "natural" food that results is under my control. There are no preservatives, no coloring agents, no flavor enhancers. What I eat is the sum total of the raw ingredients I have begun with. That, to me, is "natural."

Fresh, Frozen, and Canned Vegetables

You may be amazed as I was to learn that canned and frozen foods do *not* lack the nutrition of fresh. Once they have been boiled and drained, fresh, frozen, and canned vegetables all offer the same amounts of protein, vitamins, minerals, and fiber. Even dehydrated mashed potatoes, reconstituted with milk and butter, have the same food value as homemade.

This, however, is not the entire story. Mel Marshall, in *Real Living with Real Foods*, details the steps of the canning and freezing processes. First, the vegetable skins are loosened in a peeling bath of sodium hydroxide (lye) or methyl naphthalene sulfonate, the traces of which are then neutralized with additional chemicals. Soft vegetables, like squash or tomatoes that are to be canned, go into a firming solution of sodium hydroxide, calcium carbonate, or monobasic calcium phosphate. Most vegetables are then dunked in a chemical solution that preserves or enhances their natural colors (did you ever wonder why canned beets are so brilliantly red, while most of the color in fresh beets you cook yourself runs out into the cooking liquid?). A variety of chemicals may be used for this, many of them containing sodium. Finally, texturizers, emulsifiers, and agents to prevent clouding may be added to canned vegetables, and most are seasoned with salt and glucose.

The most worrisome result of all this processing is a tremendous increase in the quantity of sodium (the potentially harmful element in table salt) in canned vegetables. While fresh and frozen vegetables contain very little sodium (about 1 mg/100 or 1/1000 of a percent), the level in canned vegetables is 200 times as high. Thus, while frozen and canned vegetables do supply the same nutrients as fresh, they also contain much more sodium, most of which we would be wise to do without. And, of course, the taste and texture cannot compare with that of fresh. A final consideration is that processed produce generally costs more than fresh because it is you who foots the bill for packaging, processing, and advertising.

Organic Produce

While "natural" does not have a precise definition, "organic" does, and I think that *Organically Grown Foods* (Rodale Press, 1973) supplies one of the best: "Organically grown food is food grown without pesticides; grown without artificial fertilizers; grown in soil whose humus content is increased by the additives of organic matter; grown in soil whose mineral content is increased with applications of natural mineral fertilizers."

What does this mean? Basically, while farmers growing for large supermarket chains are liberal in their usage of chemical fertilizers and pesticides, the organic farmer avoids synthetic chemicals and replenishes naturally the minerals in the soil he has used. This often results in the consumer paying a higher price for the organically grown produce.

The question is, of course, whether it is worth the additional trouble to go to a health food store for your fruits and vegetables, when a supermarket is right around the corner. I must confess that despite claims attributing superior taste to organically grown produce, I am unable to detect any difference. As far as whether this growing method produces more healthful foods, no systematic studies have been done to compare the nutritive values of these versus chemically treated fruits and vegetables. It is known, however, that the mineral quality of the soil does affect the final product grown there. Too, plants may retain some residues of the various toxic chemicals and insecticides with which they are treated. It can certainly do no harm to consume organically grown food; but you may prefer to live without this extra bother and expense.

Other Sources of Fresh Produce

Of course, one of the best sources of good fresh produce is to grow your own in your backyard. More and more families are doing just that. Besides being able to eat a wealth of fruits and vegetables for very little financial output, whatever cannot be consumed during the summer months can be frozen or canned in your own kitchen without the additives of industrial processing. But many live in apartments or haven't the time or inclination for gardening.

Depending on where you live, there are many other places to go for fresh fruits and vegetables. In an area of lush backyard growth, some families seek to earn extra money by setting up roadside stands. Where I reside in New Jersey, such tempting stands dot the countryside, and I rarely pass one without stopping to buy a sack of apples, some fresh-picked corn, or a ripe, juicy cantaloupe.

Many big cities boast a Farmer's Market, where growers from miles around come to peddle their wares. The prices are generally far lower than at the supermarket, and you usually obtain superior products. Sometimes it is necessary to buy in quantity; some families even band together and divide the produce and the work of shopping among them.

One of the most enjoyable ways of obtaining fresh produce is to frequent a "pick-your-own" farm. At a low cost because you and your family are the laborers, you may climb apple, peach, or cherry trees in search of the best fruit, scour the ground for the ripest red strawberries, or fill box upon box with blueberries fresh from the bush. On a sunny spring day or during the crisp fall harvest, there are few finer ways to spend a weekend afternoon with your family than on such a country adventure. If you do not know the location of a "pick-your-own" farm near you, contact your county's Agricultural Extension Service.

Sources for Dry Goods

For flours, grains, nuts, and dried beans, you must do a bit of hunting to find the best sources and prices. In some neighborhoods, the grocery stores are well stocked with whole grains, unsalted nuts, lentils, and the like and may have the lowest prices. Other foods, such as millet, whole wheat berries, and soy flour, you may only be able to locate in health or natural foods stores.

Even in these stores, the prices differ vastly. Try to locate one that sells the food from large barrels. Generally the prices will be lower because you do not have to pay for the packaging. That way, too, you can purchase exactly the amount you need. Some stores even have huge vats of peanut butter, honey, and tahini. The price per pound is low because you fill your own jar.

Many health food stores also display large jars of herbs and spices; you may buy them by the ounce at a far lower price than you would pay for a one-ounce jar or tin at the supermarket. Or, if you use these ingredients in quantity, check the prices at a wholesale mail order house. Generally, the greatest savings are achieved when you purchase four to eight ounces of a particular herb or spice. If you know that you will not use this much before it loses its potency, why not arrange to split an order with a friend?

Now, welcome to the world of *Cashews and Lentils, Apples and Oats*, where we will adventure with delicious natural food recipes.

part 1
Dried Beans
and Peas

1
Dried Beans

In December 1977, the Senate Select Committee on Nutrition and Human Needs published a guideline of suggested changes in the American diet. It was felt that if these new eating patterns were implemented, the result would be a healthier population with a decreased risk of many major diseases, including heart attacks and strokes. Among the dietary goals proposed were the following: (1) Americans should increase their consumption of complex carbohydrates (i.e., whole grains, legumes, starchy vegetables); and (2) overall fat consumption should be lowered, particularly all saturated fats and especially cholesterol. This means that many of the calories contributed to the diet by animal foods (meats, poultry, eggs, and cheese) should be replaced by energy from carbohydrates. Today, both health and financial considerations dictate adherence to these dietary goals.

Perhaps the most versatile of such complex carbohydrates are beans in their nearly endless variety. When eaten along with dairy products (or meats), corn, spinach, sunflower or sesame seeds, nuts, wheat products, barley, millet, oatmeal, or rice, the quality of beans' protein is augmented.

The other chapters in this section will be devoted to the beans I personally find most distinctive. There exists a tremendous variety of other dried beans, all with slightly different tastes, textures, sizes, and colors. These may really all be used interchangeably, allowing for the fact that some require longer cooking times than others. I often prefer to use an assortment of dried beans, particularly in soups, when each spoonful produces a colorful array of beans and vegetables. In the recipes that follow (and also many in the succeeding chapters), use any combination of beans of your choice.

Here are some you may select:

Black-eyed peas (cowpeas—really of the bean family): small and tan with a dark spot. Eaten in the South on New Year's Eve for good luck.

Black beans (turtle beans): small with a strong flavor. Most often used in Mediterranean, Latin, and Oriental cooking.

Brown beans: about as large as kidney beans. Used in Swedish dishes.

Great Northern beans: large, flat, and white. Very tender and should be cooked gently.

Fava beans: similar to lima beans, but somewhat larger. Delicate flavor. Some people of Mediterranean extraction are unable to digest them.

Kidney beans: red or white. Probably used in more American dishes than any other bean, particularly in salads and vegetable soups.

Lima beans (butter beans): large and pale green. Very mealy. A common ingredient of succotash.

Pea beans: small and white. Often used for baked beans.

Pinto beans: small and beige. Used in chili and other Mexican foods.

Note: Dried beans should be soaked overnight before using. Rinse dried beans with water. Place in a large bowl or jar. Cover with about three times as much water as beans. Place in the refrigerator to prevent any fermentation. Unless recipe directs otherwise, use soaking liquid along with fresh water for cooking. The soaking liquid contains vitamins from the beans.

DIANA'S BASIC BEAN SOUP

This is the soup I make most frequently and most variously, depending on what fresh vegetables are available. I generally cook up a huge pot of it and serve it to guests, along with a freshly made loaf of bread, cheese wedges, and a hearty red wine. Or, if no one is expected, I freeze the soup in batches and defrost a jar whenever I want a good, wholesome meal in a hurry.

It's difficult to give an exact recipe for the soup, but this is pretty much what I do:

PREPARATION TIMES: overnight soaking of beans
½ hour kitchen work
2 hours simmering

YIELD: 10 to 12 servings

1. The night before, start soaking the beans. Use 1½ to 2 cups of an assortment of them, including some barley. Cover the beans with twice the volume of water and place in the refrigerator (I refrigerate the beans because a long soaking period at room temperature may cause some fermentation).

2. The next day, take a big pot (6 to 8 quarts). Put in the beans and any leftover soaking liquid. Then fill up the pot with:

1 onion, chopped
3 carrots, sliced
1 28-ounce can tomatoes, chopped and undrained
½ cup chopped fresh parsley
2 cloves garlic, minced
4 stalks celery, chopped
2 zucchini, sliced
½ rutabaga, diced
1 small eggplant (about ¾ pound), peeled and cubed

1 small head green or Chinese cabbage (½ to 1 pound), coarsely chopped
any other vegetables you fancy
2 teaspoons salt
½ teaspoon pepper
3 cloves
1 teaspoon curry powder
2 bay leaves

3. Fill the pot with water just to cover the vegetables. Bring the liquid to a boil. Then reduce the heat, and simmer, covered, for about 2 hours, or until the beans and all vegetables are tender. Taste for seasoning.

AMERICAN INDIAN RUTABAGA-BEAN SOUP

The American Indians often cooked with beans and rutabagas, generally in a simple manner, just simmering all ingredients together in a pot. Such a hearty bean soup as the one below is wonderful accompanied by Sunflower Seed Bread.

PREPARATION TIMES: overnight soaking of beans
½ hour kitchen work
4 hours simmering

YIELD: 10 servings

2 cups dry beans, soaked overnight in 4 cups water
1 large rutabaga (about 1½ pounds), peeled and chopped
3 cloves garlic, minced

2 teaspoons salt
7 peppercorns
3 quarts water (liquid left from soaking beans, plus fresh water)

1. Place all ingredients into a large pot. Bring to a boil. Then lower the heat and simmer, covered, 4 hours.

2. Puree the beans and rutabaga in the blender with enough cooking liquid to blend easily (this will require several batches) and return to the pot. Reheat.

SPICY BEAN AND SQUASH PUREE

A vegetable puree such as this may be served as a side dish or as a thick soup. Or, if you prefer, serve it as the (Asian) Indians do—as a moistener for rice, vegetables, or bread.

PREPARATION TIMES: overnight soaking of beans
45 minutes kitchen work
30 minutes simmering

YIELD: 4 to 6 servings

2 onions, sliced
2 cloves garlic, minced
2 tablespoons minced fresh
  ginger root
½ teaspoon cinnamon
2 tablespoons butter or
  unsaturated margarine
2 pounds banana squash (or
other winter squash),
  peeled and cubed
1 teaspoon salt
2 cups water
1 cup dry beans, soaked
  overnight in 2 cups water
1 cup milk

1. In a large, heavy pot, brown the onions, garlic, and ginger root in the butter or margarine. Add the cinnamon, squash, salt, water, and beans (use the soaking liquid to make up part or all of the water). Simmer the mixture, covered, 30 minutes or until the beans are tender.

2. Puree the mixture in the blender in batches until smooth. Return to the pan. Add the milk, and heat through.

FRIJOLES NEGROS

In Spanish, black beans become exotic-sounding **frijoles ne-gros**. A friend of mine, who lived for several months in the Caribbean, brought back the following recipe. While another variety of bean could be substituted, the taste and texture will not be authentic unless you use the black bean. The beans absorb the flavor of the wine and take on a delicious subtlety. Traditionally, black beans are served over plain boiled rice.

PREPARATION TIMES: overnight soaking of beans
15 minutes kitchen work
1¾ hours simmering

YIELD: 6 to 8 servings

1 pound black beans
4 cups water
1 large onion, finely chopped
  (about 1 cup)
1 green pepper, finely
  chopped
4 cloves garlic, minced

¼ cup olive oil
¼ teaspoon oregano
2 bay leaves
2 tablespoons sugar
salt and freshly ground black
  pepper to taste
2 cups red wine

1. Soak the beans in 4 cups water overnight. Drain; cover with fresh water, and simmer until soft (about 45 minutes), adding more water if needed.

2. Sauté the onion, green pepper, and garlic in olive oil until translucent and soft.

3. Stir the contents of the sauté pan into the cooked beans. Add the oregano, bay leaves, sugar, salt, pepper, and red wine. Simmer 1 hour or until the mixture thickens, adding more water if the liquid level becomes too low.

TOMATO SAUCED BEANS

The peppy sauce really perks up the bland flavor of beans. Serve the casserole with hot corn bread and wedges of Cheddar cheese (or try the Cheddar Corn Bread).

PREPARATION TIMES: overnight soaking of beans
20 minutes kitchen work
1 hour 35 minutes simmering and baking

YIELD: 6 servings

1½ cups dried beans, soaked overnight in 3 cups water
¼ cup catsup
2 tablespoons molasses
2 tablespoons brown sugar
1 teaspoon salt
1 tablespoon spicy brown mustard

½ teaspoon chili powder
1 small onion, minced (about ⅓ cup)
1 green pepper, minced
2 tablespoons vegetable oil

1. Cook the beans in water to cover (use any leftover soaking liquid plus fresh water) until tender, about 50 minutes. Drain. Stir in the catsup, molasses, brown sugar, salt, mustard, and chili powder.

2. Meanwhile, sauté the onion and green pepper in oil until tender. Stir the contents of this pan into the bean mixture.

3. Turn the entire mixture into a greased 1½-quart casserole. Bake in a 350 degree oven 45 minutes.

SWEET-SIMMERED SOYS

Soy beans, often so plain tasting, here absorb the full, rich flavors of molasses, apple, and raisins. The result is somewhat sweet; so the dish is best served with a plain green vegetable, such as steamed broccoli or zucchini, along with a freshly baked whole wheat loaf.

PREPARATION TIMES: overnight soaking of beans
15 minutes kitchen work
1¾ hours simmering

YIELD: 6 servings

1 cup dried soy beans, soaked overnight in 3 cups water
1 large onion, chopped (about 1 cup)
3¼ cups water
1 teaspoon salt
3 tablespoons molasses
¼ teaspoon cinnamon
¼ teaspoon cloves
¼ cup raisins
1 small apple, unpeeled, cored, and chopped (about ½ cup)
1 tablespoon lemon juice

1. Place the beans, soaking liquid, onion, additional water, salt, molasses, cinnamon, and cloves in a heavy saucepan. Simmer, covered, 30 minutes. Add all remaining ingredients and simmer 1 hour longer, or until the beans are tender.

2. Remove cover and cook until most of the liquid evaporates, about 15 minutes.

ZIPPY BEAN, RICE, AND CHEESE CASSEROLE

Here's a delicious main course casserole that combines lentils, beans, and brown rice with a variety of vegetables, crunchy nuts, cheese, and the zip of chili peppers. Altogether, it makes a very well-balanced meal that need be accompanied by only a salad.

PREPARATION TIMES: overnight soaking of beans
40 minutes kitchen work
1½ hours simmering and baking

YIELD: 8 servings

½ cup each lentils and kidney
beans, soaked overnight in
2 cups water
additional water
salt
1 cup brown rice
5 tablespoons vegetable oil,
divided usage
2 green peppers, diced
1 cup shredded cabbage
2 stalks celery, sliced

1 large onion, chopped
(about 1 cup)
2 cloves garlic, minced
1 cup tomato sauce
2 tablespoons catsup
1 4-ounce can chopped mild
green chili peppers, drained
1½ tablespoons sesame seeds
1 cup chopped walnuts
1½ cups shredded mozzarella
cheese, divided usage

1. Place the lentils and kidney beans, along with the soaking liquid, in a saucepan. Add enough additional water to cover them completely. Add ½ teaspoon salt. Simmer, covered, about 1 hour, or until tender. Drain and mash.

2. Meanwhile, in a heavy saucepan, sauté the rice in 2 tablespoons vegetable oil until golden. Add 3 cups of water and 1 teaspoon salt. Bring to a boil. Reduce heat and simmer, covered, until the rice is tender, about 40 minutes.

3. Next, in a large skillet, sauté the green peppers, cabbage, celery, onion, and garlic in the remaining oil until tender.

4. Remove from the heat and stir in the mashed beans, cooked rice, tomato sauce, catsup, chili peppers, sesame seeds, walnuts, and ½ cup cheese.

5. Turn the mixture into a greased 4-quart casserole dish. Bake in a 375-degree oven 15 minutes. Sprinkle with the remaining cheese and bake 15 minutes longer.

CORN AND BEAN PIE

Its crust is a quickly made corn meal mixture that expands when baked into a delicious, dense corn bread. The filling combines kidney beans, fresh corn, peanuts, black olives, Cheddar cheese, and zippy chili powder and cumin seeds. Altogether, the pie makes an extraordinarily nutritious and satisfying dinner.

PREPARATION TIMES: overnight soaking of beans
                   30 minutes kitchen work
                   1¾ hours simmering and baking

YIELD: 4 to 6 servings

1 cup kidney beans, soaked overnight in 2 cups water
1¾ cups cornmeal
5 tablespoons vegetable oil, divided usage
¾ cup hot water
½ teaspoon salt
1 onion, chopped
½ cup chopped celery
1 green pepper, chopped
½ cup fresh corn kernels
1 8-ounce can tomato sauce
⅓ cup chopped, lightly salted peanuts
½ teaspoon oregano
2 teaspoons chili powder
½ teaspoon cumin seeds
½ cup shredded Cheddar cheese
¼ cup sliced black olives

1. Cover the kidney beans with water (use any leftover soaking liquid plus fresh water). Bring to a boil and cook until the beans are tender, about 1 hour. Drain, reserving ¼ cup cooking liquid.

2. Meanwhile, mix together the cornmeal, 3 tablespoons oil, hot water, and salt. Press into the bottom and sides of a 9-inch pie plate.

3. In a large skillet, sauté the onion, celery, and green pepper in the remaining 2 tablespoons oil until tender. Stir in the corn, tomato sauce, peanuts, oregano, chili powder, cumin seeds, kidney beans, and reserved liquid. Turn into the corn meal pie shell.

4. Bake the pie in a 350-degree oven 30 minutes. Top with the cheese and olives and bake 10 minutes longer.

BLACK-EYED PEA TEA BREAD

Although it calls for fresh, not dried, beans, so delightful a tea bread simply had to be included in this chapter. The recipe is adapted from one that won a Texas Black-Eyed Pea recipe contest. The peas add a pleasantly chewy texture and wonderfully nutty flavor and also supply a great deal of protein, making a slice of the bread very nutritious for snacking.

PREPARATION TIMES: 15 minutes kitchen work
1 hour baking

YIELD: 1 9″ × 5″ loaf

1¼ cups black-eyed peas
¼ cup coffee (or substitute Postum)
½ teaspoon vanilla
½ cup vegetable oil
1 cup sugar
2 eggs
¾ cup unbleached white

flour
¾ cup whole wheat flour
½ teaspoon salt
¼ teaspoon baking powder
½ teaspoon baking soda
1½ teaspoons cinnamon
⅓ cup golden raisins
⅓ cup chopped walnuts

1. Place the peas, coffee, vanilla, vegetable oil, sugar, and eggs in a blender and blend until smooth.

2. In a large bowl, stir together the flours, salt, baking powder, baking soda, and cinnamon. Add the mixture from the blender and stir until just well mixed. Stir in the raisins and walnuts.

3. Turn the batter into a greased and floured 9″ × 5″ loaf pan. Bake in a 350-degree oven 55 to 60 minutes, or until the bread tests done with a toothpick. Let cool on a rack before slicing.

2
Lentils

"Rice is good, but lentils are my life"

—Hindu Proverb

Lentils are believed to be one of the first plants cultivated by man. They are mentioned in the Bible; Esau apparently sold his birthright for a bowl of lentil soup. The lentil has been and still is a major food source throughout much of the world, particularly in India, Africa, and the Middle Eastern countries.

Yet despite their long-term and widespread use, lentils are not very popular in this country. Most American cookbooks devote to lentils little more than a simple soup recipe. This is unfortunate, for lentils have a lighter texture than that of most dried beans and combine very well with a great variety of ingredients. Syrian cooks add them to meat and fruit stews. Indians season them highly, and others make them into patties, either with or without the addition of ground meats.

Lentils, so often seen only as brown, come in an assortment of colors. The most esteemed in flavor by French cooks is the red lentil. Yellow lentils are also praised. These more colorful varieties may generally be purchased in health food stores, usually for a higher price than that commanded by the common brown lentil.

But lentils, whether common or rare, are a food that should be enjoyed more often.

INDIAN LENTIL SOUP WITH VEGETABLES AND NUTS

Here's a lentil soup that's a lively change of pace from the usual. Less thick than most bean soups, it is filled with exotic spices, a variety of vegetables, and the richness of nuts. Serve the soup as a hearty appetizer, or lunch dish, or as a winter main course with hot bread. You might even accompany it with small bowls of yogurt with cooling cucumber grated into it.

PREPARATION TIMES: 30 minutes kitchen work
40 minutes simmering

YIELD: 10 servings

1 cup lentils
⅓ cup raw rice
¼ teaspoon turmeric
4½ cups water
4 onions, chopped, divided usage
4 potatoes, peeled and diced
1 large eggplant (about 1¼ pounds), unpeeled and diced
2 tomatoes, peeled and chopped

2 teaspoons mustard seeds
3 tablespoons vegetable oil
2 green peppers, chopped
4 teaspoons salt
1 teaspoon curry powder
⅛ teaspoon pepper
⅛ teaspoon chili powder
2 teaspoons sesame seeds
¾ cup finely chopped cashews
¾ cup finely chopped peanuts

1. In a large pot, begin cooking the lentils, rice, and turmeric in the 4½ cups water.

2. Meanwhile, place 2 onions, the potatoes, and eggplant in another saucepan. Add water to just cover. Cover the pan and cook until the potatoes are barely tender. Add the contents of this pan to the lentils, along with the tomatoes, and cook 10 minutes longer. (By now, the lentils should be tender; if not, continue cooking until they are.)

3. In a skillet, cook the mustard seeds in oil until they begin to pop. Add the remaining 2 onions and the green peppers. Saute until the onions are tender. Add contents of the skillet and all remaining ingredients to the lentils and heat through.

DAL

Dal is a rather plain Indian lentil dish. Generally quite thick, it is used almost as a gravy—to moisten rice, to pour over the main course, or as a dipper for bread. Made thinner with water, dal also serves as a soup. The recipe below is for a thick dal to serve with dinner, but it may also be thinned (with additional water), if you prefer.

PREPARATION TIMES: 20 minutes kitchen work
50 minutes simmering

YIELD: 4 servings

1 cup lentils	1 teaspoon salt
½ teaspoon turmeric	3 cups boiling water
½ teaspoon grated ginger root	2 tablespoons vegetable oil
	¼ teaspoon mustard seeds
1 clove garlic, pressed	1 onion, chopped

1. Place the lentils, turmeric, ginger root, garlic, and salt in the boiling water. Cook until the lentils are very soft, about 50 minutes.

2. In a skillet, cook the mustard seeds in oil until they begin to pop. Add the onion and sauté until tender. Stir into the lentils.

LENTIL LOAF

This is a flavorful, nutritious main course, given a pleasant crunch by the sunflower seeds. Because the loaf is so dense, serve it with a light soup and green vegetable or tossed salad. Since dairy products complement the protein in beans and lentils, a good choice would be a soup with milk or yogurt, such as Apple Yogurt Soup. Or, if you wish, serve a dairy dessert—Cottage Cheese Custard Pie, for example.

PREPARATION TIMES: 20 minutes kitchen work
40 minutes simmering
35 minutes baking

YIELD: 4 servings

¾ cup lentils
water
½ cup rolled oats
2 eggs, beaten
1 teaspoon salt

½ teaspoon thyme
1 cup tomato-vegetable
  cocktail juice
½ cup sunflower seeds

1. Cook the lentils in water to cover until tender, about 40 minutes, adding more water as necessary. Drain and mix with the remaining ingredients.

2. Turn the mixture into a greased 9″ × 5″ loaf pan and bake in a 350-degree oven 35 minutes.

LENTIL SALAD

So often at picnics we are served the same macaroni, sweet and sour bean, and potato salads. Tart and flavorful lentil salad makes a refreshing change. As it has a vinaigrette dressing, it complements a great variety of foods very well.

Note: The raw onion in the salad can be optional; some people dislike the taste, while others seem to dote on it.

PREPARATION TIMES: 20 minutes kitchen work
                   40 minutes simmering
                   1 to 2 hours cooling

YIELD: 6 servings

1 cup lentils
1 onion, chopped
2 cloves
1 bay leaf
3 cups water
1 teaspoon salt
¼ teaspoon pepper

2½ tablespoons salad oil
1½ tablespoons red wine vinegar
1 minced raw onion, optional
2 tablespoons minced fresh
  parsley
2 tomatoes, peeled, seeded,
  and chopped

1. Place the lentils, onion, cloves, and bay leaf in the water and simmer until tender, about 40 minutes. Drain and discard the cloves and bay leaf.

2. Stir in the salt, pepper, salad oil, and vinegar; stir in the raw onion, if desired. Let cool to room temperature or chill. Just before serving, stir in the tomatoes.

COTTAGE CHEESE-LENTIL CASSEROLE

A light main course dish that supplies complete protein, this is a handy recipe to have in your repertoire because it is so simple to put together and also contains ingredients you're likely to have on hand. Serve the casserole with a salad or vegetable and hot bread or muffins.

PREPARATION TIMES: 10 minutes kitchen work
40 minutes simmering
45 minutes baking

YIELD: 4 servings

1½ cups lentils
2 cups cottage cheese
2 eggs, beaten
1 cup shredded carrots

½ teaspoon thyme
¼ teaspoon oregano
1 teaspoon salt
¼ cup sesame seeds

1. Place the lentils in a saucepan. Add water to cover. Cook, covered, until tender, about 40 minutes, adding additional water if necessary. Drain.

2. Mix the lentils with all remaining ingredients except the sesame seeds. Turn into a greased 1½ to 2-quart casserole dish and sprinkle with the seeds.

3. Bake in a 375-degree oven 45 minutes.

3
Split Peas

Split peas are somewhat different from other dried beans and peas. To process them, ordinary green peas are divested of their skins; thus, when dried, the peas split into halves along the natural lines of division. This makes for a distinctive characteristic when cooked—the pulp, rather than remaining encased in a coating, easily flows out. The result is both a convenience and a nuisance.

In soups, this quality is marvelous. The split peas, with no pureeing required, function as a thickening agent. For this reason, split pea soups, in a myriad of forms, are popular throughout the world. In making loaves, too, the split pea mashes easily, allowing the pulp to be well mixed with the other ingredients.

However, this same trait can also make vegetable dishes made with split peas very heavy. Rather than remaining whole, in delicate little rounds, the peas tend to dissolve into a pulp. Great care in cooking must be taken if you wish to make a split pea dish that is not mushy and thick.

Split peas, with their distinctive taste and texture, are loved by some and scorned by others. I prefer to season them highly and thus offset their strong taste a bit. The recipes here are three that I especially enjoy.

INDIAN SPLIT PEA AND SPINACH SOUP

Indian split pea soups may contain a variety of ingredients such as squash, tomatoes, cauliflower, or coconut in addition to the fragrant spices. In my version, the slightly bitter taste of the spinach makes a pleasing contrast to the mealy peas.

The soup, in addition to being flavorful and easy to prepare, is quite economical. Serve it with warm pita bread and raita (yogurt to which is added grated cucumber, toasted cumin seeds, salt, and pepper, all to taste).

PREPARATION TIMES: 10 minutes kitchen work
                   1 hour simmering

YIELD: 4 servings

1 cup split peas	½ teaspoon grated ginger root
4 cups boiling water	½ teaspoon cumin seeds
1 teaspoon salt	¼ teaspoon paprika
½ teaspoon turmeric	1 10-ounce package frozen
1 teaspoon coriander	chopped spinach, thawed

1. In a saucepan, combine the split peas, boiling water, and spices. Cover, and simmer over a low heat until the peas are soft, about 40 minutes.

2. Stir in the spinach and simmer 20 minutes longer.

SPLIT PEA LOAF

Split peas make for a mealy loaf, considerably more so than do the lentils in the loaf recipe given in the preceding chapter. This is a heavy main course that is particularly satisfying during the cold months. Serve it with a cabbage salad and steamed broccoli or rutabaga.

PREPARATION TIMES: 20 minutes kitchen work
45 minutes simmering
60 minutes baking

YIELD: 4 servings

1 cup split peas
2 cups water
1 onion, chopped
2 tablespoons vegetable oil
½ cup whole wheat bread crumbs

½ cup soy nuts
1 teaspoon salt
⅛ teaspoon pepper
⅓ cup milk

1. Cook the split peas in the water 45 minutes. Puree in a blender with ⅓ cup of cooking liquid.

2. In a skillet, sauté the onion in oil until tender. Add the contents of the skillet to the split peas, along with all remaining ingredients. Mix well.

3. Turn the mixture into a greased 9″ × 5″ loaf pan. Bake in a 350-degree oven about 50 minutes or until firm.

SPANISH SPLIT PEAS IN TOMATO SAUCE

Here the peas remain mostly intact, and so have less of that mealy consistency. They're surrounded by a spicy tomato sauce that makes the casserole a pleasant side dish to a main course featuring eggs.

PREPARATION TIMES: 15 minutes kitchen work
1¼ hours simmering
15 minutes baking

YIELD: 6 to 8 servings

2 cups split peas
4 cups water
2 teaspoons salt
2 onions, chopped
2 cloves garlic, minced

2 green peppers, diced
¼ cup olive oil
2 cups tomato sauce
2 teaspoons chili powder

1. In a saucepan, simmer the split peas, water, and salt for 1 hour or until tender. Drain.

2. Meanwhile, in a skillet, sauté the onions, garlic, and green pepper in olive oil until they are browned. Stir in the tomato sauce and chili powder. Cook over low heat for 15 minutes. Stir in the split peas.

3. Turn the mixture into a greased 2-quart casserole. Bake in a 400-degree oven 15 minutes.

4
Chick-Peas

Chick-peas (or garbanzos) were for many years in this country primarily associated with minestrone soup or as one of the selections at a "make-your-own" salad bar. But, as interest in foreign foods has increased during recent years, more and more chick-pea dishes from the Mediterranean, Mid-Eastern, and Spanish cuisines have made their way here.

Chick-peas are probably second only to soy beans in their multiplicity of uses beyond that of ordinary cooked legumes. They are mashed and served in a variety of dips, most notably **hommos bi tahini**, one of the recipes here. Chick-peas are also ground into a flour and baked into breads and sweets. (Recently I encountered an Italian recipe for deep-fried pastries with chick-peas, chocolate, and pine nuts.) Finally, chick-peas may be roasted and served as a snack in much the same way as the now common soy nuts.

Chick-peas require a long cooking time (about 1 hour) even after a preliminary overnight soaking. But they have the advantage of not becoming soggy (unless you purchase the canned beans which are too soft for my taste). Chick-peas retain their crunchiness and impart a delicious flavor to all the recipes following.

HOMMOS BI TAHINI

This dip found throughout the Middle East is also great served as a sandwich filling or topping. Very rich and satisfying, a little goes far. Serve with pita bread, sesame crackers, or raw vegetable dippers.

PREPARATION TIMES: overnight soaking of chick-peas
15 minutes kitchen work
2 hours simmering
1 to 2 hours cooling

YIELD: 2½ cups

1 cup chick-peas, soaked
  overnight in 2 cups water
2 cloves garlic
2 tablespoons lemon juice
2 tablespoons olive oil
2 tablespoons water
1 teaspoon salt
¼ cup tahini (sesame seed

paste that is available in
many supermarkets, health
food stores, and Middle
Eastern groceries)
Tabasco pepper sauce,
  optional
1 tablespoon minced fresh
  parsley

1. Cook the chick-peas in water to cover (use any leftover soaking liquid plus fresh water) until very tender, about 2 hours. Drain.

2. Place the chick-peas in a blender or food processor with the garlic, lemon juice, olive oil, water, and salt. Blend until smooth. Stir in the tahini.

Note: These amounts are approximate. Some add more lemon juice for a tarter flavor, while others prefer a bit more olive oil. If too thick, add more water. If too bland for your taste, add a dash of Tabasco to perk it up. In other words, you can experiment with the dip until it suits your fancy.

3. Turn the mixture into a serving dish and sprinkle with the parsley. Serve either at room temperature or chilled.

SOPA SECA

Sopa Seca translates literally from the Spanish as "dry soup." Unlike true soups, which are liquidy, the rice and beans in a dry soup have absorbed all the cooking liquid. There are many, many recipes for dry soups; sometimes an entire chapter of a Mexican cookbook is devoted to them. This version, from South America, is one of my favorites. Serve it with a tossed green salad and cold beer or iced tea. If any is leftover, it reheats well. Or, serve it cold; it makes a delicious, crunchy bean salad.

PREPARATION TIMES: overnight soaking of chick-peas
                               15 minutes kitchen work
                               1¼ hours simmering

YIELD: 6 servings

1 cup chick-peas, soaked overnight in 2 cups water	1¾ cups peeled, seeded, and chopped tomatoes
3 tablespoons olive oil	¼ teaspoon oregano
2 onions, chopped	½ teaspoon chili powder
2 cloves garlic, minced	1 teaspoon salt
1 green pepper, chopped	¼ teaspoon pepper
1 cup raw rice	¼ cup raisins
1 cup boiling water	¼ cup sliced almonds

1. Simmer the chick-peas, uncovered, in water to cover (use leftover soaking liquid plus fresh water) for 30 minutes. Drain.

2. Meanwhile, heat the olive oil in a large skillet. Sauté the onions, garlic, green pepper, and rice until browned.

3. Add the boiling water, tomatoes, chick-peas, and spices to the skillet. Cover and simmer 40 minutes. Stir in the raisins and almonds and cook 5 minutes longer.

MUSHROOM–CHICK-PEA CASSEROLE

This is a lovely, creamy casserole, rather similar in taste and texture to scalloped potatoes. It's especially enjoyable on a cold night with a steaming bowl of vegetable soup, hot bread, and a wedge of cheese.

PREPARATION TIMES: overnight soaking of chick-peas
30 minutes kitchen work
1 hour simmering
15 minutes baking

YIELD: 6 servings

1⅓ cups chick-peas, soaked overnight, in 2⅔ cups water
1 pound mushrooms, sliced
4 tablespoons butter or unsaturated margarine, divided usage
4 tablespoons unbleached white flour

2 cups evaporated milk
1 teaspoon salt
¼ teaspoon pepper
½ teaspoon basil
½ teaspoon marjoram
6 tablespoons whole wheat bread crumbs

1. Cook the chick-peas, uncovered, in water to cover (leftover soaking liquid plus fresh water) for 1 hour. Drain.

2. Meanwhile, sauté the mushrooms in 2 tablespoons butter or margarine until tender.

3. Melt the remaining butter or margarine in a saucepan. Add the flour and cook 1 minute. Add the milk and cook, stirring with a wire whisk, until thickened and just at the boiling point. Stir in the spices, chick-peas, and mushrooms.

4. Turn the mixture into a greased 1-quart casserole dish and top with the bread crumbs. Bake in a 350-degree oven 15 minutes.

CHICK-PEA AND BLACK OLIVE SALAD

Here is a deliciously crisp salad with a distinctly Middle Eastern flavor from the olive oil, garlic, black olives, cumin seeds, and fresh tomatoes. It goes well with many main vegetarian courses, particularly eggplant dishes, and is especially delicious in the summer when fresh tomatoes are at their peak.

PREPARATION TIMES: overnight soaking of chick-peas
20 minutes kitchen work
1 hour, 20 minutes cooking
2 or more hours chilling

YIELD: 6 servings

2 cups chick-peas, soaked
  overnight in 4 cups water
2 onions, chopped
⅓ cup olive oil
3 cups peeled, seeded, and
  chopped tomatoes

2 cloves garlic, pressed
⅔ cup sliced black olives
¾ cup minced fresh parsley
2 teaspoons cumin seeds
1 teaspoon salt
¼ teaspoon pepper

1. Cover the chick-peas with water (use liquid left from soaking plus fresh water) and simmer, uncovered, until tender, about 1 hour. Drain.

2. In a large skillet, sauté the onions in olive oil until tender. Add the chick-peas, tomatoes, and garlic, and cook, covered, for 5 minutes. Remove the cover and cook 5 minutes longer, stirring occasionally.

3. Remove from the heat and stir in the olives, parsley, cumin seeds, salt, and pepper. Turn into a serving dish and chill well.

CHICK-PEA COOKIES

I was once served some marvelously flavorful and chewy cookies in an Indian restaurant. I inquired as to what was in them and was surprised to learn that the mysterious ingredient was chickpeas. After much searching and researching I have finally developed a recipe for the delicacy.

In the recipe, you must use chick-pea flour, which is generally available in health food stores. One recipe I came across in my search suggested that I grind the raw chick-peas in my blender. They didn't become fine enough, and the resulting cookies had a texture somewhat like egg shells. Made with chick-pea flour, however, the cookies really are delicious. And they are an ideal treat for anyone allergic to wheat.

PREPARATION TIMES: 15 minutes kitchen work
                   30 minutes baking

YIELD: 40 cookies

2 sticks (1 cup) butter or
   unsaturated margarine,
   softened
1 cup confectioners' sugar

1 egg
1 teaspoon cardamom
2 cups chick-pea flour
½ cup water

1. In a large bowl, cream the butter or margarine with the sugar. Beat in the egg and cardamom. Stir in the chick-pea flour and water. This requires quite a lot of elbow work. If necessary, add a little more water, but the batter should not be too soft.

2. Drop teaspoonfuls of the dough onto greased baking sheets. Bake in a 300-degree oven about 30 minutes.

5
Soy Granules

The soy bean has long been hailed as the most nutritious variety of bean. But it does have the drawback of requiring a very long period of cooking. One product that allows you to obtain the protein of soy in a very easy way is soy granules. These are dehydrated, precooked soy beans that merely need a brief soaking in water for them to be edible.

Soy granules have been available for a long time in health food stores; and early vegetarian cookbooks suggest adding them to soups, stuffings, spreads, and vegetable dishes. But within the last few years, as the price of meat has soared, soy granules have appeared on supermarket shelves as "hamburger extenders" as well. Some of these products are seasoned; some are not. Try different brands to see which you prefer. Each company also has different instructions regarding reconstitution, but generally the ratio is approximately one part soy granules to one part hot water.

For some reason, soy granules, in many cookbooks, have come

to be called soy grits (not to be confused with the well-known Southern hominy grits which are a corn derivative). Soy grits are actually the raw soy bean split into 10 pieces; and they require 45 minutes of cooking. But because cookbooks so often refer to soy granules as soy grits, many stores have also changed the name of the product. So, before buying, make certain which product you are getting.

Besides using them in the recipes following, try dropping reconstituted soy granules into soups or spaghetti sauces, adding them to a vegetable or cottage cheese casserole, or beating them into an omelette or scrambled eggs. They will add nutrition, a chewy texture, and a pleasantly salty taste to any dish.

Incidentally, soy beans and soy granules have a slightly different amino acid composition from other beans. They lack only the sulfer-containing amino acids and so are nearly a complete protein food. To complement the deficiency in soy beans and thereby achieve a superior product, combine them with dairy products (or meats), sesame seeds, Brazil nuts, millet, rice, or bran.

SOY GRANULE SOUFFLÉ

Enjoy this extremely nutritious soufflé, flecked with chewy bits of soy. If you're a novice at making soufflés, before trying this recipe, see the detailed instructions in the Egg chapter. Serve the dish with a tossed salad, sliced tomatoes, and hot bread.

PREPARATION TIMES: 15 minutes kitchen work
                   30 minutes baking

YIELD: 4 appetizer, or 2 main course servings

2 green onions, sliced
2 tablespoons butter or
  unsaturated margarine
2 tablespoons unbleached
  white flour
1 cup milk
½ cup soy granules,
  reconstituted (use 1
  tablespoon less water than
  called for)

½ teaspoon salt
¼ teaspoon pepper
4 eggs, separated
¼ cup grated Cheddar cheese
pinch salt
about 1 tablespoon Parmesan
  cheese

1. Cook the green onions in the butter or margarine in a heavy saucepan for 2 minutes. Add the flour and cook, stirring another 2 minutes. Add the milk, and cook, stirring with a wire whisk, until thick and smooth and just at the boiling point. Boil 1 minute longer.

2. Remove from the heat and stir in the soy granules, ½ teaspoon salt, pepper, and egg yolks, one at a time. Then stir in the Cheddar cheese.

3. In a large bowl, beat the egg whites with a pinch of salt until stiff. Stir one-third of the beaten whites into the soy mixture, and then fold in the rest gently.

4. Grease a 1½-quart round casserole or soufflé dish and sprinkle it with Parmesan cheese. Pour in the soufflé mixture. Bake in a 375-degree oven about 30 minutes. Serve immediately.

SOY GRANULE LOAF

Many possibilities exist for turning soy granules into an interesting baked loaf that has the appearance of meat loaf but with a milder flavor, chewier texture, and almost no fat content. This recipe is just one suggestion. You might also try adding chopped nuts or green peppers, tomato sauce, sesame or sunflower seeds.

PREPARATION TIMES: 15 minutes kitchen work
                             45 minutes baking

YIELD: 4 fairly small servings

1½ cups soy granules, reconstituted	¾ cup raisins
	2 eggs, beaten
½ cup sliced green onions	¾ cup grated Cheddar cheese
¼ cup whole wheat bread crumbs	½ teaspoon salt
	¼ teaspoon pepper
¼ teaspoon nutmeg	

1. Mix together all ingredients except the Cheddar cheese. Place half the mixture in a greased 1½-quart casserole. Sprinkle with the cheese. Repeat the layers.

2. Bake the loaf in a 350-degree oven about 45 minutes. The mixture should be fully set but not dried out.

ITALIAN STUFFED EGGPLANT

Similar to Eggplant Parmesan, this dish escapes the greasy quality so often found in other versions. Rather than eggplant slices sautéed in oil, eggplant halves are stuffed with a spicy tomato and soy mixture, then sprinkled with cheese before baking. It's definitely a dish that will impress guests, especially if you accompany it with bread sticks or hot Italian bread, a tossed green salad, and red wine.

PREPARATION TIMES: 1 hour kitchen work
                   30 minutes simmering
                   30 minutes baking

YIELD: 4 servings

1 onion, chopped	¼ teaspoon thyme
1 clove garlic, minced	¼ teaspoon marjoram
2 tablespoons olive oil	2 tablespoons minced fresh
1 cup soy granules,	parsley
reconstituted	2 tablespoons dry sherry
1 1-pound can tomatoes,	1 large eggplant (about 1¼
drained and coarsely	pounds)
chopped	1 cup grated mozzarella
1 6-ounce can tomato paste	cheese
½ teaspoon salt	½ cup grated Parmesan
¼ teaspoon pepper	cheese
½ teaspoon oregano	

1. In a large, heavy saucepan, brown the onion and garlic in olive oil. Add the soy granules, tomatoes, tomato paste, spices, and sherry. Simmer, covered, for 15 minutes.

2. Meanwhile, cut the eggplant in half lengthwise. Remove the pulp without damaging the shells and dice it. Add the pulp to the simmering mixture, and place the shells on top, so they will soften in the steam. Replace the cover, and simmer another 15 minutes.

3. Place the eggplant shells in a shallow greased baking dish. Fill with the simmered mixture, and sprinkle with the cheeses. Bake in a 350-degree oven 30 minutes.

SOY AND VEGETABLE STEW

Here's a colorful stew so thick and hearty that, served alone, it makes a complete dinner. It's inexpensive, very simple to prepare, and highly nutritious. What more could anyone ask from a dinner? The vegetables listed below are only suggestions. Substitute other favorites or those in season.

PREPARATION TIMES: 30 minutes kitchen work
$1\frac{1}{4}$ hours simmering

YIELD: 8 servings

6 cups water
2 cups soy granules
½ cup cracked wheat
1 onion, chopped
1 green pepper, chopped
2 cloves garlic, minced
2 carrots, sliced
4 potatoes, unpeeled, halved, and sliced
3 stalks broccoli, sliced

¼ cup minced fresh parsley
3 large tomatoes, peeled, seeded, and chopped (about 1½ cups) (or use 1 1-pound can)
2 teaspoons salt
¼ teaspoon pepper
1½ teaspoons turmeric
2 teaspoons chili powder
2 bay leaves

Place all ingredients in a large, heavy pot. Bring to a boil. Reduce heat, cover, and simmer until all vegetables are tender, about 1¼ hours.

SOY AND CARROT CASSEROLE

You can't beat this moist, well-flavored casserole loaf that's packed with protein and plenty of crunchy vegetables. Serve portions over whole wheat noodles and sprinkle with freshly grated Parmesan cheese for a meal with that distinctive Italian touch.

PREPARATION TIMES: 20 minutes kitchen work
                   40 minutes baking

YIELD: 6 servings

2 onions, chopped
3 tablespoons vegetable oil
1 cup soy granules, soaked in
   1½ cups hot water 10
   minutes and then drained
¼ cup minced parsley
¼ cup chopped celery
2 cups (packed down to

measure) grated carrots
2 cups tomato sauce
   (homemade or canned)
2 eggs, beaten
1 cup wheat germ
1 teaspoon thyme
1 teaspoon basil
½ teaspoon salt

1. In a skillet, sauté the onions in oil until lightly browned.

2. Mix the contents of the skillet with all remaining ingredients.

3. Turn the mixture into a greased 2-quart casserole. Bake in a 350-degree oven 40 minutes.

part 2

Grains

6
Brown Rice

There is probably no item as symbolic of natural foods cooking as brown rice. It has been made famous by those on macrobiotic diets who subsist only on this food. I have encountered people who prefer whole wheat flour to white but will gladly eat an ordinary brownie and those who praise honey but will lick a sugar-sweetened ice cream cone, yet when it comes to the eating of rice, it is brown rice or nothing for them.

But here I must make a virtually heretical statement for a natural foods cookbook. The fact is there is very little difference in nutritive value between brown rice and enriched white rice (the type most typically purchased). The major difference between these two types of rice is that the brown retains its outer coating of bran, thus supplying us with fiber (.3 gram in an average serving of brown rice compared with .1 in white), a certain amount of which is necessary in our diets. (Refer to the chapter on Bran for further details on fiber.)

There are advantages to brown rice, though. It has a heavy,

chewy texture and a satisfying fullness of flavor that particularly enhances hearty, robust dishes.

Although each culture has its own cooking method for rice (and even within a culture individuals argue vehemently over its proper preparation), there are basically two ways to cook it. It may either be simmered in water until tender or sautéed in butter or oil prior to the simmering. This latter technique produces pilaf, which may undergo innumerable variations, including using broth as the simmering liquid and adding nuts, fruits, vegetables, and/or meats to the rice. While plain boiled rice tends to be a bit sticky, the grains in a pilaf are more solid and separate. Experiment with both methods of cooking rice to see which you prefer. The majority of the recipes in this book utilize the simple boiling method.

While on the subject of cooking rice, I would like to say a word about leftover rice. There are many appropriate ways of using it; add it to soups, casseroles, or even salads. But, in my experience, recipes calling for this food in baked goods have invariably turned out badly. In quick-baking pastries, such as cookies or muffins, the cooked rice gives up its water, making the dough soggy, with hard rice kernels scattered throughout. In yeast breads, the cooked rice absorbs enormous quantities of flour when kneading; yet even so, the finished loaf is heavy, doughy, and wet. Unless your source is highly reliable, I would avoid a bread-type recipe with cooked rice as an ingredient.

One further comment on rice (both brown and white) is in order: this food is deficient in isoleucine and lysine. To make a complete protein food and thus assure yourself of necessary nutrition when eating a rice-based dinner, add dairy products (or meat, poultry, or fish), wheat germ, broccoli, cauliflower, spinach, okra, Swiss chard, or beans. Rice and beans, incidentally, form a classic combination in Latin and Creole cooking; a New Orleans dish, known as Dirty Rice, mixes rice with kidney beans.

PILAF STUFFED EGGPLANT

The rice in this dish is sautéed, simmered with herbs, and then mixed with eggplant pulp and crunchy walnuts. The mixture is stuffed into the eggplant shells, topped with cheese, and then baked. One eggplant half makes a delicious, complete meal. Steamed string beans and sliced tomatoes go well with it.

PREPARATION TIMES: 30 minutes kitchen work
1 hour simmering
30 minutes baking

YIELD: 6 servings

3 medium eggplants (about 1 pound each), halved lengthwise
1 large onion, chopped (about 1 cup)
2 tablespoons vegetable oil
1 cup brown rice
3 cups water
juice of 1 lemon

¼ cup minced fresh parsley
½ teaspoon salt
1 teaspoon oregano
½ teaspoon thyme
⅛ teaspoon pepper
1 cup chopped walnuts
6 tablespoons All-bran cereal
2 cups shredded Muenster cheese

1. Place the halved eggplants in a large pot. Cover with water and boil until tender, about 15 minutes. Drain. When cool enough to handle, scoop out and coarsely chop the pulp. Place the skins in a large, shallow, greased baking dish.

2. Meanwhile, in a large skillet, sauté the onion in vegetable oil until tender. Add the rice and cook, stirring, for 2 minutes. Add the water, lemon juice, and spices. Bring to a boil. Cover and lower the heat. Simmer 30 minutes. Add the eggplant pulp and cook 15 minutes longer. Stir in the walnuts and cereal.

3. Stuff the rice mixture into the eggplant shells. Sprinkle with the Muenster cheese. Bake in a 350-degree oven 30 minutes.

SWEET-AND-SOUR STUFFED CABBAGE

Cabbage leaves are rolled up with brown rice that's given extra crunch and protein from soy nuts and a special touch of sweetness from raisins. The rolls are then simmered in a delightful lemony tomato sauce. The dish would follow well a cold yogurt soup, such as Apple-Yogurt Soup.

PREPARATION TIMES: 45 minutes kitchen work
                   1 hour simmering

YIELD: 4 servings

3 cups water
½ teaspoon salt
1 cup brown rice
12 cabbage leaves
1 onion, chopped
2 tablespoons vegetable oil
½ cup roasted soy nuts (snack food available in supermarkets and health food stores)
1 teaspoon caraway seeds
¼ cup raisins
1 6-ounce can tomato paste
¾ cup water
1 tablespoon brown sugar
2 tablespoons lemon juice

1. Bring the 3 cups of water and the salt to a boil in a heavy saucepan. Add the rice. Lower the heat, cover, and simmer 45 minutes, or until the liquid is absorbed.

2. Meanwhile, parboil the cabbage leaves until they are pliable. You may do this in one of two ways: either boil the whole cabbage in water to cover, peeling off the outer leaves as they become soft (use any leftover cabbage for another dish). Or you may peel off 12 leaves from the raw head of cabbage and cook them in a large pot of boiling water until they wilt. Dry the leaves with paper towels and spread them out.

3. In a small skillet, sauté the onion in oil until it is tender. Add the contents of the skillet to the cooked rice, along with the soy nuts, caraway seeds, and raisins. Divide this mixture among the cabbage leaves. Roll each leaf up, and place the rolls in a single layer in a large skillet.

4. Mix together the tomato paste, ¾ cup water, brown sugar, and lemon juice. Pour over the cabbage rolls. Cover the skillet and simmer 15 minutes.

CALIFORNIA RICE CASSEROLE

Chilies help give this rice dish a refreshing zing, while tomatoes and melted Cheddar cheese add to its marvelous flavor. While the dish is nutritious enough to serve as a main course, most people would probably prefer using it as a hearty vegetable accompaniment with Carrot-Cashew Patties or Soy Granule Loaf or any other entrée that goes well with rice.

PREPARATION TIMES: 30 minutes kitchen work
45 minutes simmering
30 minutes baking

YIELD: 8 servings as a vegetable side dish

3 cups water
½ teaspoon salt
1 cup brown rice
1 28-ounce can tomatoes, drained and chopped (reserve liquid)
1 4-ounce can chopped mild green chilies
1 onion, chopped

2 tablespoons butter or unsaturated margarine
2 tablespoons unbleached white flour
1 cup milk
⅛ teaspoon pepper
1½ cups shredded Cheddar cheese

1. Bring the water and salt to a boil in a heavy saucepan. Add the rice. Lower the heat, cover, and simmer 45 minutes, or until the liquid is absorbed. Stir in the tomatoes and chilies.

2. Meanwhile, in another heavy saucepan, sauté the onion in butter or margarine until tender. Stir in the flour and cook, stirring, 2 minutes. Add the milk, reserved tomato liquid, and pepper. Cook, stirring with a wire whisk, until it just comes to the boil. Stir into the rice mixture.

3. Turn the rice mixture into a greased 9″ × 13″ baking pan and sprinkle with the Cheddar cheese. Bake in a 350-degree oven 30 minutes.

RICE AND SQUASH PIE

This easily prepared casserole combines brown rice with summer squash, herbs, and Parmesan cheese in a melange that's distinctly Italian in character. The "pie" makes a delightful main course in the summer and goes well with sliced tomatoes.

PREPARATION TIMES: 20 minutes kitchen work
45 minutes simmering
30 minutes baking

YIELD: 4 servings

1½ cups water
½ teaspoon salt
½ cup brown rice
1 small red onion, chopped
(about ½ cup)
1 clove garlic, minced
1 tablespoon vegetable oil
4 yellow summer squash, diced

½ teaspoon oregano
¼ teaspoon thyme
⅛ teaspoon pepper
3 eggs, beaten
⅓ cup plus 2 tablespoons
Parmesan cheese, divided
usage

1. In a heavy saucepan, bring the water and salt to a boil. Add the rice. Lower the heat and simmer, covered, 45 minutes, or until the rice is tender and the liquid absorbed.

2. Meanwhile, in a large skillet, sauté the onion and garlic in oil until softened. Add the squash and seasonings. Cook, stirring, 5 minutes, or until the squash is just tender. Remove from the heat.

3. Stir in the rice, beaten eggs, and ⅓ cup Parmesan cheese. Turn the mixture into a greased 8-inch pie plate and sprinkle with the 2 tablespoons Parmesan cheese.

4. Bake the pie in a 350-degree oven 25 to 30 minutes or until set and browned.

ZUCCHINI AND BROWN RICE CASSEROLE

This delicious vegetable casserole could be turned into a main course dish by the addition of more cheese. As is, it's a fine accompaniment to another entrée, such as Cottage Cheese–Lentil Casserole. It's always a good and economical idea, of course, to use the oven for double duty; in this instance, two complementary casseroles.

PREPARATION TIMES: 30 minutes kitchen work
                   45 minutes simmering
                   1 hour baking

YIELD: 8 servings

2 cups water
½ teaspoon salt
⅔ cup brown rice
1 onion, chopped
1 tablespoon vegetable oil
1 potato, unpeeled and diced
1 carrot, sliced
3 medium zucchini (about 1

    pound), shredded coarsely
1 green pepper, diced
⅛ teaspoon pepper
½ teaspoon thyme
3 eggs, beaten
¾ cup shredded mozzarella
    cheese

1. In a heavy saucepan, bring the water and salt to a boil. Add the rice. Lower the heat and simmer, covered, until the liquid is absorbed and the rice tender, about 45 minutes.

2. Meanwhile, in a small skillet, sauté the onion in oil until tender.

3. Place the potato and carrot in a saucepan. Cover with water. Boil, covered, until tender and then drain.

4. In a large bowl, toss together all ingredients. Turn into a greased 2-quart round casserole. Bake in a 350-degree oven 1 hour, or until browned on top and set.

SHERRIED MUSHROOM-RICE RING

Rice rings are customarily unmolded and filled with a well-sauced dish, such as creamed onions or eggs. Curried Eggs with Onions (from the Eggs chapter) are really a perfect accompaniment, with the sherry and mushroom flavors complementing the fragrant curry seasonings. If you've become bored with rather insipid rings made with white rice, you'll find this version a welcome change, with more body and a hearty taste.

PREPARATION TIMES: 30 minutes kitchen work
                   45 minutes simmering
                   30 minutes baking

YIELD: 6 servings

3 cups water
½ teaspoon salt
1 cup brown rice
½ pound mushrooms, sliced
2 tablespoons butter or

unsaturated margarine
2 tablespoons water
2 tablespoons dry sherry
⅛ teaspoon pepper

1. Bring the 3 cups water and salt to a boil in a heavy saucepan. Add the rice. Lower the heat, cover, and simmer 45 minutes, or until the rice is tender and the liquid absorbed.

2. Meanwhile, in a medium skillet, sauté the mushrooms in butter or margarine until softened. Stir in the 2 tablespoons water, sherry, and pepper. Stir the contents of the skillet into the rice.

3. Turn the rice mixture into a greased ring mold and set it in a pan containing 1 inch of hot water. Bake in a 350-degree oven 30 minutes.

4. To serve, invert the ring onto a warmed plate.

RICE SALAD

In winter, when leafy greens are so expensive and when hearty meals are welcome, a salad such as this is ideal. The rice is seasoned with an oil-and-vinegar dressing and enhanced with raisins, almonds, and parsley.

PREPARATION TIMES: 15 minutes kitchen work
                   45 minutes simmering
                   30 minutes drying the rice
                   2 or more hours chilling

YIELD: 6 servings

3 cups water
½ teaspoon salt
1 cup brown rice
¼ cup vegetable oil
3 tablespoons red wine
  vinegar

⅛ teaspoon pepper
¼ teaspoon cinnamon
½ cup raisins
½ cup slivered almonds
¼ cup minced fresh parsley

1. In a saucepan, bring the water and salt to a boil. Add the rice. Reduce the heat, cover, and simmer 45 minutes, or until the rice is tender. Drain any excess liquid, and spread the rice out on a large platter. Allow to dry about 30 minutes.

2. In a large bowl, mix the oil, vinegar, pepper, and cinnamon. Add the rice, raisins, almonds, and parsley, and toss well. Refrigerate until well chilled.

RICE-STUFFED PUMPKIN

Entertain with this marvelous, showy dish of Armenian origin. The pumpkin is stuffed with a spiced, fruited rice mixture and then baked until browned and tender. It's great for serving to guests because the whole stuffed pumpkin looks so dramatic.

PREPARATION TIMES: 20 minutes kitchen work
20 minutes simmering
1½ hours baking

YIELD: 4 servings (with leftover pumpkin)

⅔ cup brown rice
1 4-pound pumpkin, hollowed out and rinsed
1 teaspoon salt, divided usage
1 teaspoon cinnamon, divided

usage
¼ cup raisins
½ cup chopped dried peaches
1 apple, peeled, cored, and chopped

1. Place the rice in a saucepan. Add boiling water to cover by 2 inches. Cook, covered, 20 minutes and then drain (the rice will not be fully cooked).

2. Season the inside of the pumpkin with ½ teaspoon each salt and cinnamon.

3. Mix the half-cooked rice with the remaining salt and cinnamon and the fruits. Stuff into the pumpkin. Replace the top of the pumpkin and place it on a greased baking sheet.

4. Bake the pumpkin 1½ hours in a 350-degree oven, or until very tender. To serve, bring the stuffed pumpkin, as is, to the table. Serve each guest a portion of the rice filling. Any extra may then be scooped into a serving bowl. Then either cut the pumpkin into wedges for each serving, or simply spoon out a portion of the pulp onto each plate.

Note: There may be leftover pumpkin. Scrape it from the skin, mash it, and season it to taste with salt, pepper, cinnamon, ginger, and cloves. On another night, reheat it gently, either in a saucepan or oven, and serve as a vegetable. Or, you may leave the pumpkin unseasoned for other recipes.

7
Millet

Until I started my adventure into natural foods, I had never tasted millet. Nor had I any particular desire to do so. It was one of those foodstuffs that I knew of by name only. I think many others feel a similar hesitancy to try a food that is so unfamiliar to them that they don't even know what it looks like. Friends who were delighted to sample cream puffs I was practicing on for a cooking class or pumpkin pies I was judging for a recipe contest showed no similar eagerness to try my millet casseroles. Fortunately for me, since I had bought a large bag of it, millet tastes very good. The seeds start out as tiny, round, pale yellow balls, almost like light-colored mustard seeds. When it is cooked, the result is fluffy and chewy, a cross between brown rice and barley.

Millet is very much like rice, in fact. Except that it absorbs more liquid than rice, it is cooked in much the same way. It may be boiled, sautéed and then simmered as in a pilaf, or combined with other ingredients in a casserole. When cooked with milk and then sweetened, millet makes a delicious dessert pudding.

Because millet absorbs more liquid than rice, a cup of it cooked has fewer calories (327 for millet versus 677 for rice). A cup of cooked millet contains 9.9 grams of protein and 2.9 grams of fat. It's also high in thiamin, riboflavin, niacin, calcium, iron, and phosphorus.

Millet is deficient only in lysine, making it a nearly complete protein food. To add extra lysine through combining foods, eat millet in conjunction with dairy products (or meats, fish, or poultry), beans of all types, tofu (soybean curd), pumpkin or squash seeds, cashew or pistachio nuts, wheat germ or bran, soy flour, green peas, brussels sprouts, broccoli, mushrooms, asparagus, cauliflower, collard, spinach, turnip or mustard greens, potatoes, okra, or Swiss chard. As you can see, when a vegetable lacks only one essential amino acid, many foods are available to complement it and thus produce a highly nutritious, complete protein food.

So, if you have never sampled millet and are looking for a new food with which to occasionally replace rice or want a different tasting main course, try one of these recipes.

BASIC COOKED MILLET

Here is a plain millet recipe that goes well with many main course dishes.

PREPARATION TIMES: 5 minutes kitchen work
                   30 minutes simmering
YIELD: 4 servings

½ cup millet   1½ cups water   ½ teaspoon salt

Place all ingredients in a saucepan. Cover and cook over a low heat 30 minutes.

MILLET WITH MIXED VEGETABLES

This lovely side dish combines millet and a variety of vegetables that blend together well, yet remain as distinct tastes. An omelette, along with a wedge of cheese, would delightfully complete the meal.

PREPARATION TIMES: 15 minutes kitchen work
                   45 minutes simmering

YIELD: 4 servings

2 carrots, sliced   ¼ cup minced fresh parsley
1 onion, chopped   ½ cup millet
1 potato, unpeeled, diced   1 teaspoon salt
1 cup chopped yellow turnip   2½ cups water
1 cup shredded cabbage

Place all ingredients in a heavy pot. Bring to a boil. Then cover, reduce heat, and simmer 45 minutes.

MILLET PUDDING

Similar in taste to rice pudding but with a different texture, Millet Pudding is pleasantly chewy rather than creamy.

PREPARATION TIMES: 30 minutes kitchen work
                   1¼ hours simmering
                   2 hours or more chilling the pudding

YIELD: 6 servings

2 cups milk, divided usage   1 tablespoon whole wheat
¼ cup millet   flour
2 eggs, beaten   ½ cup raisins
¼ cup molasses

1. Scald 1½ cups of milk in the top part of a double boiler, directly on the heat. Stir the millet into the remaining ½ cup of milk, and then stir this into the hot milk.

2. Place the milk and millet, covered, over the bottom part of the double boiler, which has been filled with water. Cook 45 minutes, stirring occasionally.

3. Beat together the remaining ingredients. Add about ¼ cup of hot millet mixture to the egg mixture and beat it in. Then pour the egg mixture back into the millet. Cook over hot water for about 20 minutes longer, or until thickened. Transfer to a serving dish and chill.

MILLET CASSEROLE

Hearty and nourishing, this casserole could easily serve as a main course. The flavor is quite similar to a wheaty version of Spanish rice.

PREPARATION TIMES: 30 minutes kitchen work
30 minutes simmering
45 minutes baking

YIELD: 8 servings

2 onions, chopped
1 clove garlic, minced
2 tablespoons vegetable oil
1 cup millet
4 cups water
1 teaspoon salt
2 cups tomato puree

2 cups wheat germ
1 teaspoon marjoram
¼ cup minced fresh parsley
½ teaspoon celery seeds
1½ cups cubed Cheddar
   cheese

1. In a small skillet, sauté the onions and garlic in oil until the onions are tender.

2. Meanwhile, bring the millet, water, and salt to a boil. Lower the heat, cover, and simmer 30 minutes.

3. Mix together all the ingredients, including the contents of the skillet and the millet. Turn into a greased 1½-quart casserole dish. Cover and bake in a 350-degree oven 30 minutes. Uncover and bake 15 minutes longer.

8
Whole Wheat Berries and Cracked Wheat

For years, whole wheat flour could only be found at special health food stores. Despite the fact that it is so much more nutritious than white flour (see the chapter on Soy Flour for a comparison), the housewives of this country had been brainwashed by advertising into wanting bleached white flour and so were not demanding the whole wheat.

During the last few years, however, there has been a trend toward more health-conscious eating; and the major flour manufacturers now market whole wheat flour in five-pound bags. Some companies depict on the back of the packages, for novices, just what whole wheat flour is. The picture shows a large, round oval called the endosperm, which is turned into white flour. Surrounding this is a fibrous coating of bran, and at the bottom of the oval is the sprouting portion, which we know as wheat germ. These three parts are ground together to make whole wheat flour.

Perhaps because this picture is so greatly magnified and because bran is so rough and fibrous, it is quite surprising to see the whole wheat berries (the diagram on the flour bags) in real life. Scaled down to true size, these berries are tiny, only about ⅛-inch long, very smooth and shiny, and extremely hard.

Unfortunately, the whole wheat berry requires quite a bit of grinding to turn it into bran, flour, and wheat germ. If we choose to purchase the intact berries, we must make do with the hard and extraordinarily chewy kernel that even long periods of soaking and cooking will not much alter.

Cracked wheat, on the other hand, softens far more easily. Although it is merely the whole wheat berry cut into fairly small pieces, the inner endosperm is exposed and thus responds to heat very quickly. In fact, soaking the grain in boiling water alone is sufficient to "cook" the cracked wheat enough for use in chewy, unusual salads. Bulgar is cracked wheat that has been partially cooked before grinding and so becomes tender even more quickly than cracked wheat. For all practical purposes, though, cracked wheat and bulgar may be used interchangeably in recipes.

Nutritionally, whole wheat berries, cracked wheat, and bulgar are almost identical and supply a goodly amount of protein, fiber, calcium, phosphorus, iron, potassium, magnesium, and niacin. They, like rice, are deficient in isoleucine and lysine. (Refer to the chapter on Brown Rice for details of combining foods.)

Following are several recipes that utilize whole wheat berries, both whole and in the cracked form. I prefer the latter. But if you are one who loves to chew, you may very well become addicted to the unground berries. Either way, the resulting dishes are hearty and nutritious; and all have a wholesome, wheaty flavor.

BERRY, BRAN, AND MILLET STEW

I first concocted this stew to use up some leftover grains I had on my pantry shelf and was delighted by the result. The cooked grains make for a wonderfully thick and flavorful broth. Serve the soup as a hearty first course on a cold night, or for lunch with warm rolls and a tossed salad.

PREPARATION TIMES: overnight soaking of wheat berries
                           20 minutes kitchen work
                           3 hours simmering

YIELD: 4 servings

½ cup whole wheat berries, soaked overnight in water to cover
½ cup barley
½ cup millet
2 carrots, sliced
1 1-pound can tomatoes, chopped and undrained
1 large onion, chopped (about 1 cup)
1 clove garlic, minced
1½ cups coarsely chopped rutabaga
2 stalks celery, sliced
½ cup minced fresh parsley
2 teaspoons salt
4 peppercorns
2 cloves
water

Place all the ingredients in a large pot, fully covering them with water. Bring to a boil. Reduce the heat, cover, and simmer for 3 hours. Check the pot occasionally and add more water if necessary (the grains will absorb quite a lot of liquid).

WHOLE WHEAT BERRY BREAD

Here is a special light whole wheat bread, filled with chewy wheat berries. It makes excellent sandwiches with any filling—egg, cheese, or peanut butter.

PREPARATION TIMES: 2 hours soaking berries
$1\frac{1}{4}$ hours kitchen work
2 hours rising
65 minutes baking

YIELD: 2 very large, high loaves

2 cups boiling water
$\frac{2}{3}$ cup whole wheat berries
2 packages active dry yeast
1 tablespoon honey
$\frac{1}{2}$ cup warm water
2 cups whole wheat flour

7 cups unbleached white flour or bread flour, divided usage
1 tablespoon salt
$1\frac{1}{2}$ cups milk
$1\frac{1}{2}$ cups warm water

1. Pour the boiling water over the whole wheat berries and let sit for 2 hours. Drain.

2. Stir the yeast and honey into the $\frac{1}{2}$ cup warm water. Let sit in a warm place until bubbles form at the top, about 10 minutes.

3. In a large bowl, stir together the whole wheat flour, 5 cups white flour, and the salt. Stir in the whole wheat berries, yeast mixture, milk, and $1\frac{1}{2}$ cups warm water.

4. Turn out onto a heavily floured surface and knead until smooth and elastic, adding more white flour as needed until this texture is reached.

5. Place the dough in a greased bowl and turn once so the greased surface is on top. Cover the bowl with plastic wrap and let sit in a warm place about 1 hour or until doubled in bulk.

6. Punch the dough down. Divide into 2 equal pieces. Knead each piece a bit and then form to fit into 2 greased 9″ × 5″ loaf pans. Let rise, covered, until doubled in bulk, about 1 hour.

7. Make 3 diagonal slashes on each loaf. Brush with water. Bake in a 400-degree oven about 1 hour, or until the tops sound hollow when tapped. Tip the loaves out onto a baking sheet and bake them upside down for 5 minutes longer. Cool on a rack before slicing.

WHOLE WHEAT BERRY-RAISIN MUFFINS

These rather non-sweet muffins make a good, nutritious snack, particularly when warm. Spread them with apple butter, honey, or jam to increase the sweetness and add extra flavor.

PREPARATION TIMES: 2 hours soaking berries
                         10 minutes kitchen work
                         25 minutes baking

YIELD: 1 dozen muffins

1 cup boiling water
¼ cup whole wheat berries
1 cup whole wheat flour
1 cup unbleached white flour
5 teaspoons baking powder
1 teaspoon salt
3 tablespoons butter or

unsaturated margarine, melted
1 egg, beaten
2 tablespoons honey
1 cup milk
½ cup raisins

1. Pour the boiling water over the berries. Let sit 2 hours or overnight. Drain.

2. In a large bowl, stir together the flours, baking powder, and salt.

3. In another bowl, stir together the melted butter, egg, honey, and milk. Stir these ingredients into the dry mixture, mixing only long enough to moisten them. Fold in the raisins.

4. Fill greased muffin tins three-quarters full. Bake in a 400-degree oven 20-25 minutes. If you can't eat them immediately, the muffins taste best if briefly reheated in a hot oven.

WHOLE WHEAT BERRY CUSTARD

This distinctive two-layered dessert contains a base of chewy wheat berries topped by a delicate orange and honey custard. It makes a highly nutritious finish to any family-style meal.

PREPARATION TIMES: 15 minutes kitchen work
30 minutes simmering
1½ hours baking
optional chilling of custard

YIELD: 6 servings

1½ cups water
¾ cup whole wheat berries
3 eggs, beaten
3 cups milk
1 cup raisins

¼ cup honey
grated rind from 1 orange
⅛ teaspoon salt
¼ teaspoon nutmeg

1. Bring the water to a boil. Stir in the whole wheat berries. Cover and cook over low heat for 30 minutes. Drain.

2. Mix the berries with the remaining ingredients and turn into a greased 2-quart casserole. Bake in a 325-degree oven 1½ hours or until set. Serve warm or cold.

Note: The berries may give off a bit of their cooking liquid which should simply be poured off the top of the custard before serving.

TABBOULEH

I first tasted Tabbouleh—a hearty, grainy salad—at a friend's house several years ago as part of a Middle Eastern buffet. I loved the salad, devoured mound after mound of it, and immediately demanded the recipe. Since then, Tabbouleh has become quite popular and well-known in this country, so much so that tabbouleh mixes are available at the supermarket. But don't be tempted by the quick preparation, for the dehydrated herbs have none of the fresh, perky character of the fresh.

Tabbouleh may be served as an appetizer with romaine lettuce leaves (just roll the tabbouleh up in the leaves and eat with your fingers) or as a combination salad-starch course with the main course.

PREPARATION TIMES: 1 hour soaking the wheat
15 minutes kitchen work
1 to 2 days chilling

YIELD: 4 to 6 servings

1 cup cracked wheat
¾ cup minced onion
½ cup minced green onion
1 teaspoon salt
¼ teaspoon pepper
1½ cups minced fresh parsley

up to ½ cup lemon juice
up to ¾ cup olive oil
2 tomatoes, peeled and
chopped (when needed as
garnish)

1. Cover the cracked wheat with hot water and allow to stand 1 hour. Drain and squeeze out the extra water.

2. Add the onions, salt, pepper, parsley, and half of the lemon juice and olive oil. Very slowly, add a little more each of the juice and oil, always waiting until they are absorbed before adding more. If you add too much, the oil will float unappetizingly on the salad.

3. Turn the tabbouleh into a serving dish and chill 24 to 48 hours. Before serving, garnish with the tomatoes.

SIMPLE CRACKED WHEAT SALAD

This is a plainer and less rich Middle Eastern salad than Tabbouleh, with less calorific oil. It is enhanced with black olives, cumin seeds, and mint. The salad makes an excellent accompaniment to eggplant dishes.

PREPARATION TIMES: 20 minutes kitchen work
2 or more hours chilling

YIELD: 8 servings

2 cups cracked wheat
1¼ cups very hot water
¼ cup olive oil
¾ teaspoon salt
15 black olives

¾ teaspoon cumin seeds
1 tablespoon fresh (or 1 teaspoon dried) mint, chopped or crushed

Pour the hot water and oil over the cracked wheat in a bowl. Let stand until the liquid is absorbed and the wheat has cooled. Stir in the remaining ingredients and refrigerate until well chilled.

CRACKED WHEAT BREAD

This wonderfully light loaf has a rich, wheaty taste. As it is quite plain, the bread is perfect for nearly any type of sandwich and also makes delicious toast.

PREPARATION TIMES: 50 minutes kitchen work
2½ hours rising
35 minutes baking

YIELD: 2 loaves

1½ cups water
½ cup cracked wheat
½ stick (4 tablespoons) butter or unsaturated margarine, softened
1 tablespoon salt
2 tablespoons molasses

2 tablespoons honey
1 package active dry yeast
pinch sugar
⅓ cup warm water
1 cup whole wheat flour
4 cups unbleached white flour or bread flour

1. In a large pot, bring the 1½ cups water to a boil. Add the cracked wheat and simmer, stirring occasionally, about 10 minutes, or until all the water is absorbed. Remove from the heat and stir in the butter or margarine, salt, molasses, and honey. Let sit until lukewarm.

2. Meanwhile, dissolve the yeast and sugar in ⅓ cup warm water. Let sit about 10 minutes, or until a foam forms on the surface. Stir this into the cracked wheat mixture.

3. Stir in the whole wheat flour and then the white flour, 1 cup at a time, until the dough is fairly stiff. Turn the dough out onto a well-floured surface and knead until smooth and elastic and no longer sticky, adding more flour as necessary.

4. Place the dough in an oiled bowl, and turn once so that the greased side faces up. Cover the bowl with plastic wrap and let the dough rise in a warm, draft-free spot until doubled in bulk, about 1½ hours.

5. Knead the dough a few minutes longer, and divide in half. Shape each half into a loaf and place each in a greased 9″ × 5″ loaf pan. Cover the pans and let rise until doubled in bulk, about 1 hour.

6. Bake the loaves in a 375-degree oven 30 minutes. Tip the bread out of the pans and bake upside down on a baking sheet 5 minutes longer, or until they are crisp and browned on the bottom. Transfer the bread to racks to cool before slicing.

9
Barley

Wheat and rice we consume in great quantities. It is rather surprising then that barley, one of the world's oldest cultivated grains, is now used mainly for feeding livestock and producing beer. Why has its popularity diminished? Probably, as wheat and rice became available, people began to appreciate their unique qualities in cooking and baking. Barley flour, lacking the glutenous properties of wheat, cannot make light breads and cakes or chewy pasta. Rather, breads made with barley flour turn out heavy and are hard to digest. When compared with rice, barley again is a second choice. Cooked simply in water, barley tends to become rather slippery, while cooked rice is dry and fluffy.

Barley does, however, have a place in our kitchens. With its pleasant, rather nutty flavor, it is a common addition to soups, where the moisture of the grains is of no consequence. And it also provides an occasional vacation from rice, pasta, and other commonly eaten starches.

The barley available in stores has generally been hulled, which means that its fibrous coating has been removed. The package may also say "pearl barley" which simply indicates that the grain has been further polished. Hulled and pearl barley may be used interchangeably in the recipes in this book.

Barley, like rice, is deficient in isoleucine and lysine. To balance this lack with foods high in these amino acids, refer to the chapter on Brown Rice for nutritious food combining.

Incidentally, of all the grains discussed in this section, wheat supplies the most protein per serving (4 grams protein per 1 ounce raw grain), while the others are quite similar to each other (about 2.5 grams per ounce).

POLISH BARLEY SOUP WITH YOGURT

I am very partial to this thick, nourishing soup with a tart creaminess from the yogurt. Serve the soup as an opener to dinner or as a main course with a good whole wheat bread and a chunk of cheese.

PREPARATION TIMES: 15 minutes kitchen work
2 hours simmering

YIELD: 4 to 6 servings

2 carrots, sliced
2 onions, chopped
2 tablespoons minced fresh
   parsley
1 cup sliced mushrooms
3 potatoes, peeled and diced

½ cup barley
2 teaspoons salt
6 peppercorns
6 cups water
1 cup yogurt

1. Place all the ingredients except the yogurt in a large pot. Bring to a boil. Then reduce the heat, cover, and simmer 2 hours.

2. Just before serving, stir in the yogurt and gently heat through.

MUSHROOM, BARLEY, AND EGG CASSEROLE

The combination of mushrooms and barley has become a classic, particularly in soups. Here's a casserole that mixes these two popular ingredients with hard-cooked eggs in a creamy sauce. It's the sort of dish that is often served over toast or English muffins, although it is also fine plain on the plate accompanied by a green vegetable.

PREPARATION TIMES: 25 minutes kitchen work
                   15 minutes simmering
                   30 minutes baking

YIELD: 4 servings

¼ cup barley
2 cups boiling water
1 onion, chopped
12 ounces mushrooms, sliced
4 tablespoons butter or
   unsaturated margarine,
   divided usage
2 tablespoons flour

2 cups milk
¼ cup grated Parmesan
   cheese
3 hard-cooked eggs, coarsely
   chopped
1 teaspoon salt
¼ teaspoon pepper

1. Slowly stir the barley into the boiling water. Boil, uncovered, for 15 minutes. Drain.

2. In a skillet, sauté the onion and mushrooms in 2 tablespoons of the butter or margarine until they are softened.

3. Melt the remaining 2 tablespoons of butter or margarine in a large, heavy saucepan. Stir in the flour and cook, stirring, for 2 minutes. Add the milk, and cook, stirring with a wire whisk, until just at the boiling point. Stir in the Parmesan cheese, chopped hard-cooked eggs, barley, contents of skillet, salt, and pepper.

4. Turn the barley mixture into a greased 2-quart casserole. Bake in a 350-degree oven 30 minutes.

BARLEY WITH LENTILS

In this dish, the soy flour coats the barley grains, making them lose their slippery texture, and also adds a nutty taste. The pleasant flavor of rosemary is predominant.

PREPARATION TIMES: 20 minutes kitchen work
40 minutes simmering

YIELD: 6 servings

1 onion, chopped
2 tablespoons vegetable oil
½ cup barley
½ cup lentils
¼ cup soy flour

2½ cups boiling water
1 teaspoon salt
3 tablespoons minced fresh
  parsley
1 teaspoon rosemary

In a large, heavy saucepan, sauté the onion in oil until it is softened. Add the remaining ingredients. Stir briefly. Cover and simmer 40 minutes or until the liquid has been absorbed and the barley and lentils are tender.

BARLEY WITH TOASTED ALMONDS AND RAISINS

This is one of those sweetish grain dishes common to Middle Eastern cookery. I enjoy it served with pita bread that's been filled with a green salad and drizzled with tahini (sesame seed paste available in Middle Eastern groceries, health food stores, and many supermarkets). A dish of yogurt on the side completes the meal.

PREPARATION TIMES: 15 minutes kitchen work
                    35 minutes simmering

YIELD: 3 to 4 servings

1½ cups water
½ teaspoon salt
½ cup barley
1 onion, chopped
1 clove garlic, pressed
2 tablespoons vegetable oil

¼ cup raisins
¼ cup slivered almonds, toasted in an ungreased skillet
⅛ teaspoon pepper

1. Heat the water and salt in a saucepan to boiling. Stir in the barley. Cover and cook 35 minutes. Drain, reserving ¼ cup cooking liquid.

2. Sauté the onion and garlic in oil until the onion is softened. Stir in the barley, raisins, almonds, pepper, and reserved liquid. Cook briefly to heat through.

10
Oats

Many of us, in recent years, have gradually developed real reservations about processed foods. Thus, we shy away from canned and frozen fruits and vegetables, prefer to bake our own breads and cakes, and eat "convenience" foods only when we absolutely need their convenience.

There are some foods, however, that I have regarded as one step below convenience, these falling into the category of "instant." I avoided Minute rice, mashed potato flakes, and instant oatmeal. I also seldom purchased quick-cooking oats, under the assumption that something had been removed as part of their processing.

However, in recent researching, I have discovered several surprising (to me, at least) facts. First, the old-fashioned and the quick-cooking oatmeals are almost identical. The only difference is that for old-fashioned oatmeal, the oat groat is used intact, while for the quick-cooking oatmeal it is cut into several pieces before rolling. As a representative of the Quaker Oats Company informed me, "It's like cutting a potato into several pieces before cooking to make it cook more quickly." Thus, the nutritive values of both types of oatmeal are the same.

Instant oatmeal, which is very thoroughly processed, has added to it synthetically produced nutrients, which makes this form of oatmeal considerably more nutritious, not less! While a single serving of old-fashioned or quick-cooking oats supplies only 6 percent of our daily protein needs and 10 percent of our requirements for thiamine, iron, and phosphorus, instant oats (unsweetened variety) supply between 10 and 25 percent of most of the vitamins and minerals we need in a day.

Oatmeal also contains pectin, about .3 gram in a single serving of old-fashioned, quick-cooking, *and* instant oats. Preliminary studies have shown pectin to reduce cholesterol levels in people and animals. (See chapter on Bran for more about fiber.)

In cooking or baking, regular or quick rolled oats work best, for they have the texture necessary to give oatmeal cookies and breads their characteristic chewiness. But for breakfast oatmeal, it is certainly not necessary to abolish the instant form from your staples. Be advised, however, that you are paying for the processing and added nutrients, because the instant costs considerably more than plain rolled oats.

A Word about Cake Baking

Since this is the first chapter of the book with a cake recipe, it seems appropriate to include here some notes on cake baking (the rules, incidentally, are similar for cookies and "quick" breads). Many people believe that making a cake is a difficult feat and so resort to mixes or ready-made cakes, nearly all of which are terrible products. Containing all white flour, too much sugar, hydrogenated fats, artificial flavors, and so much leavening that they puff into airy, tasteless masses, store-bought cakes bear little resemblance to homemade. And they are also usually piled with a mound of sickeningly sugary icing. Most are products that well deserve the "empty calories" label. When you make your own cakes, you know what ingredients go into them—whole grains, dried fruits, nuts, seeds, and fresh fruits. A good, well-flavored cake really needs no ornamental frosting.

I often come across cake recipes that direct the cook to place all the ingredients in a bowl and beat well. This is *not* the way to make a good cake. The butter will not be combined well enough with the sugar, while the flour will be overbeaten. The main rule to remember when baking a cake is to beat the liquid ingredients very well, and handle the dry ingredients as little as possible.

Most recipes call for butter (or margarine), which should be softened so that the sugar can be thoroughly incorporated. The beating of sugar into the butter is generally the first step in making a cake. When done, the mixture should be of a uniform consistency and very soft. The eggs are beaten in next, and again this must be done very well. (Some recipes direct you to separate the eggs, folding the stiffly beaten egg whites into the batter last. This produces a light, fine-textured cake. While this step is essential for certain types of cakes, particularly tortes, for the ordinary cake it is usually unnecessary.) At this point, other wet ingredients such as vanilla, cooked pumpkin, melted chocolate, or mashed bananas, are generally added.

In another bowl, the dry ingredients are stirred together. Unless the cake is very delicate, or the dry ingredients are lumpy, it is not necessary to sift them. These are beaten into the butter mixture, either all at once, or alternately with a liquid, such as water or milk. The idea is to beat in the flour as quickly as possible and to stop beating as soon as all the dry ingredients are completely moistened. Finally, any hard extras, such as raisins, nuts, chocolate chips, or apple pieces are stirred into the batter.

The batter is turned into a greased and floured pan and baked until a toothpick inserted in the center comes out clean. Let the baked cake cool on a rack until it has nearly come to room temperature. Run a knife around the edge to loosen it, and carefully tip the cake out onto a serving dish. (Or you may, of course, serve the cake directly from the baking pan.)

A second major type of cake, calling for liquid shortening (oil, melted butter or margarine), requires a slightly different procedure. First the eggs are beaten very well. Then the sugar is added gradually, beating all the while. When done, the mixture will be thick and pale yellow. This thorough beating is essential in achieving the desired chewy texture of brownies and other cakes following this rule. After this step, the liquid shortening is added, and the rest of the directions are as for the first type of cake just described.

Since fats play so predominant a role in baking, it is important to discuss the issue of butter versus margarine versus oil. Few nutritionists would question the fact that cold-pressed, unsaturated oils are far better for our bodies than cholesterol-containing butter. Cholesterol and other saturated fats have been implicated as a causative or exacerbating factor in the onset of heart and other disorders. In much cooking, oil does work beautifully. For sautéing vegetables or when baking breads that require only small amounts of shortening, oil is ideal. But few cakes taste good when made with oil. The texture is greasier, and a bite leaves an unpleasant, oily aftertaste. The flavor and consistency of butter is essential to most cakes.

An alternative to high cholesterol butter is the use of polyunsaturated margarine. When margarine was first developed as a cheap substitute for butter, it was high in saturated fats, containing such substances as lard and palm and coconut oils. Even today, the less expensive margarines are based on these oils and should be avoided. But polyunsaturated margarines, containing such oils as corn and safflower, though nearly as costly as butter, do have a lower saturated fat content. To be certain of what you are purchasing, check the label: a good quality margarine should contain at least twice the amount of polyunsaturated fats as saturated.

To discuss margarine in this manner does not, however, present the entire story. In order for margarine to be made hard and firm, some oil, even if it is unsaturated to begin with, must undergo hydrogenation. This turns the oil into a solid and also makes it saturated. (In case you are unfamiliar with the meaning of saturated, it is essentially the adding of hydrogen atoms onto the carbon atoms in oil. The more the carbon has become "saturated" with hydrogen, the worse it is supposed to be for our bodies.) This new saturated fat has a molecular structure unlike any found in nature, a fact that causes many who espouse natural foods to avoid margarine. Too, margarines contain a variety of preservatives, antioxidants, and artificial flavors. Butter, on the other hand, is colored only with annatto or carotene, two very common natural vegetable dyes.

What is the solution then? Make baked foods that are less tasty with a pure oil? That is one option. Another is to use butter, but use it sparingly because of its cholesterol content. Cakes, cookies, and other goodies contain, in addition to fats, plenty of sugar. They should be regarded as special treats, not as foods to be gobbled by the handful. Or finally, you may choose to use a high quality margarine. However, in exchange for obtaining much of the flavor and texture of butter, with less saturated fat, you will necessarily be forced to consume a variety of chemical additives.

My recipes specify "butter or unsaturated margarine" when that is the taste required for the dish to turn out best. I have presented the facts as I see them. There are no simple solutions; we must always weigh a desired flavor in a balance with good health. You must decide which fat is the one best for you

OAT CRACKERS

These homemade crackers are thin, delicate, and quite crisp. As they are mild in flavor, don't serve them with a too highly seasoned dip. An herbed cheese spread would go well. The crackers also make great snacks even unadorned.

PREPARATION TIMES: 20 minutes kitchen work
20 minutes baking

YIELD: about 70 crackers

1½ cups rolled oats	2 tablespoons honey
1 tablespoon vegetable oil	¾ cup hot water
¾ teaspoon salt	¼ cup whole wheat flour

1. In a bowl, stir together the oats, oil, salt, honey, and hot water. Let sit 10 minutes. Stir in the whole wheat flour.

2. Grease 11" × 16" jelly roll pan. Place the dough on it, and roll out, using a floured rolling pin or plain drinking glass, to ⅛-inch thick. Cut into 1½-inch squares. Bake in a 350-degree oven about 20 minutes or until crisp and pale brown.

FRUIT AND NUT, HOT OR COLD CEREAL

Many feel that breakfast is the most important meal of the day; and for those who want to start off the morning well, a hearty cereal makes an excellent choice. My version is highly nutritious, supplying protein, fats, sugars, and all vitamins, except vitamin C. It's so good for you, in fact, you could probably live on this cereal alone, if you occasionally ate an orange or two.

The cereal has other advantages. It is nearly as sweet as the "natural food" cereals on the market but contains no added sugar or honey: the sweetness is obtained from the dried fruits. Also, as it contains dry milk powder, you need add only water. Add boiling water, and you have a mixture similar to oatmeal, but much chewier. With cold water, you have a great bowl of cold cereal.

Needless to say, the cereal is ideal for camping trips. I also take it along with me, plus a couple of bowls, when staying at a motel. It's amazing how much money you can save on a trip just by eating breakfasts in the motel room instead of in a restaurant.

PREPARATION TIME: 10 minutes kitchen work

YIELD: 2 quarts, or 10 servings

1½ cups quick-cooking rolled oats
1 cup wheat flake cold cereal (such as Wheaties)
1½ cups dry milk powder
¾ cup wheat germ, preferably raw
¼ cup each: dark raisins, golden raisins, chopped dates, and diced dried peaches or apricots
⅓ cup unsalted sunflower seeds
⅓ cup chopped walnuts or slivered almonds

Simply mix all ingredients in a large container. Store in the refrigerator.

PINEAPPLE-ALMOND SNACK

A cross between a bar cookie and a granola bar, this Pineapple-Almond Snack is highly nutritious, thanks to the nuts, whole wheat flour, oats, bran, and raisins it contains. Note that it has no added sugar, all the sweetness being derived from the pineapple and raisins. A bar of the "cake" makes ideal fare for breakfast for those who dote on rather sweet, hearty goodies to munch with morning coffee or milk. It is also an especially healthful after-school treat for youngsters. The bars are best kept refrigerated; this protects from spoilage and also makes them exceptionally chewy.

PREPARATION TIMES: 20 minutes kitchen work
                    1 hour baking

YIELD: 12 bars

1 cup whole wheat flour	1½ cups crushed, juice-packed canned pineapple, drained
½ teaspoon salt	
¾ cup rolled oats	
¼ cup All-bran cereal	½ cup raisins
1 stick (½ cup) butter or unsaturated margarine, melted	¼ cup chopped walnuts
	¼ cup slivered almonds, toasted in an ungreased skillet until golden
1 teaspoon vanilla	
1 egg, beaten	

1. In a bowl, stir together the flour, salt, oats, and All-bran.

2. In another bowl, mix well the melted butter or margarine, vanilla, egg, and pineapple. Add the dry ingredients and mix until moistened. Stir in the raisins and nuts.

3. Spread the batter evenly in a greased and floured 8″ × 8″ baking pan. Bake in a 350-degree oven 1 hour, or until browned on top (it will still be a little moist if tested with a toothpick).

4. Let cool on a rack. Then cut into bars and chill.

MOLASSES OATMEAL BREAD

A lovely, chewy bread, well flavored with oats and molasses, this makes great eating just plain, as a between-meal snack or with dinner. It is also a fine bread for sandwiches or toast.

PREPARATION TIMES: 50 minutes kitchen work
                   1 hour 35 minutes rising
                   40 minutes baking

YIELD: 2 loaves

2 cups boiling water
2 cups rolled oats
2 teaspoons salt
⅓ cup molasses
1 tablespoon vegetable oil
2 packages active dry yeast

pinch sugar
½ cup warm water
2 cups whole wheat flour
about 2½ cups unbleached
    white flour or bread flour

1. In a large mixing bowl, pour the boiling water over the oats. Stir in the salt, molasses, and oil. Let sit until lukewarm.

2. Meanwhile, dissolve the yeast and sugar in the warm water. Let sit about 10 minutes, or until a foam forms on the surface. Then stir into the oat mixture. Add the flour, 1 cup at a time, beginning with the whole wheat, until the dough is stiff.

3. Turn the dough out onto a floured surface and knead until smooth, elastic, and no longer sticky, adding more flour as needed. Place in a greased bowl, and turn once so that the greased side faces up. Cover the bowl with plastic wrap and let sit in a warm, draft-free spot until doubled in bulk, about 1 hour.

4. Knead the dough a few minutes longer. Divide in half. Shape each half into a loaf and place in a greased 9″ × 5″ baking pan. Cover and let rise again until doubled in bulk, about 35 minutes.

5. Bake the loaves in a 375-degree oven 35 minutes. Tip out onto a baking sheet and bake upside down 5 minutes longer, or until the bottoms are crisp and browned. Let cool thoroughly on a rack before slicing.

RAISIN AND NUT OATMEAL BREAD

This slightly sweet, well-textured loaf that's flecked with raisins and pecans is ideal for cheese or peanut butter sandwiches. It also makes a satisfying between-meal snack.

PREPARATION TIMES: 1 hour kitchen work
2 hours rising
30 minutes baking

YIELD: 2 loaves

1½ cups milk
¼ cup dark brown sugar
1 tablespoon salt
3 tablespoons butter or
  unsaturated margarine,
  softened
2 packages active dry yeast
pinch sugar

½ cup warm water
2 cups rolled oats
½ cup golden raisins
½ cup chopped pecans
2 cups whole wheat flour
2½ to 3 cups unbleached
  white flour or bread flour
about ¼ cup sesame seeds

1. In a large pot, scald the milk. Remove from heat and add the brown sugar, salt, and butter or margarine. Let sit until lukewarm.

2. Meanwhile, dissolve the yeast and sugar in the warm water. Let sit 10 minutes, or until a foam forms on the surface. Add the yeast, oats, raisins, and pecans to the milk. Add the flour, 1 cup at a time, beginning with the whole wheat, until the dough is stiff.

3. Turn the dough out onto a floured surface and knead until smooth, elastic, and no longer sticky, adding more flour as needed. Place in a greased bowl, and turn once so that the greased side faces up. Cover the bowl with plastic wrap and let sit in a warm, draft-free spot until doubled in bulk, about 1 hour.

4. Knead the dough a few minutes longer. Divide in half. Shape each half into a loaf and place in a greased 9" × 5" loaf pan. Cover and let rise until doubled in bulk, about 1 hour.

5. Brush the top of each loaf with water and sprinkle with sesame

seeds. Bake in a 400-degree oven 25 minutes. Tip out onto a baking sheet and bake upside down 5 minutes longer, or until the bottoms are crisp and browned. Let cool thoroughly on a rack before slicing.

OATMEAL RAISIN MUFFINS

Extremely light muffins, these display a golden color and a delicate molasses flavor. They are rather crumbly; so serve them plain, preferably hot from the oven.

PREPARATION TIMES: 10 minutes kitchen work
25 minutes baking

YIELD: 1 dozen muffins

1 cup unbleached white flour
¼ cup sugar
1½ teaspoons baking powder
1 teaspoon salt
½ teaspoon baking soda
1⅓ cups rolled oats
1 teaspoon lemon juice plus

enough milk to make 1 cup liquid
½ stick (4 tablespoons) butter
or unsaturated margarine,
melted
¼ cup molasses *maple syrup*
1 egg, beaten
¾ cup golden raisins
½ " dark "

1. In a large bowl, stir together the dry ingredients.

2. In another bowl, stir together the lemon-milk mixture, melted butter or margarine, molasses, and egg. Stir these liquid ingredients into the dry ones, mixing only until the dry ones are moistened. Stir in the raisins.

3. Pour the batter into greased or paper-lined muffin tins, filling each about ¾ full. Bake in a 400-degree oven 25 minutes.

APPLESAUCE-OATMEAL BREAD

I have seldom sampled a moister quick bread. This has a wonderful spicy flavor and is sweet enough to be eaten as a cake with tea. It can also be used to make marvelous cream cheese sandwiches for a special picnic lunch.

PREPARATION TIMES: 20 minutes kitchen work
                   1 hour baking

YIELD: 1 loaf

1¼ cups unbleached white flour
1¼ cups whole wheat flour
1½ cups rolled oats
1 teaspoon baking powder
1 teaspoon baking soda
½ teaspoon salt
1 teaspoon cinnamon
½ teaspoon nutmeg

⅓ cup (5⅓ tablespoons) butter or unsaturated margarine, softened
⅔ cup brown sugar
2 eggs
1 cup thick applesauce, preferably homemade
1 cup dried currants (or substitute raisins)

1. In a bowl, stir together the flours, oats, baking powder, baking soda, salt, and spices.

2. In a large bowl, cream the butter or margarine with the brown sugar. Beat in the eggs, then the applesauce. Stir in the dry ingredients, mixing only enough to moisten them. Stir in the currants.

3. Turn the batter into a greased and floured 9″ × 5″ loaf pan. Bake in a 350-degree oven about 1 hour or until a toothpick inserted in the center comes out clean. Cool thoroughly before slicing.

OATMEAL PANCAKES

Very light and delicate and bearing little resemblance to ordinary pancakes, which tend to be rather spongy, these are really quite impossible to resist. You'll enjoy one after another.

PREPARATION TIMES: overnight soaking of oats
                   15 minutes kitchen work

YIELD: 24 small pancakes, or 4 to 6 servings

2 cups rolled oats
2 tablespoons lemon juice
  plus enough milk to equal 2
  cups liquid
½ cup unbleached white
  flour
2 tablespoons sugar

1 teaspoon baking powder
1 teaspoon baking soda
2 eggs, beaten
½ stick (4 tablespoons) butter
  or unsaturated margarine,
  melted

1. Stir together the oats and lemon-milk mixture in a large bowl. Cover and refrigerate overnight.

2. The next morning, stir together in a small bowl, the flour, sugar, baking powder, and baking soda. Stir this into the oat mixture, along with the eggs and melted butter or margarine.

3. Place a lightly greased skillet over a moderately high heat (375 degrees on an electric skillet) and let remain over the heat for 2 to 3 minutes or until hot. Keeping the skillet on the heat, drop the batter, 2 tablespoons at a time, for each pancake. Brown on one side, turn, and brown the other side. Serve with applesauce, honey, jam, or maple syrup.

PRIZEWINNING OATMEAL CAKE

When I wrote a weekly cooking column for the *Trenton Times*, one of my readers sent me this recipe with which her daughter-in-law had once captured the grand prize in a local bake-off. Oatmeal in baked goods tends to make them light and chewy, and this cake is no exception. The crisp crumb topping will win over any who are addicted to those crumb-topped snack cakes.

PREPARATION TIMES: 30 minutes kitchen work
                   1 hour baking

YIELD: 1 9" × 13" cake

Cake:

1¼ cups boiling water
1 cup rolled oats
1¼ cups unbleached white flour
1 cup whole wheat flour
1½ teaspoons baking soda
¾ teaspoon salt
1 teaspoon cinnamon
½ teaspoon nutmeg
1½ sticks (¾ cup) butter or unsaturated margarine, softened
1 cup granulated sugar
1 cup brown sugar

3 eggs
1½ teaspoons vanilla
½ cup chopped walnuts
½ cup raisins

Topping: (Mix all ingredients together with a fork)

6 tablespoons unbleached white flour
1 teaspoon cinnamon
½ cup granulated sugar
½ stick (4 tablespoons) butter or unsaturated margarine, softened

1. Pour the boiling water over the oats and let stand while preparing the other ingredients.

2. In a bowl, stir together the flours, baking soda, salt, cinnamon, and nutmeg.

3. In a large bowl, cream the butter or margarine with the sugars. Beat in the eggs, then the vanilla and oatmeal. Beat in the dry ingredients only until they are moistened. Stir in the raisins and walnuts.

4. Turn the batter into a greased and floured 9" × 13" baking pan and spread the topping over the batter. Bake in a 350-degree oven 55 minutes, or until a toothpick inserted in the center comes out clean. Let cool on a rack. Do not try to tip the cake out of the pan or the topping will come off. Slice in pan to serve.

FRUITED OATMEAL BARS

Although definitely dessert fare, these bars provide plenty of nutrition. They are easy to prepare, chewy, and deliciously flavored. But be forewarned. They are hard to resist!

PREPARATION TIMES: 15 minutes kitchen work
                   20 minutes baking

YIELD: 20 bars

⅓ cup molasses
⅓ cup honey
1 stick (½ cup) butter or
   unsaturated margarine,
   melted
1½ cups rolled oats
1 cup whole wheat flour

½ cup wheat germ
½ teaspoon baking soda
¼ teaspoon salt
½ cup dark raisins
½ cup golden raisins
½ cup chopped walnuts

1. Beat together the molasses, honey, and melted butter or margarine.

2. In a large bowl, stir together the oats, flour, wheat germ, baking soda, and salt. Add the molasses-honey mixture and mix well. Stir in the raisins and nuts.

3. Spread the batter in a greased 9″ square baking pan. Bake in a 375-degree oven about 18 minutes, or until a toothpick inserted in the center comes out clean. Let cool on a rack and then cut into bars.

part 3
Nuts and Seeds

11
Walnuts

Many cookbooks suggest using black walnuts whenever possible. The flavor is said to be finer and fuller than that of English walnuts, and the nutritional value is indisputably better. Black walnuts contain somewhat more protein, phosphorus, and magnesium, twice the iron, and ten times more vitamin A than English walnuts. Incidentally, English walnuts, also called Persian walnuts, were originally imported into this country. Now, with more than 100,000 acres in California devoted to the growth of walnut trees, you will often see English walnuts referred to as "California" walnuts.

Of course I felt that I could not possibly pursue my natural foods adventure without at least sampling the black walnut. In my quest for this rarity, I learned why I had not previously encountered it. My search through multitudes of groceries and fancy food shops failed to unearth such an item. Finally, at a natural foods store I did locate a small cache of the prized unshelled black walnuts. I was warned that this was a "tough nut to crack."

I bought a few and quickly discovered why all books suggest buying them already shelled. Neither a nutcracker nor a hammer could mar the incredibly hard black shell. Finally, my strong husband managed to crack one, nearly losing a finger in the process. The nut was open, but no nutmeats came out. These were encased in membranes nearly as hard as the original shell. Eventually, with the kitchen littered with bits of shell and membranes, with sore wrists and broken thumb nails, I was finally able to taste the black walnut. I have to admit it was good. The flavor was indeed more pungent, almost winey. But was it worth it? I answer a firm "No."

So if you choose to buy black walnuts for any of these recipes, buy them shelled, and be advised that you will pay considerably more for them. Fortunately, though, the recipes also taste marvelous made with the "everyday" English walnuts which I heartily recommend.

Since nuts and seeds are rich, caloric, and expensive, few people make a main course of them. However, as their crunch and unique flavors are unsurpassed, and because they are highly nutritious, nuts and seeds may be used to impart a fine taste and to augment the protein value of more mundane foods. Rice with the bite of cashews, bread with the savor of walnuts, vegetables sprinkled with pungent peanuts—all are great combinations.

NUTTY DIP

An unusual, blender-made dip, with a pale green color and a distinctive taste, this always inspires people to ask what's in it. Don't overpower the flavor with a too highly seasoned dipper. I suggest a wheat thin type cracker, wedges of pita bread, or raw vegetable sticks.

PREPARATION TIMES: 20 minutes kitchen work
                   1 to 2 hours chilling

YIELD: 1½ cups

2 onions, chopped
2 tablespoons butter or
  unsaturated margarine
3 hard-cooked eggs,
  quartered
1 tablespoon milk

½ cup chopped walnuts
½ cup non-fat dry milk
  powder
½ cup very well-cooked sliced
  green beans
½ teaspoon salt

Sauté the onions in butter or margarine until softened. Then place in a blender along with the remaining ingredients. Blend until smooth. Turn into a serving dish and chill well.

WALNUT CHEESE OLIVES

These appetizers are fairly simple to make but do require a bit of patience, for the cheese mixture tends to stick to your fingers as you wrap it around the olives. The tidbits are ultrarich, with their coating of butter, cream cheese, and blue cheese, but well worth any extra calories. Count on two or three per person.

PREPARATION TIMES: 20 minutes kitchen work
                   30 minutes chilling

YIELD: 24

½ stick (4 tablespoons) butter
  or unsaturated margarine
4 ounces cream cheese
4 ounces blue cheese
2 tablespoons minced green
  onion
2 teaspoons brandy

¼ teaspoon dry mustard
½ teaspoon salt
⅛ teaspoon pepper
about 24 small pimiento-
  stuffed green olives
about 1 cup finely chopped
  walnuts

1. In a bowl, cream together the butter or margarine, cheeses, green onion, brandy, mustard, salt, and pepper. Place in the refrigerator until firm enough to handle.

2. Coat each olive with a small amount of the cheese mixture and roll in walnuts. Serve on toothpicks.

SUMMERTIME VEGETABLE CASSEROLE

Here, the produce of summer is imbedded in a delicate custard-like casserole. The smoothness of the eggs and minced greens contrasts well with the crunchy walnuts scattered throughout. Serve with warm pita bread and a dish of tahini on the side. Sliced tomatoes, also in season, go nicely, too.

PREPARATION TIMES: 20 minutes kitchen work
1 hour baking

YIELD: 4 to 6 servings

1 10-ounce package chopped frozen spinach, thawed and squeezed dry
2 cups chopped green onions
1 cup chopped lettuce
1 cup chopped fresh parsley
1 cup chopped leeks (if too expensive, use another cup of green onions or omit altogether)

2 tablespoons unbleached white flour
¾ cup coarsely chopped walnuts
1½ teaspoons salt
¼ teaspoon pepper
8 eggs, beaten

1. Stir together the vegetables, flour, nuts, salt, and pepper. Mix in the eggs.

2. Turn the mixture into a well-greased 2-quart round casserole. Bake in a 325-degree oven 1 hour or until set and browned on top.

PEAS WITH WALNUTS

It never ceases to amaze me that people will go out and spend so much extra money on a package of frozen peas with a few mushrooms or pearl onions, on green beans with slivered almonds, or on seasoned rice mixtures, when it is really so very easy to fancy up plain vegetables oneself. Try my green pea recipe, for example, with sautéed onions, delicate lettuce, and crunchy walnuts all adding that extra flair to a plain cooked vegetable.

PREPARATION TIMES: 30 minutes kitchen work
15 minutes simmering

YIELD: 4 servings

1 onion, chopped
2 tablespoons vegetable oil
1 cup water
1½ pounds green peas, shelled (about 1½ cups after shelling

½ teaspoon salt
¼ teaspoon pepper
2 cups shredded lettuce
½ cup chopped walnuts

1. Sauté the onion in oil in a small skillet until it is softened. Set aside and keep warm.

2. Meanwhile, place the water, peas, salt, pepper, and lettuce in saucepan. Boil gently, covered, until the peas are tender, about 15 minutes. Drain and toss with the sautéed onion and the walnuts.

SUMMER SQUASH WITH WALNUTS

Here is another easily prepared vegetable dish, to which honey adds a faint sweetness, and walnuts, a crunchy texture.

PREPARATION TIMES: 10 minutes kitchen work
10 minutes simmering

YIELD: 4 servings

3 good-sized yellow summer squash, cut into ⅓-inch slices (about 3 cups)
1 small red onion, chopped (about ½ cup)
1 clove garlic, minced
1 tablespoon vegetable oil
2 tablespoons water

1 tablespoon honey
½ teaspoon salt
2 tablespoons minced fresh parsley
1 tablespoon whole wheat flour
¼ cup chopped walnuts

1. Place all the ingredients except the flour and walnuts in a large skillet. Bring to a boil. Cover and reduce the heat. Cook about 10 minutes, or until the squash is just tender.

2. Stir in the flour and walnuts. Cook, stirring, until the flour is dissolved and the liquid thickens.

POTECA

This Swiss coffee cake is for those who really enjoy putting a lot of effort into baking. The batter requires three risings, which adds to the time needed to make the cake. It is also rather sticky and painstaking to roll out. But the results are superb! The dough is tender and rich, and the walnut filling unbelievably delicious.

PREPARATION TIMES: 1¼ hours kitchen work
2½ hours rising
40 minutes baking

YIELD: 1 coffee cake, serving 12 to 15

Dough:
½ cup yogurt
2 tablespoons milk
⅓ cup plus ½ teaspoon sugar
½ teaspoon salt
1 package active dry yeast
¼ cup warm water
1½ cups whole wheat flour
2 egg yolks
4½ tablespoons very soft butter or unsaturated margarine

about 1½ cups unbleached white flour

Filling:
2 egg whites
pinch salt
⅓ cup sugar
8 ounces finely chopped walnuts (about 2 cups after chopping)
½ teaspoon grated lemon rind

1. In a small saucepan, heat the yogurt, milk, ⅓ cup sugar, and salt, stirring constantly until it begins to bubble. Pour into a large bowl, and let cool to lukewarm.

2. Meanwhile, dissolve the yeast and ½ teaspoon sugar in the warm water. Let sit until a foam forms on the surface, about 10 minutes. Stir this and the whole wheat flour into the yogurt mixture very well. Cover the bowl with plastic wrap and let sit in a warm, draft-free spot for 45 minutes.

3. With a heavy wooden spoon, beat the egg yolks and soft butter or margarine into the batter after it has risen for the 45 minutes. Stir in enough unbleached white flour to make a stiff dough. Turn out onto a floured surface and knead until smooth and elastic, adding more flour until it is no longer sticky. Place

the dough in an oiled bowl, and turn once so the greased side faces up. Let rise, covered, about 1 hour.

4. Knead the dough a few minutes longer. Let rest 5 minutes. Meanwhile, make the filling: Beat the egg whites until stiff with a pinch of salt. Gradually beat in the sugar until the mixture is glossy. Stir in the walnuts and lemon rind.

5. Roll out the dough into a rectangle 24″ × 10″. Spread the filling evenly over the surface, and starting with a long edge, roll up, jelly roll style. Place, seam side down, in a greased tube pan. Pinch the edges to seal. Let rise, covered, 40 minutes.

6. Bake the cake in a 350-degree oven 35 minutes. Turn out onto a baking sheet, and bake upside down, 5 minutes longer. Let cool on a rack.

WALNUT SLICES

These very rich cookies, made mostly of ground nuts, seem to crumble in your mouth. The dough may be made ahead and refrigerated for several days or frozen for a month or two.

PREPARATION TIMES: 20 minutes kitchen work
2 or more hours chilling the dough
12 minutes baking

YIELD: 4 dozen

1 stick (½ cup) butter or unsaturated margarine
⅓ cup sugar
¼ teaspoon salt
1 teaspoon vanilla

1¼ cups unbleached white flour
1⅓ cups finely ground walnuts

1. Cream the butter or margarine with the sugar. Beat in the salt, vanilla, flour, and then the walnuts.

2. Form the dough into 1 or 2 long rolls, about 1½ inches in diameter. Wrap in plastic wrap and refrigerate until firm, at least 2 hours.

3. To bake, slice ¼-inch thick and place on lightly greased cookie sheets. Bake in a 350-degree oven 10 to 12 minutes, or until pale brown. Let cool on racks and then store in a tightly sealed container.

CHOCOLATE-NUT TORTE

Few people are conversant with the true meaning of the word *torte*. Part of the reason for mixup is that the word sounds like tart; and one true tart, a jam-filled pie, has even been given the misnomer, *Linzer Torte*. Another cause of confusion is that many cookbook authors, restaurateurs, food advertisers, and magazine writers commonly name any fancy cake a torte in order to make it more enticing.

Despite this, there is a real, although somewhat complex, definition of a torte. Basically, it is a fairly heavy cake of European origin. Usually most, if not all, of the flour which would ordinarily be used in a cake has been replaced by other finely ground substances, such as nuts, chocolate, bread or cookie crumbs, or even carrots. Tortes generally contain many eggs, usually at least six; and the egg whites are beaten separately. The cake will rise, almost soufflé-like, as it bakes and fall to a rich, dense mass as it cools. My Chocolate-Nut Torte is very rich with ground walnuts and well-flavored with cocoa. The lemon rind, though faint, lends an exotic touch.

You may perhaps wonder why this recipe, and a few others scattered throughout the book, contain cocoa or chocolate; after all, this is not a food commonly found in health or natural foods cookbooks. Nearly every writer substitutes carob. Why haven't I?

Carob is said to be more nutritious than chocolate. A comparison with cocoa, the powdery form of chocolate most like carob, reveals that carob does indeed supply about twice the fiber and calcium of cocoa, with slightly fewer calories and sixteen times less fat. However, cocoa contains about three times the protein, two times the phosphorus, and significant quantities of vitamin A and potassium, which carob lacks altogether. Clearly, then, carob is not the hands-down winner!

Then, of course, one must consider the taste of what you are making. For similar as carob is to cocoa, it is not the same. Personally, I am not fond of carob, finding it lacking in flavor, yet leaving a too-sweet aftertaste. Once, I made two batches of brownies, identical except that one contained cocoa, the other carob. I brought them into my office (at a newspaper) and asked the other staff members to sample one from each batch, not informing them as to what I was surveying. Fourteen out of nineteen tasters preferred the cocoa brownies, claiming the others were not sufficiently chocolaty. As one editor remarked, "When I eat a brownie, I know that I'm consuming a whole lot of calories, and so I should be eating the best, most chocolaty brownie I can eat."

I do agree. I believe you will, too, when you have tried this Chocolate-Nut Torte.

PREPARATION TIMES: 15 minutes kitchen work
30 minutes baking

YIELD: 1 8″ × 10″ torte, or 10 servings

4 eggs, separated	⅓ cup cocoa
¾ cup sugar	1 teaspoon vanilla
1¼ cups ground walnuts	1 teaspoon grated lemon rind

1. Beat the egg whites until stiff and set aside.

2. Beat the egg yolks in a large bowl. Gradually beat in the sugar. When done, the mixture should be thick and pale yellow. Stir in the walnuts, cocoa, vanilla, and lemon rind. Gently fold in the egg whites.

3. Turn the batter into a greased and floured 8″ × 10″ baking pan. Bake in a 350-degree oven 30 minutes, or until it tests done with a toothpick. Transfer to a rack. The torte may be served warm or at room temperature, either plain or with whipped cream, ice cream, or frozen yogurt.

WALNUT BREAD

Most walnut breads are nearly sweet enough to classify them as cakes. Here is a version that's quite different—chewy, wheaty, rather salty, and so full of nuts that you almost seem to be munching on a handful of salted nuts. The bread makes fantastic cheese sandwiches!

PREPARATION TIMES: 40 minutes kitchen work
$2\frac{1}{2}$ hours rising
1 hour baking

YIELD: 2 large, round loaves

2 packages active dry yeast
$\frac{2}{3}$ cup warm water
3 cups whole wheat flour
2 tablespoons salt
3 cups warm milk
$1\frac{1}{2}$ cups coarsely chopped walnuts

1 cup (2 sticks) butter or
    unsaturated margarine, at
    room temperature
about 6 cups unbleached
    white flour or bread flour

1. Dissolve the yeast in the warm water. Let sit for a few minutes.

2. Meanwhile, place the whole wheat flour and salt in a very large bowl. Add the yeast mixture and milk and stir thoroughly. Add the walnuts and butter or margarine. Stir in enough unbleached white flour to make a stiff dough. Turn the dough out onto a heavily floured board or counter and knead until smooth and elastic, incorporating as much additional white flour as is necessary.

3. Place the dough in a large, oiled bowl and turn once so the oiled side faces up. Cover the bowl with plastic wrap and let the dough rise in a warm, draft-free spot until doubled in bulk, about 2 hours.

4. Knead the dough a few minutes longer and divide into 2 equal pieces. Shape each into a large round loaf and place each on a greased baking sheet. Cover and let rise until doubled in bulk, about 20 minutes longer.

5. Bake the loaves in a 425-degree oven with a pan of hot water on the bottom of the oven for 30 minutes. Reduce the heat to 300 degrees, remove the water, and bake for about 30 minutes longer.

12
Cashew Nuts

The cashew is not a true nut. Rather, it is the fruit of a tree cultivated in tropical areas. Surrounding this hard fruit is a fleshy portion that is eaten raw, made into preserves, or fermented to produce wine and vinegar.

But the firm part of the fruit is generally eaten as we do all nuts—out of hand for munching or cooked into dishes. Unfortunately, cashew nuts are fairly expensive, considerably more so than peanuts or walnuts. I have found the most economical way of buying them is in the form of raw pieces. (Unless you are serving the cashews as part of an attractive bowl of nuts, the fact that the nutmeats are broken is of little consequence.) These can usually be found in natural foods stores.

A note of caution: The raw cashew causes dermititis in some people (similar to the effects of poison ivy), but a brief cooking destroys the toxins in the nut. If the dish is not to be cooked, you may wish to roast the nuts. To do this, spread them in a shallow pan and bake in a 300-degree oven until lightly browned. The roasting also serves to enhance the flavor of the cashew.

CARROT-CASHEW PATTIES

The patties take only a few minutes to fix and make a great lunch or light dinner dish. The flavor is wonderful—just carrots, cashews, and sautéed onions. Serve the patties with a scoop of brown rice and a platter of sliced tomatoes and cucumbers.

PREPARATION TIMES: 20 minutes kitchen work
                   25 minutes baking

YIELD: 2 servings

1 onion, chopped	½ cup finely chopped cashew nuts
1 tablespoon vegetable oil	1 egg, beaten
1 cup grated carrots	½ teaspoon salt

1. In a small skillet, sauté the onion in oil until tender.

2. Mix the remaining ingredients in a bowl and add the contents of the skillet.

3. Form the mixture into 6 small patties. Place on a greased baking sheet and bake in a 350-degree oven 25 minutes.

CASHEW AND EGG STUFFED EGGPLANT

This delicious main course dish needs no accompaniment save a tossed salad. The nuts add a flavorful crunch that makes a good contrast to the bland rice and eggs. Melted cheese over the top adds a rich and pleasant chewiness.

PREPARATION TIMES: 30 minutes kitchen work
                   1 hour simmering
                   30 minutes baking

YIELD: 4 servings

3 cups water	1 clove garlic, minced
1 cup brown rice	2 tablespoons vegetable oil
2 medium-sized eggplants	½ cup finely chopped cashews
(about 1 pound each),	4 hard-cooked eggs, chopped
halved lengthwise	1 1-pound can tomatoes,
1 onion, chopped	undrained and chopped

1 teaspoon salt
¼ teaspoon pepper
2 tablespoons minced fresh
 parsley

2 cups shredded Muenster
 cheese

1. Bring the water to a boil in a saucepan. Add the brown rice and simmer over a low heat, covered, until the water is absorbed, about 45 minutes.

2. Meanwhile, in another saucepan, cook the eggplant in boiling water to cover just until tender, about 15 minutes. Drain. Scoop out the pulp, being careful not to damage the skins, and chop the pulp. Place the skins, shiny side down, in a greased, shallow baking pan.

3. In a small skillet, sauté the onion and garlic in oil until tender. Add the contents of the skillet to the rice, along with the eggplant pulp, cashew nuts, eggs, tomatoes, and seasonings.

4. Stuff the eggplant-rice mixture into the eggplant skins and sprinkle with the cheese. Bake the eggplants in a 350-degree oven until very hot, about 30 minutes.

CASHEW-DATE BALLS

Crunchy, chewy, fruity confections, these contain only a small amount of honey, since the dried fruits supply plenty of sweetness. They are great for snacks and especially good to take on camping trips or hikes.

PREPARATION TIME: 30 minutes kitchen work

YIELD: 50 balls

1 cup finely chopped cashew
 nuts
½ pound finely chopped dates
½ pound finely chopped
 dried apricots

1 cup wheat germ
¼ teaspoon salt
½ cup honey
toasted sesame seeds or
 shredded coconut

Mix all ingredients together thoroughly. Form into one-inch balls and roll in sesame seeds or shredded coconut. Store in a tightly covered container.

CASHEW SLICES

I have known guests to stand by a plate of these incredibly rich and delicious bar cookies and surreptitiously devour one after another until all had disappeared.

PREPARATION TIMES: 30 minutes kitchen work
40 minutes baking

YIELD: 36 bars

Dough:
1 stick (½ cup) butter or unsaturated margarine
¼ cup sugar
1 egg
1¼ cups unbleached white flour
⅛ teaspoon salt
½ teaspoon vanilla

Topping:
2 eggs, beaten
1½ cups brown sugar
1½ cups chopped cashew nuts

2 tablespoons unbleached white flour
½ teaspoon baking powder
½ teaspoon salt
1 teaspoon vanilla

Lemon glaze:
1 cup sugar
⅓ cup milk
2 tablespoons butter or unsaturated margarine
¼ teaspoon salt
1 teaspoon grated lemon peel

1. Make the dough: Cream the butter and sugar well. Beat in the egg, then the flour, salt, and vanilla. Pat evenly into a greased 9″ × 13″ pan. Bake in a 350-degree oven 15 minutes.

2. Mix together the topping ingredients and spread evenly over the dough. Bake 25 minutes longer.

3. When cool, ice with the lemon glaze. Place all ingredients except the lemon peel in a saucepan. Bring to a boil over a medium heat and then boil 1 minute. Cool to lukewarm and then stir in the lemon rind. Beat with a spoon until the glaze is thick enough to drizzle over the bars. The glaze may be either drizzled in an attractive pattern or spread in a very thin layer. When it has set, cut the bars.

13
Peanuts

I, like many other adults (and hundreds of children, too) in this country, am addicted to peanut butter sandwiches. In fact, about half the peanuts grown in the United States go into peanut butter, and most of this into sandwiches. The consumption of these sandwiches is one of the few of our country's food habits that is highly commendable. Peanut butter constitutes a very economical and nutritious lunch. It also makes the only commonly eaten sandwich that is free of cholesterol.

The people of this country did not always feel such a fondness for peanut butter. During the eighteenth and nineteenth centuries, peanuts, actually a type of legume rather than a true nut, were grown mainly to feed hogs, particularly those raised to be the famous Smithfield hams. But the slaves from Africa had used peanuts in their cooking at home, especially in soups, and snitched handfuls of the animal food for their own consumption in the slave cabins.

From here, slave cooks then developed dishes fit for the plantation dining tables. Not only were there peanut soups and stews, but peanuts were mixed with mashed yams, formed into cakes, and deep-fried. They were also blended into cream sauces for vegetables, made into salad dressings, spread on corn in place of butter, and, of course, made into a myriad of desserts including pies, cakes, cookies, and candies.

It was not, however, until the 1890s, when the boll weevil destroyed the South's cotton crops, that Dr. George Washington Carver, looking for another major crop for the South, decided on the peanut. Not only did Carver find gastronomic uses for the peanut in soups, vegetables, salads, breads, and desserts, but he also utilized it in salves, bleaches, wood and plastic fillers, cosmetics, paints, dyes, and oils. And since that time, the peanut, and particularly peanut butter, have been consumed in increasing amounts. More recently the election of a President linked to Georgia's peanut industry focused even more attention on this nutritious nut.

The recipes here make use of peanuts in cereal, bread, cookies, and candy. They are all nutritious and, I think, quite irresistible.

Incidentally, if you are a peanut fan, as I obviously am, one of the best ways to buy the nuts is raw. Roast them on a cookie sheet in a 350-degree oven, turning them occasionally, until they begin to brown and emit a wonderful aroma. They are marvelous eaten hot or used in these recipes, particularly if you own a machine that can turn them into peanut butter.

PEANUT GRANOLA

Granola is one of those foods I eat by the handful, absolutely unable to stop. Besides eaten plain, there are many other uses for it. With milk, it makes a great breakfast cereal or snack. It's also good sprinkled on ice cream, frozen yogurt, or atop a frosted cake. For a quick dessert, place apple slices in a greased shallow oven dish, add one-half inch of apple juice, cover with a layer of granola, and dot with butter. Bake at 350 degrees until the apples are tender. Delicious warm or cold!

PREPARATION TIMES: 10 minutes kitchen work
25 minutes baking

YIELD: 5 cups

½ cup peanuts
½ cup sunflower seeds
2 cups rolled oats
½ cup wheat germ

¼ cup vegetable oil
¼ cup honey
½ teaspoon vanilla
½ cup raisins

1. In a large bowl, combine the peanuts, sunflower seeds, oats, and wheat germ.

2. In a small saucepan, heat the oil and honey to just below boiling. Stir in the vanilla. Add to the bowl with the dry ingredients and toss well.

3. Spread the mixture evenly in an 11″ × 16″ jelly roll pan. Bake in a 300-degree oven about 25 minutes, or until slightly brown, stirring occasionally. Mix in the raisins. Let cool fully and then store in a tightly covered container.

PEANUT BUTTER CORN MUFFINS

Nothing beats these hearty nutritious muffins served hot from the oven with a big bowl of hot soup or a crisp, vegetable-laden salad for dinner. Since they really are best served warm, if you are unable to eat them all at once, reheat them before serving a second time.

PREPARATION TIMES: 15 minutes kitchen work
                   15 minutes baking
YIELD: 10 large muffins

2 cups whole wheat flour
2 tablespoons baking powder
1 teaspoon salt
1 cup cornmeal

½ cup peanut butter
¼ cup honey
2 eggs, beaten
1⅓ cups milk

1. In a large bowl, stir together the whole wheat flour, baking powder, salt, and cornmeal.

2. In another bowl, mix together the peanut butter, honey, eggs, and milk. Add the contents of this bowl to the dry ingredients and stir only until the dry ingredients are fully moistened.

3. Fill greased muffin tins nearly full. Bake the muffins in a 450-degree oven 15 minutes, or until they test done with a toothpick.

PEANUT BUTTER–BANANA BREAD I (QUICK)

This moist bread reminds me of the peanut butter and banana sandwiches I consumed in great quantities as a child. As it is so rich and flavorful, it is best served plain, with a glass of milk or hot tea.

PREPARATION TIMES: 15 minutes kitchen work
                               1 hour baking

YIELD: 1 loaf

6 tablespoons butter or unsaturated margarine, softened

1 cup peanut butter, preferably chunk style

1¼ cups sugar

1¼ cups mashed ripe bananas

2 eggs

1 cup whole wheat flour

1 cup plus 2 tablespoons unbleached white flour

2½ teaspoons baking powder

¼ teaspoon baking soda

½ teaspoon salt

½ cup raisins or chopped dates

1. In a large bowl, cream together the butter or margarine, peanut butter, and sugar. Beat in the bananas and eggs very well.

2. In another bowl, stir together the flours, baking powder, baking soda, and salt. Beat these dry ingredients into the peanut butter–banana mixture only until they are fully moistened. Stir in the raisins or dates.

3. Turn the batter into a greased and floured 9″ × 5″ loaf pan. Bake the bread in a 350-degree oven about 1 hour, or until a toothpick inserted in the center comes out clean. Let cool on a rack before slicing.

PEANUT BUTTER–BANANA BREAD II (YEASTED)

Here is a yeasted version of the preceding bread. The texture is lighter and more delicate but the taste is very similar. It is delicious plain or toasted and mades a perfect bread for cream cheese sandwiches.

PREPARATION TIMES: 45 minutes kitchen work
2¼ hours rising
45 minutes baking

YIELD: 2 loaves

2 packages active dry yeast
⅓ cup warm water
½ cup dark brown sugar
¾ cup peanut butter,
    preferably chunk style
¾ cup mashed ripe bananas

1 egg
1 cup lukewarm milk
1½ teaspoons salt
2 cups whole wheat flour
3 to 4 cups unbleached white
    flour or bread flour

1. Dissolve the yeast in the warm water, adding a pinch of the brown sugar. Let sit about 10 minutes, or until a foam appears on the surface.

2. Meanwhile, in a large bowl, cream the peanut butter with the remaining brown sugar. Beat in the bananas, egg, milk, and salt. Beat in the yeast mixture and the whole wheat flour. Stir in enough white flour to make a stiff dough.

3. Turn the dough out onto a floured surface and knead until smooth, elastic, and no longer sticky, adding more flour as needed. Place the dough in a greased bowl and turn once so the greased side faces up. Cover the bowl with plastic wrap and let rise in a warm, draft-free spot until doubled in bulk, about 1½ hours.

4. Knead the dough a few minutes longer. Divide in half. Roll each half to a ¾-inch rectangle, and roll up, jelly roll style. Place each loaf in a greased 9″ × 5″ pan. Cover and let rise until doubled, about 40 minutes.

5. Make three diagonal slashes across the top of each loaf and brush with water. Bake in a 350-degree oven 40 minutes. Turn the loaves out onto a baking sheet and bake upside down 5 minutes longer, or until the bottoms are crisp. Let cool on racks before slicing.

PEANUT BUTTER ROLL-UPS

A delightful honeyed peanut mixture fills simple yeasted whole wheat dough crescents. The roll-ups are delicious warm or at room temperature and may be served anytime you'd ordinarily enjoy a coffee cake.

PREPARATION TIMES: 1¼ hours kitchen work
1½ hours rising
15 minutes baking

YIELD: 16 roll-ups

½ cup milk, scalded
1 stick (½ cup) butter or
  unsaturated margarine
⅓ cup sugar
¾ teaspoon salt
1 package active dry yeast
½ cup warm water
1 egg, beaten

2 cups whole wheat flour
about 2 cups unbleached
  white flour or bread flour
⅓ cup peanut butter,
  preferably chunk style
⅓ cup honey
½ teaspoon cinnamon

1. Pour the scalded milk into a large bowl. Add the butter or margarine, sugar, and salt. Stir until the butter has melted and let sit until lukewarm.

2. Meanwhile, dissolve the yeast in the warm water. Add this, the egg, and the whole wheat flour to the milk mixture. Beat with an electric mixer until well mixed. Stir in enough white flour to make a stiff dough.

3. Turn the dough out onto a floured surface and knead until smooth elastic, and no longer sticky, adding more flour as needed. Place the dough in a greased bowl and turn once so that the greased side faces up. Cover the bowl with plastic wrap and let rise in a warm, draft-free spot until the dough has doubled in bulk, about 1 hour.

4. Meanwhile, in a small bowl, mix together the peanut butter, honey, and cinnamon.

5. Knead the dough a few minutes longer. Divide in half and let rest 10 minutes. Roll each half into a 12-inch circle. Spread evenly with the peanut mixture. Cut each circle into 8 equal

wedges. Roll up each wedge from the wide end, and curve to make a crescent. Place the rolls, pointed side down, on greased baking sheets. Let rise, covered, until doubled in bulk, about 30 minutes.

6. Bake the roll-ups in a 400-degree oven about 15 minutes, or until golden brown. Place on racks to cool.

CRUMB-TOPPED PEANUT CAKE

Peanut butter and cinnamon flavor both the batter and crumb topping of this creamy, moist cake which, while still sweet, offers more protein than most cakes.

PREPARATION TIMES: 30 minutes kitchen work
                   40 minutes baking

YIELD: 1 9″ × 13″ cake

Batter:
½ cup peanut butter, preferably chunk style
⅓ cup butter or unsaturated margarine, softened
1½ cups brown sugar
2 eggs
1 cup unbleached white flour
1 cup whole wheat flour
1 teaspoon cinnamon
2 teaspoons baking powder
½ teaspoon salt
1 cup milk

Topping: (Mix all ingredients until crumbly)
¼ cup peanut butter
½ cup brown sugar
½ cup whole wheat flour
2 tablespoons butter or unsaturated margarine
½ teaspoon cinnamon

1. In a large bowl, cream the peanut butter, butter or margarine, and brown sugar well. Beat in the eggs.

2. In another bowl, stir together the flours, cinnamon, baking powder, and salt. Beat these dry ingredients into the creamed mixture alternately with the milk.

3. Turn the batter into a well-greased 9″ × 13″ baking pan. Sprinkle with the topping mixture. Bake the cake in a 375-degree oven 35 to 40 minutes, or until it tests done with a toothpick. Let the cake cook on a rack. Do not try to tip it out of the pan, or the topping will fall off. Slice for serving in the pan.

PEANUT BUTTER COOKIES

These rich and crumbly cookies keep very well if stored in a tightly covered container. They are the traditional peanut butter cookies, with a crisscross design on top.

PREPARATION TIMES: 20 minutes kitchen work
15 minutes baking

YIELD: 3 dozen cookies

½ cup butter or unsaturated margarine
½ cup brown sugar
½ cup granulated sugar
1 egg
1 cup peanut butter,

preferably chunk style
½ teaspoon salt
½ teaspoon baking soda
1½ cups unbleached white flour
½ teaspoon vanilla

1. In a large bowl, cream the butter or margarine with the sugars. Beat in the egg and peanut butter, then the dry ingredients and finally the vanilla.

2. Form the batter into one-inch balls and place on greased cookie sheets. Press the cookies into flat patties using a fork to make a crisscross design.

3. Bake in a 375-degree oven about 15 minutes or until the edges just begin to brown.

PEANUT BUTTER BALLS

This highly nutritious confection makes a great snack for camping trips or hikes. It's also an ideal candy to feed children.

PREPARATION TIME: 15 minutes kitchen work

YIELD: 2 dozen balls

½ cup peanut butter
½ cup honey
¾ cup dry milk powder

½ cup wheat germ
chopped peanuts, sesame seeds, or shredded coconut

In a bowl, mix together the peanut butter, honey, dry milk, and wheat germ. Form into small balls and roll in the peanuts, sesame seeds, or coconut. Store in a tight-fitting container.

14
Sunflower Seeds

The foods that Americans customarily eat are derived from a variety of sources. There are, of course, the foods native to the land and sea—the corn, beans, squash, fish, etc. Then there is the tremendous array of foods brought by people of different cultures as they migrated to the United States. So ginger root, soy sauce, snow peas, and macadamia nuts have become as familiar as any native food.

These sources account for nearly all the foods we eat. Yet a few edibles seem to have become popular solely through people involved with health and natural foods. The sunflower seed is one such example.

No so many years ago, sunflower seeds were used solely as bird feed and were sold unhulled in giant bags in pet shops. The tiny nuggets inside did not seem worth the human effort to get to them.

Eventually, of course, sunflower seeds were sold hulled; and with the increasing awareness of the nutritional value of seeds, their popularity grew. The dishes featuring sunflower seeds reflect their background, for they are generally found in "vegetarian" foods—whole grain breads, honey-sweetened candies, vegetable casseroles, and atop cottage cheese and bean sprout salads.

Now the sunflower seed has become so common that it may be purchased, dry-roasted and salted, in jars (although except for snacking, I recommend that you buy them for cooking raw and unsalted).

CASSEROLE WITH A CRUNCH

Here is a casserole that combines many flavors and textures. The lentils and millet give it body; the onions, mushrooms, and tomatoes add a good vegetable taste; the chili powder supplies a foreign accent; and the sunflower seeds lend a pleasant crunchiness. The casserole is easy to assemble and goes well with a variety of foods. Try it with hot bread, Cheddar cheese, and a green vegetable or tossed salad.

PREPARATION TIMES: 20 minutes kitchen work
30 minutes simmering
1 hour baking

YIELD: 4 servings

⅓ cup millet
⅓ cup lentils
1½ cups water
2 onions, chopped
½ pound mushrooms, sliced
2 tablespoons vegetable oil

1 cup sunflower seeds
1 28-ounce can tomatoes, drained and chopped
1 teaspoon chili powder
1 teaspoon salt

1. Place the millet, lentils, and water in a saucepan. Simmer, uncovered, 30 minutes. Drain any water that has not been absorbed.

2. In a medium skillet, sauté the onions and mushrooms in oil until they are tender.

3. In a large bowl, mix together the millet-lentil mixture, the contents of the skillet, and all other ingredients. Turn into a greased 2-quart casserole dish. Bake in a 350-degree oven 1 hour.

CAULIFLOWER WITH SUNFLOWER SEEDS

If you've ever thought cauliflower a mundane vegetable, here's a marvelous spicy and crunchy dish that will dispel that image forever. Although it's easy to prepare, the casserole certainly makes for party fare.

PREPARATION TIMES: 15 minutes kitchen work
15 minutes simmering
10 minutes baking

YIELD: 4 servings

1 head cauliflower
¼ cup sunflower seeds
½ teaspoon cumin seeds
½ 4-ounce can diced green chili peppers
1 clove garlic

4 tablespoons minced fresh parsley
¾ cup water
½ cup shredded mozzarella cheese

1. Cook the cauliflower until just tender and then break it into flowerettes. The vegetable will be most tasty if you cook it in a vegetable steamer; but if you do not have one, boil it in a small amount of water. Either way, it should take about 10 minutes to cook.

2. Meanwhile, place the sunflower and cumin seeds in a blender and blend until gritty. Add the chilies, garlic, parsley, and water and blend until smooth. Place in a saucepan and simmer 5 minutes. Add the cauliflower and toss to coat well.

3. Transfer the cauliflower and sauce to a greased 8″ × 8″ baking dish. Sprinkle with the mozzarella cheese. Bake in a 350-degree oven 10 minutes, or until the cheese is melted.

SUNFLOWER SEED BREAD

The nutty flavor of sunflower meal and the crunchiness of sunflower seeds combine here to produce an unusually tasty loaf. The bread is delicious plain or with butter, cheese, or peanut butter and also goes very well with soups.

Note: You may purchase the sunflower meal at health food stores, or make your own by grinding the raw seeds in a blender.

PREPARATION TIMES: 50 minutes kitchen work
1¾ hours rising
50 minutes baking

YIELD: 2 large, high loaves

2½ packages active dry yeast
¾ cup honey
3 cups warm water
¼ cup vegetable oil
3½ cups whole wheat flour
1 cup sunflower meal

¾ teaspoon salt
5 tablespoons sunflower seeds
about 3 cups unbleached white flour or bread flour

1. In a large mixing bowl, stir together the yeast, honey, and water. Let sit 5 to 10 minutes or until a foam appears on the surface.

2. Stir in the oil, whole wheat flour, sunflower meal, salt, sunflower seeds, and ½ cup white flour. Beat 100 strokes. Stir in about another 1½ cups white flour.

3. Turn the dough out onto a heavily floured board or counter and knead until smooth and elastic, adding more white flour as necessary until it is no longer sticky.

4. Place the dough in a greased bowl. Turn the dough once so the greased side faces up. Cover the bowl with plastic wrap and let rise in a warm, draft-free spot until doubled in bulk, about 1 hour.

5. Knead the dough a few times. Divide in half and place each half in a greased 9″ × 5″ loaf pan. Cover and let rise again until doubled in bulk.

6. Bake the loaves in a 350-degree oven 45 minutes. Turn the loaves out and bake upside down on a baking sheet 5 minutes longer or until crisp on the bottom. Let cool on a rack before slicing.

SUNFLOWER-OATMEAL MUFFINS

These exceptionally rich and light muffins contain no flour. Instead they offer the chewiness of oats and the richness of sunflower meal. The sunflower seeds add crunchiness and additional flavor. Because the muffins are somewhat crumbly, they are best served plain, either warm or at room temperature.

PREPARATION TIMES: 15 minutes kitchen work
15 minutes baking

YIELD: 10 large muffins

3 tablespoons honey
3 tablespoons butter or
  unsaturated margarine,
  melted
1 egg, beaten
⅔ cup milk

1⅓ cups rolled oats
¾ cup sunflower meal (see
  note on previous page)
¾ teaspoon salt
1 tablespoon baking powder
½ cup sunflower seeds

1. In a large bowl, stir together the honey, melted butter or margarine, eggs, and milk.

2. In another bowl, stir together the oats, sunflower meal, salt, and baking powder. Mix these ingredients into the liquid ones, stirring only enough to moisten. Stir in the sunflower seeds.

3. Turn the batter into papered or greased and floured muffin tins. Bake in a 375-degree oven 15 minutes.

SUNFLOWER MACAROONS

The classic macaroon is made with ground almonds, sweetened with sugar, and bound with egg white. Modifications on the original, though, are prolific, often including coconut, chocolate, and a variety of nuts. The cookie recipe here, with sunflower seeds, is quite sweet and very delicate. Making macaroons is an excellent way to use up leftover egg whites (the whites may be frozen until you are ready to make the cookies; defrost before using).

PREPARATION TIMES: 10 minutes kitchen work
                    30 minutes baking

YIELD: 50 cookies

3 egg whites
⅛ teaspoon salt
1 cup sugar

1 teaspoon vanilla
¾ cup sunflower seeds
½ cup raisins

1. Beat the egg whites with the salt until stiff. Gradually beat in the sugar until the mixture is very glossy. Beat in the vanilla and stir in the sunflower seeds and raisins.

2. Drop the batter by teaspoonfuls onto greased baking sheets. Bake in a 300-degree oven about 30 minutes.

HONEY SUNFLOWER CAKE

This is most likely the best spice cake you'll ever bite into. It is rich, hearty, and well-flavored with honey and sunflower seeds. As a bonus, it's also highly nutritious.

PREPARATION TIMES: 15 minutes kitchen work
                               30 minutes baking

YIELD: 1 9″ × 13″ cake, or 12 to 16 servings

2 cups whole wheat flour
½ cup wheat germ
½ cup sunflower seed meal
¼ cup dry milk powder
¼ teaspoon cinnamon
¼ teaspoon nutmeg
½ teaspoon salt
1 teaspoon baking soda
1 stick (½ cup) butter or unsaturated margarine, softened

1 cup honey
2 eggs
1 teaspoon vanilla
1 cup coffee (or substitute Postum)
¾ cup sunflower seeds
½ cup dark raisins
½ cup golden raisins

1. In a bowl, stir together the flour, wheat germ, sunflower meal, dry milk, cinnamon, nutmeg, salt, and baking soda.

2. In a large bowl, cream the butter or margarine with the honey until very smooth. Beat in the eggs well. Beat in the vanilla. Beat in the dry ingredients alternately with the coffee. Stir in the sunflower seeds and raisins.

3. Turn the batter into a greased and floured 9″ × 13″ baking pan. Bake in a 350-degree oven 30 minutes, or until it tests done with a toothpick. Let cool on a rack.

15
Sesame Seeds

O pen sesame!" was the magical incantation that allowed Ali Baba to enter the robbers' jewel-filled cave. Although this is from a story book, sesame seeds were long thought to possess mystic powers; and Carolina slaves from the upper Niger River sprinkled these seeds on their doorsteps to bring luck to the house. Slave cooks also planted them in their gardens, adding them to their simple hominy for extra nutrition. As was the case for peanuts, sesame seeds, too, eventually made their way into plantation kitchens—in soups, as a coating for chicken, and particularly in cookies and candies.

Southern cooking was slow to influence the mainstream of American food preparation, and sesame seeds were virtually ignored except as a topping on breads, hamburger buns, and crackers. During the last two decades, however, there has been a surge of interest in foreign cuisines, including the use of sesame seeds in a variety of foods. One of the most popular uses for sesame seeds is in tahini, first made in the Middle East. The seeds are ground into a paste which is used alone as a spread or sandwich topping or mixed into other foods, usually mashed eggplant or ground chick-peas, to make dips (see chapter on Eggplant for one such dip). From Jewish cuisine comes Halvah, a sweetened sesame paste that is dried, formed into bars, and sold at candy counters everywhere. Many Oriental recipes call for sesame seeds sprinkled on dishes or for foods to be stir-fried in sesame oil. Natural foods cooks, realizing the nutritional value of sesame seeds, have developed uses for them in a tremendous variety of baked goods and candies.

Sesame seeds have a subtly nutty taste and are highly nutritious. A pound of them supplies 2,640 calories, 83 grams of protein, 242 grams of fat, 500 milligrams of calcium, 2,685 milligrams of phosphorus, and 24.5 milligrams of niacin. They do, however, have one drawback. They can be quite expensive, particularly if purchased in small boxes or jars at the grocery store. Tahini, too, is exorbitant when compared with peanut butter.

The most economical way to purchase sesame seeds is in bulk from a wholesale spice market or from bins in a health food store. One store I frequent also sells "used" sesame seeds, which have fallen from loaves of bread during the baking process. They brown in the oven and are gathered from a tray placed below the bread. Tahini is most inexpensively purchased from a store that carries it in a huge tin from which you fill your own jar which you bring with you. Not only are you eliminating the cost of the filling procedure and a glass jar, but you also may purchase exactly the amount you need for a particular recipe.

VEGETABLE MORSELS

These little tidbits are flavored with sesame and cumin seeds. Also containing crunchy green beans and carrots, they are served stuffed into pita bread pockets and topped with tahini (sesame seed paste available in Middle Eastern groceries, health food stores, and many supermarkets), yogurt, or both. The sandwiches make an ideal lunch dish or may be served for dinner, accompanied by baked eggplant slices and brown rice.

PREPARATION TIMES: 20 minutes kitchen work
                  30 minutes baking

YIELD: 4 servings

3 eggs
½ teaspoon salt
1 teaspoon cumin seeds
¼ teaspoon pepper
3 tablespoons sesame seeds
3 tablespoons wheat germ
3 tablespoons whole wheat
  flour
2 cups grated carrots
1 10-ounce package frozen,
chopped spinach, thawed
and squeezed dry
1 10-ounce package frozen,
sliced green beans, thawed
and patted dry with paper
towels
4 rounds pita bread, sliced in
half crosswise
yogurt and tahini, optional

1. In a large bowl, beat the eggs with the salt, cumin seeds, pepper, sesame seeds, wheat germ, and flour. Stir in the vegetables.

2. Form the mixture into 1½-inch mounds on a greased 11″ × 16″ jelly roll pan. There should be about 20 rounds. Bake them in a 350-degree oven about 30 minutes or until set and browned. Use to fill pita bread halves. Then top with the tahini and yogurt, if desired.

SESAME BREAD

This easy-to-make quick bread is delicious to snack on plain or with butter, cheese, or jam. The seeds give it a good nutty taste.

PREPARATION TIMES: 30 minutes kitchen work
$\qquad\qquad\qquad$ 1 hour 10 minutes baking

YIELD: 1 loaf

1 stick (½ cup) butter or
$\quad$ unsaturated margarine
⅔ cup brown sugar
2 eggs
2 teaspoons grated lemon
$\quad$ rind
1½ cups milk
1½ cups whole wheat flour
1½ cups unbleached white
$\quad$ flour

1 teaspoon salt
2½ teaspoons baking powder
½ cup sesame seeds, toasted
$\quad$ in an ungreased skillet
$\quad$ until browned
1 tablespoon untoasted
$\quad$ sesame seeds

1. In a large bowl, cream the butter or margarine with the brown sugar. Beat in the eggs and lemon rind. With the mixer on "low," beat in the milk.

2. In another bowl, stir together the flours, salt, baking powder, and toasted sesame seeds. Add this to the liquid ingredients, mixing only until they are moistened.

3. Turn the batter into a greased and floured 9″ × 5″ loaf pan. Sprinkle with the untoasted sesame seeds. Bake in a 350-degree oven about 1 hour 10 minutes, or until a toothpick inserted into the middle comes out clean. Cool before slicing.

RYE, WHEAT, AND SESAME BREAD

Most rye breads are round and quite dense. Here's a recipe, however, that produces a loaf-shaped, lighter bread, with a pleasant sesame flavor.

PREPARATION TIMES: 45 minutes kitchen work
1¾ hours rising
35 minutes baking

YIELD: 2 loaves

2 tablespoons active dry
   yeast
½ cup warm water
¼ cup plus ½ teaspoon honey
1 cup wheat germ
1 tablespoon salt
¼ cup vegetable oil

½ cup sesame seeds
1½ cups hot water
2 eggs
1½ cups rye flour
2 cups whole wheat flour
about 2½ cups unbleached
   white flour or bread flour

1. Dissolve the yeast in the warm water with the ½ teaspoon honey. Let sit 10 minutes, or until a foam forms on the surface.

2. Meanwhile, in a large bowl, stir together the ¼ cup honey, wheat germ, salt, oil, sesame seeds, and hot water. Add the eggs and yeast mixture. Stir in the rye flour, then the whole wheat flour, and finally, enough unbleached white flour to make a stiff dough.

3. Turn the dough out onto a floured surface and knead until smooth and elastic, adding more flour until it is no longer sticky. Place the dough in a greased bowl, and turn once so that the greased side faces up. Cover the bowl with plastic wrap and place in a warm, draft-free spot until the dough has doubled in bulk, about 1 hour.

4. Knead the dough a few minutes longer. Divide in half. Shape each to fit into a greased 9″ × 5″ loaf pan. Let rise, covered, until doubled in bulk, about 40 minutes. Make 3 deep diagonal gashes across the top of each loaf, being careful not to deflate the loaves. Brush the tops with water.

5. Bake the loaves in a 400-degree oven 30 minutes. Turn out onto

a baking sheet and bake upside down 5 minutes longer, or until the bottoms are crisp. Let cool on racks before slicing.

SESAME BREADSTICKS

Breadsticks you make yourself bear little resemblance to store-bought. Far chewier, more flavorful, and less hard, they make perfect accompaniments to Italian appetizers or to soups.

PREPARATION TIMES: 1 hour kitchen work
1¼ hours rising time
30 minutes baking

YIELD: 24 bread sticks

1½ cups whole wheat flour
1 package active dry yeast
1 teaspoon salt
2 teaspoons sugar
½ teaspoon thyme
⅛ teaspoon pepper
1 tablespoon Parmesan
cheese

1½ cups warm water
3 tablespoons vegetable oil
about 3 cups unbleached
white flour
1 egg white, beaten with 1
tablespoon water
½ cup sesame seeds

1. In a large bowl, stir together the whole wheat flour, yeast, salt, sugar, spices, and Parmesan cheese. Add the water and oil. With an electric mixer, beat well. Stir in enough unbleached white flour to make a stiff dough.

2. Turn the dough out onto a floured surface and knead until smooth and elastic, adding more flour until it is no longer sticky. Place the dough in a greased bowl and rotate it so that the greased side faces up. Cover the bowl with plastic wrap and place in a warm, draft-free spot until the dough has doubled in bulk, about 1¼ hours.

3. Knead the dough a few minutes longer. Divide into 24 equal pieces. Roll each into a 10-inch-long rope. Place on 2 greased baking sheets. Brush with the egg white mixture and sprinkle with the sesame seeds.

4. Bake the breadsticks in a 400-degree oven 25 to 30 minutes, or until a deep golden brown. Let cool on racks.

BEENE WAFERS

Slaves from the upper part of the Niger River called sesame seeds *beene*; and beene (or sesame) cookies, created by black cooks of Charleston, South Carolina, have become a tradition. They are soft and rich on the inside, with a crunchy coating outside.

PREPARATION TIMES: 20 minutes kitchen work
15 minutes baking

YIELD: 3 dozen

1 cup unbleached white flour
1 cup whole wheat flour
½ cup brown sugar
1½ teaspoons baking powder
¼ teaspoon salt

1 stick (½ cup) butter or
   unsaturated margarine
1 egg, beaten
¼ cup milk
sesame seeds

1. In a large bowl, stir together the flours, brown sugar, baking powder, and salt. With the mixer at low speed, beat in the butter or margarine until the mixture is in coarse pea-size bits. Stir in the egg and milk.

2. Form the dough into 1-inch balls and roll in sesame seeds, coating them well.

3. Place the cookies on greased baking sheets. Bake in a 375-degree oven about 15 minutes.

SESAME-OATMEAL COOKIES

Here are delightful nibbles that offer the chewiness of traditional oatmeal cookies, with the added nutrition and nutty taste of sesame seeds.

PREPARATION TIMES: 20 minutes kitchen work
10 minutes baking

YIELD: 40 2-inch cookies

1 stick (½ cup) butter or
  unsaturated margarine
½ cup granulated sugar
⅓ cup brown sugar
1 egg
¼ cup milk
1¼ cups rolled oats

1¼ cups whole wheat flour
1 teaspoon cinnamon
¼ teaspoon salt
½ teaspoon baking powder
½ teaspoon baking soda
¾ cup sesame seeds
½ cup raisins

1. In a large bowl, cream the butter or margarine with the sugars. Beat in the egg, then the milk.

2. In another bowl, stir together all the remaining ingredients except the raisins. Add this mixture to the butter mixture, beating until fully incorporated. Stir in the raisins.

3. Drop heaping teaspoonfuls of the batter, about 2 inches apart, onto greased baking sheets. Bake in a 375-degree oven about 10 minutes.

ORIENTAL SANDWICH SPREAD

This uniquely flavored sandwich spread combines the smoothness of cream cheese with the nutrition of peanut butter and sesame seeds. Soy sauce and ginger give it zip. The spread is also ideal appetizer fare stuffed into celery stalks or raw mushroom caps.

PREPARATION TIME: 15 minutes kitchen work

YIELD: ¾ cup, or enough for 4 sandwiches

1 3-ounce package cream
  cheese, softened
¼ cup peanut butter
2 tablespoons sesame seeds,
  toasted in an ungreased

  skillet until golden
1 tablespoon yogurt
1 teaspoon soy sauce
⅛ teaspoon ginger

Place all ingredients in a bowl and mix well. Store, covered, in the refrigerator.

part 4

Flours

INTRODUCTION

About Bread Baking

This book contains a number of yeasted bread recipes. For a long time, I was afraid to attempt this sort of baking, not certain of what standard phrases like "proof the yeast" or "let rise in a draft-free spot" meant exactly. (I once asked my grandmother, a remarkable cook, how I should let my dough rise, and she told me to aim the steam from a boiling tea kettle at the dough; the complexity of this task halted any attempts at bread-making for several years.) I have now grown to love the feeling of baking my own bread and find it the most relaxing of pastimes.

I have long since learned a number of special secrets that help make bread-making a pleasure. I'm happy to share these hints with my readers.

The dry yeast is dissolved in *warm* water (or milk), just a little hotter than the temperature of your hand when you place your finger under the faucet to test it. Generally, a little sugar, honey, or molasses is added to feed the yeast cells. This mixture should sit for about 10 minutes, until some foam forms on the top of the liquid, which indicates that the yeast cells have begun to grow. This step is known as proofing the yeast.

Occasionally, a recipe will instruct you to stir the yeast into flour and other dry ingredients, after which the warm liquid is added. Thus, the yeast is not proofed. Because yeast today is so healthy and reliable (unlike in our grandparents' time when it was apt to have "died"), such shortcut bread recipes almost always turn out fine.

Just as dry milk powder costs considerably more when purchased in premeasured packets rather than in bulk, so, too, does yeast when bought in individual envelopes. The major yeast companies—Red Star, Fleishman's, and El Molino—all put out small jars or packages of yeast, which are far more economical than the premeasured envelopes (2½ teaspoons equals one envelope). Unfortunately, most supermarkets do not stock yeast in this form. Ask the store manager to order it, or look for it in health food stores. Remember to keep the container tightly sealed and refrigerated.

In mixing the bread dough, I have found that if I add to the liquid ingredients all the flour called for in the recipe, the batter becomes so stiff that my arm muscles are overly taxed when trying to stir it in. Therefore, I add only about three-quarters of the amount of flour specified. The dough will be firm but very sticky. Then I spread a half-inch layer of flour on my counter and pile the dough on top. This I cover with another layer of flour. I knead the flour into the dough, adding more as needed until the proper texture is reached. Determining this point is quite simple. When you knead the dough with the heel of your hand, it should not be at all sticky; if it is, sprinkle it with more flour and continue kneading. The dough should be smooth; if you poke your finger into it, it will spring back. If you wish to knead beyond this point, the dough will become elastic and difficult to work with. However, increased kneading, although unnecessary, may result in a slightly lighter loaf.

When making yeasted breads, I nearly always start with the specialty flours (whole wheat, rye, oat, corn meal, etc.) and then add any white flour called for. For a long time, I used unbleached white flour in bread recipes. But recently, a major manufacturer has come out with 5-pound sacks of bread flour, and other companies will undoubtedly follow suit. Bread flour has for a long time been available (at a rather premium price) in health food stores; I had just never gotten around to trying it. Be assured, though, that it is well worth purchasing. With a higher gluten and protein content than all-purpose or unbleached white flour, bread flour produces loaves that are lighter, yet chewier, close to the ideal texture. Do not use bread flour when baking cakes, cookies, pie crusts, or "quick" breads; unkneaded, its high gluten content is apt to make them tough.

Place the kneaded dough in an oiled bowl, and turn once so the greased side faces up; this prevents the top of the dough from drying out. Cover the bowl with plastic wrap, and place it in a warm, draft-free place to rise. I use the unlit oven of my gas stove, which contains a pilot light. If you have an electric stove, when just beginning to make your bread, preheat the oven to 200 degrees. When it reaches this temperature, turn it off. The oven should stay warm for about three hours. Or, if your kitchen is warm, just place the bowl on top of the refrigerator. If the spot in which you place your dough is rather cool, it will just take longer to rise. A cold spot, though, will inhibit the rising altogether.

When the dough has properly risen, it will have doubled in bulk. It will also have a light texture. Stick your finger deep into the dough; if a hole remains, it is light enough.

My final hint concerns the baking of the bread. I have found that after I bake a loaf, the top is nice and crunchy, but the bottom remains a bit soggy. Therefore, when the requisite time has elapsed, I tip the loaves out onto a baking sheet and bake them upside down for 5 to 10 minutes longer, or until the bottom is crisp, firm, and lightly browned.

My first loaf of homemade bread was a tremendous success and gave me a great feeling of pride and accomplishment. I hope that yours will be also. However, whether you have never made a loaf of bread before or have made hundreds, I know you will enjoy my favorite breads, presented in this chapter and throughout the book.

About Food Processors for Bread Baking

Since food processors are taking the place of arm muscles in many kitchens these days, I want to add instructions for preparing bread dough in this marvelous invention.

First, what are the advantages of kneading dough in a food processor? (1) Obviously, the time involved and the effort expended amount to but a fraction of that required for hand-kneaded dough. The dough is kneaded in 40 seconds, without the use of arm muscles. (2) The kneading is very thorough; you will probably find that your finished loaf has a better texture than when made by hand. (3) There is no sticky mess on the counter to clean up. (4) Any hard ingredients, such as butter, cheese, peanuts, etc., become instantly incorporated into the dough.

Now, what are the disadvantages? (1) The main one, unless you possess the new, bigger Cuisinart, is that you can make only one loaf of bread at a time. (2) More kneading is required after the first rising than when kneaded by hand the first time. (3) The steel blade, being very sharp, is rather difficult to wash free of the sticky dough.

Next, the method: Directions for food processor dough are almost identical to hand-kneaded dough, except that all mixing is done in the work bowl. The confusing part is to know when to stop adding flour. Once all the other ingredients are mixed, add flour, about one-fourth cup at a time. As you first add the flour, processing will incorporate it into the dough immediately. After a few additions of flour, however, you will notice that not all the flour becomes quickly mixed in; after processing, white powder will dust the top of the dough. At this point, stop adding flour, and process the dough for 40 seconds (this is the kneading).

Turn the dough into an oiled bowl. It will be very sticky and you will not be able to turn the greased side up. Cover with plastic wrap and let rise as usual.

The dough is now punched down and then kneaded by hand, adding flour as necessary, until it is no longer sticky. From this point on, the procedure is the same as that detailed for hand-kneaded breads.

16
Whole Wheat Flour

Whole wheat flour does not need much of an introduction, as its good, wholesome flavor is known to us all. (For information regarding its composition and nutritive values, refer to the chapters on Soy Flour and Whole Wheat Berries.)

So I would like to make just two special points about it:

1. If you have a recipe calling for all white flour, you may substitute whole wheat—cup for cup. I do this with all my sweet, "quick" bread recipes and many of my cakes. The whole wheat flour adds more body, flavor, and nutritive value. If you use all whole wheat flour, the result may be heavier than desired. I generally use about half of each type.

2. Whole wheat flour is the same as graham flour. Ever since Sylvester Graham zealously promoted its use in this country more than 150 years ago, it has retained his name. Many people think graham flour tastes like graham crackers; these, however, obtain much of their characteristic flavor from additional ingredients, such as molasses and rye flour.

PAUL'S BREAD

As soon as I had mastered the art of bread baking, the first recipe I wanted to try was that for Paul's bread. Paul, a friend from Los Angeles, is a most particular baker. For example, he would make only one type of cake, a plain yellow one with chocolate frosting, but he made it over and over again to perfect its texture, butteriness, and quality of the icing. And when it came to bread, Paul was positively fanatic! Here is his recipe:

PREPARATION TIMES: 1 hour kitchen work
1¾ hours rising
1 hour baking

YIELD: 2 large loaves

4 cups rolled oats
½ cup honey
2 tablespoons salt
1 teaspoon cinnamon
1 teaspoon nutmeg
1 cup raisins
4 tablespoons butter or
  unsaturated margarine

3½ cups boiling water
¼ cup warm water
2 packages active dry yeast
2 eggs
6 cups whole wheat flour
about 2 cups unbleached
  white flour

1. Place the oats, honey, salt, cinnamon, nutmeg, raisins, and butter or margarine in a large bowl. Add the boiling water and mix well. Let sit until it cools to just warm. (To speed this up, you may beat this mixture with a wooden spoon.)

2. Meanwhile, in the cup in which you measured the honey, stir together the warm water and yeast. (The honey left on the side of the cup is needed to feed the yeast cells.)

3. When the oat mixture has cooled, beat in the eggs, then the yeast mixture. Stir in the whole wheat flour.

4. For this step, use unbleached white flour as needed. Turn the dough out of the bowl onto a heavily floured board or counter. With floured hands, knead the dough, incorporating flour as needed until the dough is no longer sticky.

5. Place the dough in a large, oiled bowl. Turn once so the oiled side is on top. Cover the bowl with plastic wrap, and let rise in a warm place 1 hour, or until doubled in bulk.

6. Knead the dough a little. Place in 2 greased 9″ × 5″ loaf pans. Let rise again, about 45 minutes, until double in size. Make 3 diagonal slashes across the top of each loaf. Brush with water. Bake in a 350-degree oven about 1 hour. If the aroma isn't too much for you to resist, let cool before slicing.

Paul also insisted that his bread be absolutely fresh, which meant that he never ate the last two to three inches of a loaf (although these heels always more than met my standards of excellency). So the bits and ends of this bread could be snitched to make delicious bread crumbs or even some other wonderful dish, such as a special bread pudding. The bread pudding recipes following don't have to be made with Paul's Bread, but they will come out especially delicious if you do. Or you may use a firm whole wheat bread, preferably one that lists honey as one of its ingredients.

BANANA BREAD PUDDING

Another custardy pudding, this one is wholesomely flavored with bananas, honey, and lemon peel.

PREPARATION TIMES: 10 minutes kitchen work
50 minutes baking

YIELD: 6 servings

2 cups milk, scalded
1 cup mashed, ripe bananas
½ teaspoon salt
1 teaspoon grated lemon peel
2 eggs, beaten

⅓ cup honey
½ cup raisins
4 slices whole wheat bread, cubed (this should not be stale bread)

Mix all ingredients together and turn into a greased 1-quart casserole. Bake in a 350-degree oven about 50 minutes or until set. Serve warm or cold, plain or with whipped cream.

SHERRIED BREAD PUDDING

This light, lovely pudding with bread cubes and raisins suspended in a delightful sherry-flavored custard is indeed very special.

PREPARATION TIMES: 15 minutes kitchen work
                   1 hour baking

YIELD: 4 to 6 servings

½ stick (4 tablespoons) butter
  or unsaturated margarine
3½ cups milk
2 cups dry bread cubes, from
  a firm, whole wheat bread
½ cup sugar

2 eggs, beaten
½ cup dry sherry
1 teaspoon cinnamon
1 teaspoon nutmeg
1 cup raisins

1. Melt the butter or margarine in the milk, heating the milk just to the scalding point. Stir in the bread cubes and let sit 5 minutes. Then stir in the remaining ingredients.

2. Pour the mixture into a greased 1-quart casserole. Set in a pan of hot water. Bake in a 375-degree oven about 1 hour or until set. This is best eaten warm.

COCOA-HONEYED SPIRAL BREAD

Try this unusual loaf, with a bittersweet honey and cocoa filling. The bread is so flavorful, it is marvelous just eaten plain, although it is also great for peanut butter or cream cheese sandwiches. Plan to serve these tiny sandwiches at your next lunch.

PREPARATION TIMES: 1 hour kitchen work
                   1¾ hours rising
                   40 minutes baking

YIELD: 2 loaves

Bread:

2 packages active dry yeast
2 teaspoons salt
2 tablespoons honey
2 cups warm water
½ cup dry milk powder
¼ cup vegetable oil
1 cup All-bran cereal

3 cups whole wheat flour
about 3 cups unbleached
   white flour or bread flour

Filling:
⅓ cup honey
⅓ cup cocoa

1. In a large bowl, stir together the yeast, salt, honey, and water. Let sit a few minutes. Add the milk powder, oil, bran, and whole wheat flour, 1 cup at a time, mixing in each cup after it is added. Add enough unbleached white flour to make a stiff dough.

2. Turn the dough out onto a floured surface, and knead until smooth, elastic, and no longer sticky, adding more white flour as necessary.

3. Place the dough in an oiled bowl, and turn once so that the greased side faces up. Cover the bowl with plastic wrap, and place in a warm, draft-free spot until the dough has doubled in bulk, about 1 hour.

4. Knead the dough a few minutes longer. Divide in half. Roll each half to a 14″ × 7″ rectangle. Spread each with half of the filling (just mix the honey and cocoa together until the cocoa has dissolved). Roll up, jelly roll style, beginning with a narrow side. Place each loaf in a greased 9″ × 5″ loaf pan. Cover and let rise until doubled in bulk, about 40 minutes.

5. Bake in a 350-degree oven 35 minutes. Turn out onto a baking sheet and bake upside down 5 minutes longer. Cool thoroughly on a rack before slicing.

KAISER ROLLS

These quickly made yeasted rolls require only one rising of the dough. The rolls are plain-tasting but good and chewy, making them perfect for nearly any type of sandwich.

PREPARATION TIMES: 50 minutes kitchen work
40 minutes rising
35 minutes baking

YIELD: 8 rolls (recipe may be doubled, if desired)

1 package active dry yeast
1½ cups warm water
pinch sugar
2 teaspoons salt
3 tablespoons melted butter

or unsaturated margarine, divided usage
2 cups whole wheat flour
about 2½ cups unbleached white flour or bread flour

1. In a large bowl, dissolve the yeast in the warm water with the pinch of sugar. Let sit 10 minutes, or until a foam forms on the surface. Add the salt, 2 tablespoons melted butter or margarine, whole wheat flour, and enough unbleached white flour to make a stiff dough.

2. On a floured surface, knead the dough until it is smooth and elastic, adding more white flour as needed until the dough is no longer sticky.

3. Divide the dough into 8 equal pieces. Roll each into a ball and then flatten to 1-inch thick. Place, 2 inches apart, on greased baking sheets. Cover and let rise in a warm, draft-free spot until doubled in size, about 40 minutes.

4. Make 5 curved cuts in the tops of each roll (see diagram) and brush with the remaining melted butter. Bake the rolls in a 350-degree oven 30 to 35 minutes, or until crisp. Let cool on racks.

THIS AND THAT BREAD

Here's a favorite hearty, flavorful loaf that combines a variety of flours with sesame and sunflower seeds. The result is highly nutritious and extraordinarily tasty. The bread is great with dinner and goes especially well with soups. Or it may be used for sandwich making.

PREPARATION TIMES: 1 hour kitchen work
1¾ hours rising
50 minutes baking

YIELD: 2 loaves

3 tablespoons active dry
  yeast
4 cups warm water
⅔ cup molasses
2 tablespoons vegetable oil
1 cup rye flour
1 tablespoon salt
1 cup dry milk powder

½ cup cornmeal
½ cup rolled oats
½ cup sesame seeds
½ cup sunflower seeds
3 cups whole wheat flour
about 3 cups unbleached
  white flour or bread flour

1. In a large bowl, dissolve the yeast in the water. Stir in the molasses, oil, rye flour, salt, dry milk powder, cornmeal, oats, and seeds. Stir in the whole wheat flour, 1 cup at a time. Add enough unbleached white flour to make a stiff dough.
2. Turn the dough out onto a floured surface and knead until smooth, elastic, and no longer sticky, adding more unbleached white flour as needed. Place the dough in an oiled bowl, and rotate it so that the greased side faces up. Cover the bowl with plastic wrap, and let the dough rise in a warm, draft-free spot until doubled in bulk, about 1 hour.
3. Knead the dough a few minutes longer. Divide in half and shape each half into a loaf shape. Place each in a greased 9″ × 5″ loaf pan. Let rise, covered, until doubled in bulk, about 45 minutes.
4. Brush the tops of the loaves with water. Bake in a 375-degree oven 40 minutes. Turn out of the pans onto a baking sheet and bake upside down about 10 minutes longer, or until the bottoms are crisp. Let cool thoroughly on racks before slicing.

WHOLE WHEAT YEASTED CARROT BREAD

Carrot breads and cakes are becoming increasingly popular, as they are moist and highly flavored. Here's a yeasted carrot bread that is less sweet than the usual quick bread and has a marvelous texture and a glorious orange-brown color. The bread is delicious when used for Muenster cheese sandwiches.

PREPARATION TIMES: 1 hour kitchen work   1 hour baking
                           1¾ hours rising

YIELD: 1 very large, round loaf

1 package active dry yeast
¼ cup warm water
1 tablespoon honey
2¼ cups (about 4 medium) grated, peeled carrots
1½ tablespoons lemon juice plus enough milk to equal 1½ cups altogether

1½ teaspoons salt
1 teaspoon cinnamon
2½ cups whole wheat flour
2½ cups unbleached white flour or bread flour, divided usage
½ cup raisins

1. Stir together the yeast, water, and honey. Let sit in a warm place until foam appears at the surface, about 10 minutes.

2. Heat the carrots and lemon-milk mixture in a large pot until lukewarm. Stir in the yeast mixture, then the salt, cinnamon, whole wheat flour, and 1½ cups of the white flour. Stir in the raisins.

3. Turn the dough out onto a heavily floured board or counter. Knead until smooth and elastic, incorporating more of the white flour as needed.

4. Place the dough in a large, oiled bowl and turn once so the oiled side faces up. Cover the bowl with plastic wrap and place in a warm, draft-free spot until the dough has doubled in volume, about 1 hour.

5. Knead the dough another few minutes and form into a large round loaf. Place on a greased baking sheet. Let rise until doubled in bulk.

6. Bake the bread in a 375-degree oven about 50 minutes, turning

it upside down on the baking sheet for the last 5 minutes of cooking time. Let cool before slicing.

BUTTERSCOTCH MARBLE CAKE

Most marble cakes have little flavor; a tasteless white batter is merely swirled with a bit of chocolate. But here's a cake with a wholesome wheaty, butterscotch batter that is marbled with a lovely, slightly bitter chocolate mixture. Truly, it's irresistible.

PREPARATION TIMES: 30 minutes kitchen work
                                    50 minutes baking

YIELD: 1 tube cake, about 12 servings

Batter:

6 eggs, separated	½ teaspoon salt
1½ cups brown sugar	
½ cup water	*Marble mixture: (Mix all*
½ cup vegetable oil	*ingredients together)*
2 teaspoons vanilla	6 tablespoons cocoa
1¼ cups whole wheat flour	¾ cup brown sugar
1 cup unbleached white flour	1 teaspoon vanilla
2½ teaspoons baking powder	½ cup boiling water

1. In a large bowl, beat the egg whites until stiff, and set aside.

2. In another large bowl, beat the egg yolks. Gradually beat in the brown sugar. When done, the mixture should be very thick. Beat in the water, oil, and vanilla.

3. In another bowl, stir together the flours, baking powder, and salt. Add to the batter and beat only until moistened. Gently fold in the egg whites.

4. Turn the batter into a greased and floured tube pan. Pour the marble mixture over the batter, and cut into the batter with a knife to create a swirled effect.

5. Bake the cake in a 325-degree oven 30 minutes. Raise the heat to 350 degrees and bake 20 minutes longer, or until the cake tests done with a toothpick. Let cool on a rack before removing from the pan and slicing.

STUFFED PIZZA

This Italian dish makes for exotic eating, either for lunch or dinner. The dough is filled with escarole, olives, almonds, and raisins. The effect is that of a chewy bread with a surprising and unusual flavor. It may be served hot or lukewarm and is excellent when accompanied by a full-bodied red wine.

PREPARATION TIMES: 1¼ hours kitchen work
2 hours rising
40 minutes baking

YIELD: 4 servings

Pastry:
1 package active dry yeast
½ teaspoon sugar
¾ cup warm water
1 cup whole wheat flour
⅓ cup melted butter or unsaturated margarine, divided usage
1 teaspoon salt
½ teaspoon pepper
1 cup unbleached white flour or bread flour

Filling:
2 tablespoons vegetable oil

3 to 4 very small heads escarole or other leafy lettuce, shredded (about 2½ to 3 cups)
½ cup raisins, soaked in warm water to cover and then drained
¼ cup slivered almonds
1 clove garlic, minced
3 tablespoons minced fresh parsley
1 cup black olives, chopped
⅛ teaspoon pepper

1. Dissolve the yeast and sugar in the warm water. Let sit about 10 minutes, or until a foam forms on the surface. Stir in the whole wheat flour, 3 tablespoons melted butter or margarine, salt, and pepper. Add enough white flour to make a stiff dough.

2. Turn the dough out onto a floured surface and knead until smooth, elastic, and no longer sticky, adding more white flour as needed.

3. Place the dough in an oiled bowl, and turn once so that the greased side faces up. Cover the bowl with plastic wrap. Let the dough rise in a warm, draft-free spot until doubled in bulk, about 1 hour.

4. Meanwhile, make the filling: Heat the oil in a skillet. Add the escarole and cook, stirring, 10 minutes. Add the remaining filling ingredients and cook 10 minutes longer, stirring often. Place in a colander to drain and let cool

5. Knead the dough a few minutes longer, working in the remaining melted butter or margarine. Divide the dough in half. Press one half into the bottom of a deep, greased 9- or 10-inch round cake pan or casserole. Spread the filling over the dough, and cover with the remaining half of dough.

6. Cover the pan and let rise until nearly doubled in bulk, about 1 hour.

7. Bake the pizza in a 375-degree oven 35 minutes. Tip it out onto a baking sheet and bake upside down 5 minutes longer, or until crisp on the bottom.

17
Bran

There has been so much talk about fiber these days, I would like to share some of my personal thoughts regarding it.

The way I see it, man evolved to survive in a nontechnological environment. The air was clean, the seas plentiful, and the food unprocessed. And while many of the advances we now have make our lives considerably more comfortable, they may also endanger our well-being. Thus, the air we breathe contains toxins, the fish we catch poisons, and the food we eat chemical additives that give it a longer shelf life and improved palatability and appearance but also pose the ever-present question of potential harm.

The processing of foods is another aspect of the same problem. Humans thrived on the diet that was available when the species began. There has been a trend, mostly during the present century, to remove nutrients and other natural substances from food. Bran, the outer coating of the wheat kernel, is discarded prior to the milling of white flour. Some are now linking this lack of fiber, supplied by bran and other foods, to the increasing incidence of cancer of the colon and heart disease.

It is somewhat amusing, somewhat dismaying that American industries are so ready to cash in on the replacement of what they so willingly removed from our foods. Thus, we now may purchase a bread containing processed cellulose derived from wood pulp, that is unbelievably tasteless and yet proudly advertises itself as having four times the fiber content of whole wheat bread. And the number of new bran cereals on the supermarket shelves has proliferated.

This current fiber fad began as a result of a study published in 1970 by Dr. Dennis Burkitt, a London physician. He found that in rural Africa, where a high fiber diet is consumed, there is a very small incidence of cancer of the colon and coronary heart disease, both of which are prevalent in Western society. Dr. Burkitt correlated the customary fiber-free diet (particularly the preponderance of white flour) of Americans and Europeans with the high incidence of such diseases.

Studies subsequent to Dr. Burkitt's now suggest that the action of fiber within the body is highly complex. For one thing, dietary fiber is not a single entity. Bran, alfalfa, pectin, oatmeal, and cellulose each behave differently in our systems. For example, the consumption of bran produces no change in cholesterol levels, while vegetable pectins, rye, oats, and the outer coating of corn kernels may be effective in lowering them. So it now appears that, throughout the world, high rates of colon cancer and coronary heart disease are not so much correlated with diets low in fiber but rather with those high in fats and protein. Hereditary factors also play a role in the development of these and other diseases.

Does this evidence indicate that we should return to a white bread, fiber-free diet? I think not. After all, our bodies evolved consuming whole grains, beans, and fresh produce, all of which are high in fiber. It stands to reason then that there are probably substances in these foods that our systems need. While dietary fiber probably will not protect you from colon or heart disease (particularly if you consume large quantities of animal fats), consuming such foods in a moderate quantity will be a return to the eating of what your body was designed to eat.

Beyond this, many high fiber foods taste good. Bran, in particular, adds a hearty texture and good flavor to many dishes. In testing these recipes, I used All-bran cereal, not bran flakes, nor the very fine miller's bran.

Just one further note on bran: Recent studies suggest that this food can block the absorption of iron and may hinder the absorption of calcium. If you take vitamin supplements, then, it is best to do so several hours after eating a bowl of bran cereal or a food containing it in large quantities.

CARROT-BRAN BREAD

This bread is quite different from the usual carrot breads and cakes because carrot juice, rather than the grated vegetable, is used. The bread is very dark and moist, with a strong molasses flavor and excellent keeping qualities. Serve it plain or with butter or cream cheese.

PREPARATION TIMES: 15 minutes kitchen work
                   30 minutes soaking
                   1 hour baking

YIELD: 1 loaf

2 cups All-bran cereal
1 12-ounce can carrot juice
½ cup sour cream
½ cup molasses
1 egg, beaten
1 cup unbleached white flour
1 cup whole wheat flour

1 teaspoon baking soda
4 teaspoons baking powder
1 teaspoon salt
1 teaspoon cinnamon
½ cup raisins, chopped dates,
   or prunes

1. Stir together the bran and carrot juice in a large bowl. Let sit 30 minutes. Then beat in the sour cream, molasses, and egg.

2. In another bowl, stir together the flours, baking soda, baking powder, salt, and cinnamon. Stir this into the bran mixture, mixing only until the dry ingredients are moistened. Fold in the raisins, dates, or prunes.

3. Turn the batter into a greased and floured 9″ × 5″ loaf pan. Bake in a 375-degree oven 1 hour. Let cool before slicing.

BANANA-BRAN BREAD

This is a delicious cross between a sweet, rich banana bread and a hearty, chewy bran muffin. Be sure to use very ripe bananas, as these are the most flavorful.

PREPARATION TIMES: 15 minutes kitchen work
                   1 hour baking

YIELD: 1 loaf

½ cup butter or unsaturated margarine
1 cup brown sugar
2 eggs
4 medium-sized bananas, mashed (about 1½ to 2 cups)
1 tablespoon lemon juice

¾ cup unbleached white flour
¾ cup whole wheat flour
1 cup All-bran cereal
1 teaspoon baking powder
¼ teaspoon salt
¼ teaspoon nutmeg
½ cup raisins

1. In a large bowl, cream together the butter or margarine and sugar. Beat in the eggs well. Then beat in the bananas and lemon juice.

2. In another bowl, stir together the flours, bran, baking powder, salt, and nutmeg. Stir this into the banana mixture, stirring only until the dry ingredients are moistened. Stir in the raisins.

3. Turn the batter into a greased and floured 9″ × 5″ loaf pan. Bake in a 350-degree oven about 1 hour. Let cool before slicing. It is delicious plain or spread with cream cheese.

MINCEMEAT TEA LOAF

Here's a rich quick bread that can also double as a spicy, unfrosted loaf cake. The apples and raisins in the mincemeat make it very moist. It is an excellent gift from your kitchen during the Christmas season.

PREPARATION TIMES: 15 minutes kitchen work
1 hour baking

YIELD: 1 loaf

1 9-ounce package dry condensed mincemeat
1¼ cups water
¼ cup apple jelly
¼ cup raisins
1 cup unbleached white flour
1 cup whole wheat flour
½ cup wheat germ
½ cup All-bran cereal
1 tablespoon baking powder
¼ teaspoon salt
1 egg, beaten
¾ cup milk
2 tablespoons lemon juice
¼ cup brown sugar

1. Break the mincemeat into a saucepan. Add the water and heat until it reaches boiling. Boil and stir 1 minute. Stir in the jelly and raisins and set aside.

2. In a bowl, stir together the flours, wheat germ, bran, baking powder, and salt.

3. In a large bowl, mix together the egg, milk, lemon juice, and brown sugar. Stir in the mincemeat mixture, then the dry ingredients, stirring just until they are moistened.

4. Turn the batter into a greased and floured 9″ × 5″ loaf pan. Bake in a 350-degree oven 50 to 60 minutes. Let cool before slicing.

BRAN MUFFINS

Many bran muffin recipes yield light, delicate muffins. But to my way of thinking, bran muffins should be dark and hearty, with a good molasses flavor. I developed the following recipe and find it ideal. Perhaps a bit too sweet to accompany most dinners, the muffins are perfect for breakfast or lunch box treats.

PREPARATION TIMES: 15 minutes kitchen work
20 minutes baking

YIELD: 1 dozen large muffins

1 cup white flour,
   unbleached
½ cup whole wheat flour
1 teaspoon salt
1½ teaspoons baking soda
2½ cups All-bran cereal
2 eggs, beaten
½ cup sugar
¼ cup molasses

1½ tablespoons lemon juice
   plus enough milk to equal
   1½ cups liquid
2½ tablespoons butter or
   unsaturated margarine,
   melted
½ cup raisins or diced
   bananas

1. In a bowl, stir together the flours, salt, baking soda, and bran.

2. In another bowl, mix well the eggs, sugar, molasses, lemon-milk mixture, and melted butter or margarine. Add the dry ingredients and mix only until they are moistened. Stir in the raisins or bananas.

3. Pour the batter into 12 greased muffin tins, filling them nearly to the top. Bake in a 400-degree oven 20 minutes, or until muffins test done with a toothpick. They are best served warm but are also fine at room temperature.

BRAN-DATE BREAD

A rather sweet yeasted loaf, this is delicious plain or spread with peanut butter or cream cheese. The bread is dark, heavy, and pleasantly chewy. Rolling the dates into the dough makes for a particularly attractive loaf when sliced.

PREPARATION TIMES: 50 minutes kitchen work
3 hours rising
40 minutes baking

YIELD: 2 loaves

2 cups whole wheat flour
about 2 cups unbleached
white flour or bread flour,
divided usage
1 teaspoon cinnamon
2 packages active dry yeast
1 tablespoon salt
1½ cups milk

½ cup honey
½ stick (4 tablespoons) butter
or unsaturated margarine
1 egg
2 cups All-bran cereal
1 8-ounce package dates,
coarsely chopped

1. In a large bowl, stir together the whole wheat flour, 1 cup of white flour, cinnamon, yeast, and salt.

2. In a saucepan, heat the milk, honey, and butter or margarine just until the milk is lukewarm (the butter need not melt completely). Add to the dry ingredients and beat well with an electric mixer. Add the egg and beat it in well. Stir in the bran and then enough additional white flour to make a stiff dough.

3. Turn the dough out onto a floured surface and knead until smooth and elastic, adding flour until it is no longer sticky. Place in an oiled bowl, and turn once so that the greased side faces up. Cover the bowl with plastic wrap and let sit in a warm, draft-free spot until the dough has doubled in bulk, about 2 hours.

4. Knead the dough a few minutes longer. Divide in half. Roll each half to a 12″ × 8″ rectangle. Sprinkle with the dates. Roll each up, jelly roll style, beginning with a short edge. Place each loaf in a greased 9″ × 5″ loaf pan. Cover and let rise until doubled in bulk, about 1 hour.

5. Brush the loaves with water. Bake in a 350-degree oven 35 minutes. Tip the loaves out onto a baking sheet and bake upside down 5 minutes longer or until the bottoms are crisp. Let cool on racks before slicing.

BRAN BREAD

A simple, hearty, country-style loaf, this is perfect for morning toast or sandwiches of any type. The flecks of bran add an unusual texture, and the soy flour gives the loaf an extra nutritional boost. Since the bread requires only one rising, it is more quickly made than most yeasted loaves.

PREPARATION TIMES: 40 minutes kitchen work
40 minutes rising
45 minutes baking

YIELD: 1 large, round loaf

1 package active dry yeast
½ teaspoon sugar
2½ cups warm water,
   divided usage
3 cups whole wheat flour

¼ cup soy flour
1½ teaspoons salt
1 cup All-bran cereal
about 3 cups unbleached
   white flour or bread flour

1. Dissolve the yeast and sugar in ½ cup warm water. Let sit until a foam forms on top, about 10 minutes.

2. Meanwhile, in a large bowl, stir together the whole wheat flour, soy flour, salt, and bran. Add the yeast mixture and the remaining water. Beat well. Stir in enough white flour to make a stiff dough.

3. Turn the dough out onto a floured surface and knead until smooth and elastic, adding enough flour so that it is no longer sticky. Shape into a round loaf and place on a greased baking sheet. Cover and let rise until almost doubled in bulk, about 40 minutes.

4. Bake the loaf in a 375-degree oven 40 minutes. Turn upside down and bake 5 minutes longer. Let cool on a rack before slicing.

PEACHY BRAN COFFEE CAKE

Here's a wholesome coffee cake that tastes not only of bran, but of sweet, chewy dried peaches as well. The cake is very attractive—brown and gold, with a crunchy topping. It is absolutely delicious either warm or chilled (because it is so moist, it should be stored in the refrigerator).

PREPARATION TIMES: 30 minutes kitchen work
                                40 minutes baking

YIELD: 1 8″ × 10″ cake, or 8 servings

Cake:
¾ cup chopped dried peaches
½ cup unbleached white
  flour
½ cup whole wheat flour
¾ teaspoon baking powder
¾ teaspoon baking soda
½ teaspoon salt
1½ teaspoons cinnamon
1 cup All-bran cereal
9 tablespoons butter or
  unsaturated margarine,
  softened
⅔ cup sugar

2 eggs
1 cup yogurt

Topping: (Mix all ingredients together)
3 tablespoons whole wheat
  flour
½ cup brown sugar
1 teaspoon cinnamon
½ cup All-bran cereal
3 tablespoons butter or
  unsaturated margarine,
  softened

1. Pour hot water to cover the peaches and let stand while you are preparing the rest of the cake. Before using, drain well.

2. In a bowl, stir together the flours, baking powder, baking soda, salt, cinnamon, and bran.

3. In a large bowl, cream the butter or margarine with the sugar well. Beat in the eggs and then the yogurt. Beat in the dry ingredients until they are moistened.

4. Turn the batter into a well-greased 8″ × 10″ baking pan.

Sprinkle with the peaches and then the topping mixture. Bake the cake in a 350-degree oven 35 to 40 minutes, or until it tests done with a toothpick. Transfer to a rack to cool.

BRANNIES

For those who love rich, chewy, fudgy brownies, these bars are even better, because the bran and whole wheat flour lend even more body and flavor. As an added benefit, brannies are also better for your body.

PREPARATION TIMES: 15 minutes kitchen work
30 minutes baking

YIELD: 1 8″ × 8″ pan, or 16 squares

⅓ cup sifted cocoa
½ cup whole wheat flour
¾ cup All-bran cereal
½ teaspoon baking powder
2 eggs
1 cup sugar

1 stick (½ cup) butter or
unsaturated margarine,
melted
1 teaspoon vanilla
½ cup chopped walnuts
(optional)

1. In a bowl, stir together the cocoa, flour, bran, and baking powder.

2. In a large bowl, beat the eggs. Gradually beat in the sugar. The mixture should be thick and pale yellow. Beat in the melted butter or margarine and vanilla. Add the dry ingredients and beat until moistened. Stir in the nuts, if desired.

3. Spread the batter evenly in a greased and floured 8″ × 8″ baking pan. Bake in a 375-degree oven 30 minutes, or until they test done with a toothpick. Transfer to a rack to cool and then cut into 2-inch squares.

PUMPKIN-BRAN CAKE

I prefer dense, well-flavored cakes that require no thick, sweet icing. And here's a cake that marvelously answers that craving. Filled with the fragrance of spices, the moisture of pumpkin, and the textures of bran, nuts, and raisins, it's a sure winner in any home.

PREPARATION TIMES: 20 minutes kitchen work (except the cooking of the pumpkin if you use home-cooked)
1 hour baking

YIELD: 1 9″ × 5″ loaf cake, or about 8 servings

1 cup unbleached white flour
1 teaspoon baking powder
½ teaspoon baking soda
¼ teaspoon salt
¾ teaspoon cinnamon
¼ teaspoon cloves
⅛ teaspoon nutmeg
⅛ teaspoon ginger
2 eggs
1 cup sugar

1 cup cooked pumpkin (either canned or home-cooked)*
1 stick (½ cup) butter or unsaturated margarine, melted
1 cup All-bran cereal
⅓ cup chopped walnuts
⅓ cup raisins

1. Stir together the flour, baking powder, baking soda, and spices.

2. In a large bowl, beat the eggs very well. Beat in the sugar gradually until the mixture is thick and pale. Beat in the pumpkin and melted butter or margarine. Stir in the bran, then the dry ingredients, stirring only enough to moisten them.

3. Turn the batter into a 9″ × 5″ greased and floured loaf pan. Bake in a 350-degree oven about 1 hour.

*If you wish to cook your own pumpkin, follow the directions given for winter squash (part 6, Chapter 30), allowing a somewhat longer cooking time for larger pumpkins.

18
Soy Flour

I had heard from many sources that soy flour is highly nutritious. But until I checked the tables in my nutrition handbook, I had no idea of the extent of the difference between soy and wheat flours. Nearly every listing showed soy values to be at least two, three, or four times higher than those of whole wheat and white flours. For example, a pound of enriched white flour contains 430 milligrams of magnesium, whole wheat 1,680 milligrams, and soy flour 7,800 milligrams. Looking at phosphorus levels, the difference again stands out: 400 milligrams in white flour, 1,700 milligrams in whole wheat flour, and 2,700 milligrams in soy flour. Protein differences are considerable, too. White flour supplies 50 grams of protein per pound, whole wheat 60 grams, and soy 190 grams.

Soy flour is deficient only in the sulfur-containing amino acids, which means that it completes the protein in wheat, rye, buckwheat, peanut, and barley flours, as well as in oats and cornmeal.

I was at first hesitant to begin baking with soy flour. Friends informed me that it made heavy, unappealing breads. I was surprised, then, to discover that soy flour has a pleasant, nutty taste; but the texture it produces can indeed be less than desirable. Soy flour, if used in too great a proportion to wheat, makes loaves that are very dense and moist, even unappetizingly wet. For this reason, it is best used in fairly small quantities, about one fourth cup per loaf of yeasted bread. Even this small amount produces a loaf with a moister, chewier texture and far greater food value. In non-yeasted breads, such as my corn bread and gingerbread recipes, the extra moistness from the soy flour is an asset. Both are hearty, chewy, and full-flavored.

Incidentally, soy flours may be found in full-fat, high-fat, low-fat, or defatted forms. If you buy yours in a natural foods store, you will be likely to find the full-fat type, for that is the most natural. If you choose to make your purchase in a health food store, you are more apt to find the soy flour defatted, presumably because fats are less healthy. In general the defatted flour offers more vitamins, minerals, and protein with less calories. In terms of baking with soy flours, if you mix them with other flours, the fattiness of the type you use does not much affect the finished product.

MODIFIED CORNELL BREAD

A bread formula developed by Dr. Clive McCay at Cornell did much to enrich the nutritional value of white bread. For each cup of flour called for, the baker added one tablespoon each of soy flour, dry milk powder, and wheat germ. The recipe here goes beyond the Cornell loaf in flavor and food value, including eggs, honey, and part whole wheat flour in the dough. This is a simple, tasty bread for all purposes, from morning toast to noontime sandwiches.

PREPARATION TIMES: 50 minutes kitchen work
2¼ hours rising
45 minutes baking

YIELD: 2 loaves

2 tablespoons active dry yeast	2 teaspoons salt
1 tablespoon honey	4 cups whole wheat flour
3 cups warm water	½ cup soy flour
¼ cup vegetable oil	3 tablespoons wheat germ
¼ cup honey	½ cup dry milk powder
2 eggs, beaten	about 4 cups unbleached white flour or bread flour

1. In a large bowl, dissolve the yeast and 1 tablespoon honey in the warm water. Let sit about 10 minutes, or until a foam forms on the surface.

2. Add the oil, ¼ cup honey, eggs, salt, whole wheat and soy flours, wheat germ, and dry milk powder. Mix well. Add enough white flour to make a stiff dough.

3. Turn the dough out onto a floured surface and knead until smooth, elastic, and no longer sticky, adding more white flour as needed. Place the dough in an oiled bowl, and turn once so the greased side faces up. Cover the bowl with plastic wrap, and let rise in a warm, draft-free spot until the dough has doubled in bulk, about 1 to 1½ hours.

4. Knead the dough a few minutes longer. Divide in half and shape into two loaves. Place each in a greased 9″ × 5″ loaf pan. Let rise, covered, until doubled in size, about 45 minutes.

5. Place the loaves in a cold oven. Turn the temperature to 400 degrees. After 15 minutes, reduce the heat to 375 degrees. Bake 25 minutes. Tip the bread out onto a baking sheet and bake 5 minutes longer, or until the bottoms are browned. Let cool on a rack.

OATMEAL SOY BREAD

The oats and soy flour combine here to produce a wonderfully chewy bread that toasts excellently. It also makes great grilled cheese sandwiches that, from my experience, guests will greedily devour.

PREPARATION TIMES: 45 minutes kitchen work
                   1½ hours rising
                   1 hour baking

YIELD: 2 loaves

2½ packages active dry yeast
1¼ cups warm water
¼ cup honey
2 cups rolled oats
2¼ cups boiling water
3 tablespoons vegetable oil
1 tablespoon salt

2½ cups whole wheat flour
½ cup soy flour
¼ cup wheat germ
¾ cup dry milk powder
about 2½ cups unbleached
    white flour or bread flour

1. In a small bowl, dissolve the yeast in the warm water with the honey.

2. In a large bowl, pour the boiling water over the oats. Add the oil and salt and let cool to lukewarm. Add the yeast mixture, whole wheat flour, soy flour, wheat germ, and milk powder. Mix well. Stir in enough white flour to make a stiff dough.

3. Turn the dough out onto a surface floured with white flour, and knead until smooth, elastic, and no longer sticky, adding more flour as needed. Place the dough in an oiled bowl, and turn once so that the greased side faces up. Cover the bowl with plastic wrap and let the dough rise in a warm, draft-free spot until doubled in bulk, about 1 hour.

4. Knead the dough a few minutes longer. Divide in half. Shape into two loaves and place each in a greased 9″ × 5″ loaf pan. Let rise, covered, until doubled in bulk, about 30 minutes.

5. Bake in a 350-degree oven 45 minutes. Turn out of the pans

onto a baking sheet and bake upside down 10 minutes longer, or until the bottoms are crisp and browned. Let cool on a rack before slicing.

SOY CORN BREAD

This tasty, easy-to-fix soy corn bread has a far greater nutritional value than ordinary corn bread. It goes well with creamed dishes and Mexican foods and also makes a good hot breakfast bread, especially when spread with a bit of honey. You will find this loaf moister than most corn breads; in fact, you may wish to eat it with a fork.

PREPARATION TIMES: 20 minutes kitchen work
25 minutes baking

YIELD: 8 servings

1 cup cornmeal
1 cup soy flour
2 teaspoons baking powder
2 tablespoons brown sugar
1 teaspoon salt
3 eggs, separated

1½ tablespoons lemon juice
plus enough milk to make
1½ cups liquid
3 tablespoons butter or
unsaturated margarine,
melted

1. In a large bowl, stir together the cornmeal, soy flour, baking powder, sugar, and salt.

2. In another bowl, beat the egg whites until stiff.

3. In a third bowl, beat the egg yolks with a fork. Stir in the lemon-milk mixture and the melted butter or margarine. Stir these liquid ingredients into the dry ingredients. Fold in the egg whites gently but thoroughly.

4. Turn the batter into a greased and floured 9″ × 9″ pan. Bake the bread in a 375-degree oven 20 to 25 minutes, or until a toothpick inserted in the center comes out clean. Serve warm from the oven. Any leftovers may be reheated.

PUFFED SOY CASSEROLE

The best attributes of soy flour are apparent in this casserole that's similar to a soufflé, with a nutty taste, rather like the toasted soy nuts so popular as a snack food. The casserole is substantial enough to serve as a main course; a big tossed salad makes a welcome accompaniment.

PREPARATION TIMES: 35 minutes kitchen work
                   35 minutes baking

YIELD: 4 main course servings

1 cup soy flour	1 teaspoon salt
3 cups milk	3 eggs, separated
2 tablespoons butter or	
unsaturated margarine, softened	

1. Place the soy flour in a heavy saucepan. Blend in 1 cup of the milk until no lumps of flour remain. Stir in the remaining milk. Cook, stirring, until hot but not boiling. Cook 5 minutes longer.

2. Remove from the heat and beat in the butter or margarine, salt, and egg yolks.

3. Beat the egg whites until stiff and fold them into the soy mixture gently but thoroughly.

4. Turn the mixture into a greased 2-quart casserole. Bake in a 375-degree oven 35 minutes or until puffed, browned, and set. Serve immediately.

SOY GINGERBREAD

The next time you get a craving for a sweet treat, whip up a quickly made, extremely nutritious gingerbread. Since this type of cake is best when moist and hearty, the addition of soy flour is a definite boon. Serve warm from the oven or at room temperature, plain or with a topping of homemade applesauce.

PREPARATION TIMES: 20 minutes kitchen work
                   40 minutes baking

YIELD: 1 8" × 10" cake, or about 8 servings.

2 eggs
½ cup sugar
1 stick (½ cup) butter or
   unsaturated margarine,
   melted
1 cup molasses
2 teaspoons baking soda
1 teaspoon cinnamon

1 teaspoon cloves
1 teaspoon ginger
¼ teaspoon salt
1½ cups whole wheat flour
½ cup wheat germ
½ cup soy flour
1 cup hot water

1. In a large bowl, beat the eggs. Beat in the sugar very well. Beat in the molasses and melted butter or margarine.

2. In another bowl, stir together the dry ingredients. Beat into the molasses mixture alternately with the hot water.

3. Turn the batter into a greased and floured 8" × 10" baking pan. Bake in a 350-degree oven 35 to 40 minutes, or until the cake tests done with a toothpick. Transfer to a rack to cool.

19
Cornmeal

Corn formed the basis of the American Indian diet, supplying complete protein when eaten with the available beans. (Dairy products, nuts, and grains also substantially complement the protein in corn.) The early New England settlers learned from the Indians how to pound dried corn kernels with a stone pestle in a mortar made from a hollowed-out log. They first ate the resulting meal as the Indians did—as a mush made from boiling the cornmeal in water.

But the colonists were not content for long with the dish. They missed their chewy European wheat and rye loaves and were determined to make similar breads with this new grain. However, each time the women tried, they failed. They did not know that cornmeal contains almost no gluten. It therefore could not hold the bubbles formed during yeast fermentation. The bread did not rise but simply became rather sour-tasting. When baked, it had a wet, crumbly, and thoroughly unappetizing texture.

The colonial women eventually learned not to even attempt the thick loaves of their European homelands. They fried or baked thin patties made from mixing the cornmeal and water and achieved the long-keeping johnnycakes (journey cakes), which are much like our present-day cornmeal pancakes. Also, they let the mush cool, sliced it, and made fried mush, which was served with molasses or maple syrup.

Some other dishes were invented. One that is still loved today is Indian pudding, so named because the colonists often termed cornmeal "Indian" or "Injun." The pudding is a mixture of milk, molasses, and cornmeal, and may also contain eggs, butter, spices, and raisins. The batter undergoes a long, slow baking and becomes thick with a browned crust on top.

Steamed Boston brown bread was another delight. For this, the cornmeal had to be supplemented with a bit of expensive wheat. But the results were worth it. Molasses was added, as was sour or buttermilk, which caused a release of the carbon dioxide in the baking soda, making the bread rise. Today we steam breads in molds or empty coffee cans. But then the batter was wrapped in cloth and dropped into a kettle of water hanging over the fire. Sometimes, if another pot was not available, a piece of meat would be stewing in the same pot.

Today we accept cornmeal as a regular part of our lives. We eat hot corn breads and muffins, tortillas, and corn chips. The early colonial dishes like Indian pudding and Boston brown bread are also enjoyed. The fact that cornmeal bakes differently from wheat flour rarely occurs to us. We just follow the recipes. But it required years to develop the proper cooking of cornmeal, and we are fortunate in being able to so easily reap the rewards of this work. Here are a few modern innovations on traditional cornmeal dishes.

Incidentally, the colonists were not so unfortunate as to find packaged cornmeal with the germ removed. The degerminated cornmeal most widely available in supermarkets today lacks the flavor and texture of the stone-ground whole kernel. And it is far less nutritious. Whole grain cornmeal, which can be purchased at health food stores and some supermarkets, contains two and a half times the fiber, calcium, phosphorus, potassium, and magnesium, and slightly more protein and vitamin A than degerminated and enriched meal.

CORN CRACKERS

I enjoy making my own crackers for dips or just to snack on. These are very crisp. Someone tasting one for the first time is apt to bite into one, say, "Oh, they're *so* hard!" and then go on to eat several more; they're that good.

PREPARATION TIMES: 10 minutes kitchen work
20 minutes baking

YIELD: about 50 crackers

½ cup cornmeal
1½ cups whole wheat flour
1 teaspoon salt

2½ tablespoons vegetable oil
1½ tablespoons honey
⅓ to ½ cup water

1. In a bowl, stir together the cornmeal, flour, and salt. With a fork, stir in the oil, honey, and just enough water to bind the mixture.

2. Roll out the dough as thinly as possible with a floured short rolling pin (or round drinking glass) on a greased 11" × 16" jelly roll pan. Cut the dough into 1½-inch squares.

3. Bake the squares in a 375-degree oven for 15 to 20 minutes or until crisp and just beginning to brown. When cool, store in an airtight container.

POLENTA

I first learned about polenta, hearing my husband rave about his mother's recipe. His family hails from the far north of Italy, where great quantities of this food are consumed. Polenta, a cornmeal dish, is the customary starch of the dinner (Northern Italians do not eat much pasta). It may be served plain, sautéed, baked, or covered with a rich sauce. It is often accompanied by Asiago cheese, a hard grating cheese similar to Parmesan.

When I decided to make this unfamiliar food, I was a bit apprehensive, having been told about long stirrings with a "polenta paddle," a utensil shaped much like a small oar. But learning that a heavy wooden spoon works equally well, I set out to make this dish.

Basic polenta is really quite simple to prepare, being merely cornmeal cooked in boiling water until very thick. I was surprised to learn that polenta is exactly the same food that the Indians first taught the colonists to make, that the Mexicans have consumed for centuries, and that many in the South still eat for breakfast today. Exotic-sounding polenta is none other than cornmeal mush.

But while mush is spooned up plain or with syrup as one would eat oatmeal, polenta is usually served in other guises. Following is the basic recipe with several suggested serving variations.

PREPARATION TIME: 30 minutes kitchen work

YIELD: 4 servings

1 cup cornmeal	1 teaspoon salt
1 cup cold water	butter, grated Parmesan or
3½ cups boiling water	Cheddar cheese (optional)

1. Combine the cornmeal, cold water, and salt. Gradually add to the boiling water (which should be in a heavy saucepan), stirring constantly to avoid lumps.

2. Cook this mixture, stirring constantly with a heavy wooden spoon, until it becomes very thick. The mixture should be kept almost to the boiling point throughout. Too hot, and it will splatter; too cold, and it will take too long to thicken. The process will take about 20 minutes.

3. To eat the polenta, you may: (1) eat it just as is, either plain or enriched with butter or cheese to taste; (2) layer it in a baking dish with butter and/or cheese and bake it in a 375-degree oven about 15 minutes; (3) serve it for breakfast, accompanied by maple syrup or honey; (4) spread it in a shallow pan and chill it. It is then cut into squares and baked or sautéed and served either for breakfast or as a side dish with dinner.

BAKED LAYERED POLENTA

This Northern Italian recipe makes use of polenta much as the Southern Italians use pasta in lasagna. The polenta is layered with tomato sauce and mozzarella cheese and then baked. It is marvelously different from the usual lasagna, though, because the cornmeal and Parmesan cheese give the starch layers far more taste than ordinary noodles offer.

PREPARATION TIMES: 40 minutes kitchen work (plus 30 minutes
                   to make polenta)
                   1 hour chilling
                   1 hour simmering
                   35 minutes baking

YIELD: 6 servings

1 recipe basic polenta (recipe above)
½ cup grated Parmesan cheese
4 ounces mushrooms, sliced
1 onion, chopped
1 clove garlic, minced
2 tablespoons olive or salad oil
1 1-pound can tomatoes, undrained and chopped
1 6-ounce can tomato paste
¼ cup water
2 tablespoons dry sherry
1 teaspoon oregano
½ teaspoon thyme
½ teaspoon salt
⅛ teaspoon pepper
1 10-ounce package frozen chopped spinach, thawed and squeezed dry
1½ cups shredded mozzarella cheese

1. Stir the Parmesan cheese into the polenta. Spread evenly in a lightly greased 9″ × 13″ baking pan. Chill for at least 1 hour. When firm, cut into 4 quarters, each 4½″ × 6½″.

2. Meanwhile, sauté the mushrooms, onion, and garlic in oil. Stir in the remaining ingredients, except the spinach and mozzarella cheese. Simmer, partially covered, 1 hour. Stir in the spinach.

3. Lightly grease an 8″ × 10″ baking dish. Place two polenta quarters in it, side by side. Cover with half the sauce and sprinkle with half the mozzarella cheese. Repeat these layers. Secure with toothpicks.

4. Bake the dish in a 350-degree oven about 35 minutes, until very hot and bubbly.

SOUFFLÉED SPOON BREAD

This wonderfully puffy casserole has only one drawback. It must be served as soon as it comes from the oven or it will fall. Spoon bread is the Southern version of corn bread and is somewhat more custardy, containing a larger quantity of eggs and milk. The spoon bread here is baked in a casserole. With the beaten egg whites, it's exceptionally light and delicate. Serve it as an accompaniment to any entrée. Or it can even be a lunch course, along with a tossed salad.

PREPARATION TIMES: 45 minutes kitchen work
                     45 minutes baking

YIELD: 4 servings

2 cups milk
1 cup cornmeal
2 tablespoons butter or
  unsaturated margarine
1 teaspoon salt

½ teaspoon baking powder
4 eggs, separated
¾ cup shredded Cheddar
  cheese
pinch salt

1. In a large, heavy saucepan, scald the milk. Stir the cornmeal gradually into the milk. Cook, stirring, until the mixture is thick and smooth and the milk just reaches boiling.

2. Remove the mixture from the heat and add the butter or margarine, 1 teaspoon salt, and baking powder. Stir until the butter melts. Beat in the egg yolks, one at a time, and then stir in the cheese.

3. In a bowl, beat the egg whites with a pinch of salt until stiff. Stir one third of the whites into the corn mixture. Then fold in the rest gently.

4. Turn the batter into a well-greased 2-quart round casserole. Bake in a 375-degree oven 45 minutes.

INDIAN PUDDING

Indian Pudding is without question one of the most wholesome of desserts. It is particularly satisfying on a cold evening following a light dinner.

PREPARATION TIMES: 15 minutes kitchen work
20 minutes simmering
1½ hours baking

YIELD: 6 servings

1 quart milk, scalded
½ cup cornmeal
2 tablespoons butter or
  unsaturated margarine, melted
½ cup molasses

1 teaspoon salt
1 teaspoon cinnamon
½ teaspoon ginger
2 eggs, beaten
⅓ cup raisins

1. In the top part of a double boiler, pour the milk slowly over the cornmeal, stirring as you do so. Cook over boiling water 20 minutes, stirring occasionally.

2. Stir together the butter or margarine, molasses, salt, cinnamon, ginger, and eggs. Add to the cornmeal mixture. Stir in the raisins.

3. Pour the batter into a greased, 2-quart round casserole, and place it in a pan containing 1 inch of hot water. Place in a 350-degree oven and bake about 1½ hours or until set. Serve hot with whipped cream or vanilla ice cream.

MOLASSES APPLE MUFFINS

These golden, light-textured muffins are filled with juicy apple pieces. They are delightful warm or cold, with a meal or as a snack.

PREPARATION TIMES: 20 minutes kitchen work
25 minutes baking

YIELD: 1 dozen muffins

1 cup cornmeal
1½ cups unbleached white
  flour

3 tablespoons sugar
½ teaspoon salt
1 tablespoon baking powder

1 cup milk
1 egg, beaten
2 tablespoons molasses

4 apples, peeled, cored, and
diced

1. In a large bowl, stir together the cornmeal, flour, sugar, salt, and baking powder.

2. In another bowl, mix together the milk, egg, and molasses. Stir into the dry ingredients, mixing only until they are moistened. Fold in the apples.

3. Fill greased muffin tins two-thirds full. Bake in a 400-degree oven 20 to 25 minutes.

AFRICAN BRANDIED CORN CAKE

Here is an unusual cake from Ghana that uses cornmeal in the batter. The texture is somewhat heavy, rather like a coarse pound cake. The flavor is really quite extraordinary, with corn, raisins, brandy, and peanuts all lending their distinctive tastes.

Note: If you use unsalted peanuts, add ⅛ teaspoon salt to the batter along with the dry ingredients.

PREPARATION TIMES: 15 minutes kitchen work
                   1 hour 20 minutes baking
YIELD: 1 tube cake, or about 12 servings

2 sticks (1 cup) butter or
   unsaturated margarine,
   softened
1 cup sugar
4 eggs
¼ cup brandy
½ cup milk

1 cup unbleached white flour
1 cup cornmeal
¼ teaspoon nutmeg
1 cup golden raisins
1 cup dark raisins
¼ cup lightly salted peanuts

1. In a large bowl, cream the butter or margarine with the sugar. Beat in the eggs, then the brandy and milk. Beat in the flour, cornmeal, and nutmeg until moist. Stir in raisins and peanuts.

2. Turn the batter into a greased and floured tube pan. Bake in a 325-degree oven 1 hour 20 minutes, or until it tests done with a toothpick. Let cool on a rack before removing from the pan and slicing.

BOSTON BROWN BREAD

If you've never tried a steamed bread, you are missing a great treat. The texture is moist and spongy, absolutely marvelous hot with plenty of butter. Serve it for breakfast, for lunch with cheese, or for dinner with a stew.

PREPARATION TIMES: 15 minutes kitchen work
3 hours simmering

YIELD: 2 loaves, each serving 8

2 cups cornmeal
½ cup wheat germ
1 cup whole wheat flour
½ cup All-bran cereal
2 teaspoons salt
2 teaspoons baking powder

1 teaspoon cinnamon
1 teaspoon nutmeg
¾ cup molasses
2½ cups buttermilk
⅔ cup raisins

1. In a large bowl, stir together the cornmeal, wheat germ, flour, bran, salt, baking powder, cinnamon, and nutmeg.

2. In another bowl, mix together the molasses and buttermilk. Add these to the dry ingredients, mixing only enough to moisten them. Stir in the raisins.

3. Turn the batter into 2 well-greased, empty 1-pound coffee tins. Cover with the plastic lid, which has been greased (if you don't have the lids, use greased foil, and tie it on with string). Set the tins in a large pot. Fill the pot halfway up the height of the tins with boiling water. Cover the pot and simmer for 3 hours. If steam escapes, it may be necessary to periodically add more boiling water. When done, remove the bread from the tins and serve hot with butter.

20
Rye Flour

For a long time, I avoided using rye flour in baking. I thought that the sour flavor present in delicatessen and bakery rye bread was indigenous to the flour, and it was not a flavor that I was particularly fond of. But I learned that these breads could more properly be called sourdough rye and get their characteristic taste from a fermentation process in which a mixture of rye flour, water, and yeast is allowed to sit at eighty degrees Fahrenheit for a day or two.

So I bought a bag of rye flour and tried a bread recipe that looked appealing. The result was sweet and delicious. Rye flour actually tastes very similar to whole wheat, with the same sort of dark, hearty, wholesome flavor. If you've never sampled honest rye taste, I suggest you give one of the following recipes a try.

Rye flour, like other whole grain flours, is highly nutritious. A pound contains 1,588 calories, 51.7 grams protein, 7.7 grams fat, 122 milligrams calcium, 1,188 milligrams phosphorus, 11.8 milligrams iron, 5 milligrams sodium, 921 milligrams potassium, and

11.2 milligrams niacin, these values being only slightly lower than those of whole wheat flour.

The gluten in rye flour is sticky but does not become elastic as does wheat flour gluten. For this reason, when making a yeasted bread, both types of flour are used. This is not essential for "quick" breads, in which the rye flour may predominate.

HERBED RYE BREAD

Herb breads seem to go particularly well with soups and stews. They are also ideal for sandwiches when a sweet flavor is not desired, such as with cheese or egg salad fillings. This bread is attractively dark in color, with a hearty, chewy texture.

PREPARATION TIMES: 50 minutes kitchen work
                   2¼ hours rising
                   40 minutes baking

YIELD: 2 loaves

3 packages active dry yeast
4 teaspoons sugar
2⅔ cups warm water
4 cups whole wheat flour
1½ cups rye flour
⅓ cup vegetable oil

4 teaspoons salt
1½ teaspoons freshly ground
   black pepper
4 teaspoons dried parsley
about 2 cups unbleached
   white or bread flour

1. Dissolve the yeast and sugar in the warm water in a large bowl. Let sit 10 minutes, or until a foam forms on the surface. Stir in the whole wheat flour, rye flour, oil, salt, pepper, and parsley. Add enough white flour to make a stiff dough.

2. Turn the dough out onto a surface floured with white flour. Knead until smooth, elastic, and no longer sticky, adding more flour as needed. Place the dough in an oiled bowl and turn once so that the greased side faces up. Cover the bowl with plastic wrap and let the dough rise in a warm, draft-free spot until doubled in bulk, about 1½ hours.

3. Knead the dough a few minutes longer. Divide in half. Shape

each half into a loaf, and place each in a greased 9″ × 5″ loaf pan. Let rise, covered, until doubled in bulk, about 45 minutes.

4. With a sharp knife, make three diagonal slashes across each loaf. Bake the bread in a 400-degree oven 20 minutes. Reduce the heat to 350 degrees and bake 15 minutes longer. Tip the loaves out onto a baking sheet and bake upside down 5 minutes more, or until the bottoms are crisp. Let cool thoroughly on racks before slicing.

RAISIN RYE BREAD

This quick bread will give you an opportunity to sample the taste of rye flour without taking the time to make a yeasted loaf. The bread is dark, with a coarse texture and a good, wholesome flavor. It is also considerably less sweet than many other quick breads. Serve it as a snack or spread with cream cheese to make sandwiches.

PREPARATION TIMES: 1 hour soaking
15 minutes kitchen work
1 hour baking

YIELD: 1 loaf

2½ cups rye flour
½ cup unbleached white
  flour
1 teaspoon salt
4 teaspoons baking powder
1 egg

⅓ cup molasses
1½ tablespoons lemon juice
  plus enough milk to equal
  1½ cups liquid
½ cup golden raisins, soaked
  in ¼ cup brandy for 1 hour

1. In a bowl, stir together the flours, salt, and baking powder.

2. In another bowl, beat the egg with the molasses. Stir in the lemon-milk mixture, then the dry ingredients, mixing only until they are moistened. Fold in the raisins and any brandy that was not absorbed.

3. Turn the batter into a greased and floured 9″ × 5″ loaf pan. Bake in a 350-degree oven about 1 hour. Cool before slicing.

RUSSIAN RYE BREAD

This rye bread has a deep, lovely color from coffee, molasses, and toasted pumpernickel crumbs. It is great for cheese sandwiches and goes especially well with hearty soups.

PREPARATION TIMES: 50 minutes kitchen work
2 hours rising
45 minutes baking

YIELD: 1 large, round loaf

3 cups pumpernickel bread crumbs (make by whirling bread in blender or food processor)
3 packages active dry yeast
4 teaspoons molasses
½ cup warm water
2 cups water
4 teaspoons freeze-dried

coffee granules, divided usage
½ stick (4 tablespoons) butter or unsaturated margarine
1 cup All-bran cereal
2 cups rye flour
¼ teaspoon ginger
2 teaspoons salt
2 cups unbleached white flour or bread flour

1. Spread the bread crumbs on an 11″ × 16″ jelly roll pan and bake in a 350-degree oven about 8 minutes, or until they begin to brown. Don't let them burn.

2. Stir the yeast and molasses into the warm water and let sit about 15 minutes, or until a foam forms on the surface.

3. Heat the water, 3 teaspoons coffee, and butter or margarine in a very large pot until the coffee dissolves and the water is just hot to the touch (the butter need not melt completely). Stir in the bread crumbs, yeast mixture, bran, rye flour, ginger, and salt.

4. Spread most of the white flour out on a board or counter. Place the rye mixture on it and begin kneading in the white flour. Knead until the dough is smooth and stiff, using more white flour if necessary.

5. Place the dough in a greased bowl and turn once so the greased side is on top. Cover the bowl with plastic wrap and let rise until doubled in bulk, about 1½ hours.

6. Knead the dough a few minutes longer. Shape into a large round loaf on a greased baking sheet. Cover and let rise 30 minutes.

7. Mix the remaining 1 teaspoon coffee with 2 teaspoons hot water. Brush over the loaf. Bake in a 400-degree oven 45 minutes.

RYE PANCAKES

These small, light pancakes are perfect for anyone allergic to wheat. Spread them with apple butter, jam, honey, or maple syrup.

PREPARATION TIME: 30 minutes kitchen work

YIELD: 15 2-inch pancakes

1 cup rye flour
1 teaspoon baking powder
1 teaspoon salt
3 tablespoons brown sugar
1 egg, beaten
2 tablespoons butter or

unsaturated margarine, melted
4 teaspoons lemon juice plus enough milk to equal 1¼ cups liquid

1. In a large bowl, stir together the rye flour, baking powder, salt, and brown sugar.

2. In another bowl, mix the egg, melted butter or margarine, and lemon-milk mixture. Stir these ingredients into the dry ones.

3. Drop the batter by tablespoonfuls onto a greased, medium-hot griddle or skillet. Cook on one side, turn, and cook on the other side.

PUMPERNICKEL

Here is an old-fashioned, hearty, dense pumpernickel loaf with a perfect texture and flavor. The addition of cornmeal and molasses is classic.

PREPARATION TIMES: 50 minutes kitchen work
2½ hours rising   45 minutes baking
YIELD: 2 round loaves

2¼ cups cold water	1 tablespoon active dry yeast
⅔ cup cornmeal	¼ cup warm water
2 teaspoons salt	2 teaspoons honey
2 tablespoons butter or	3 cups rye flour
unsaturated margarine	about 3 cups whole wheat
½ cup molasses	flour

1. Place the water, cornmeal, and salt in a large pot. Cook, stirring, just until thickened. Remove from the heat and stir in the butter or margarine and molasses. Let cool to lukewarm.

2. Meanwhile, dissolve the yeast in the warm water with the honey. Let sit 10 minutes, or until a foam forms on the surface.

3. Add the yeast mixture to the cornmeal mixture along with the rye flour and mix well. Add enough whole wheat flour to make a stiff dough.

4. Turn the dough out onto a well-floured surface and knead until smooth, elastic, and no longer sticky, adding more whole wheat flour as necessary. Place the dough in an oiled bowl and turn once so the greased side faces up. Cover the bowl with plastic wrap and let the dough rise in a warm, draft-free spot until doubled in bulk, about 1½ hours.

5. Knead the dough a few minutes longer. Divide in half and shape each into a round loaf. Place, diagonally opposite, on a greased baking sheet sprinkled with cornmeal. Let rise, covered, until doubled in bulk, about 1 hour.

6. Bake in a 375-degree oven 40 minutes. Turn upside down and bake 5 minutes longer, or until the bottoms are crisp. Let cool on a rack before slicing.

part 5
Dairy Dishes

21
Eggs

The egg is one of the best foods we can eat. It's an economical source of high quality protein, containing a near-perfect balance of essential amino acids. And eggs combine well with nearly every imaginable food.

The only drawback is that eggs do contain a great deal of cholesterol (about 250 milligrams per egg). Although the link between coronary heart disease and high cholesterol diets has not been definitively established, enough evidence has been mounted supporting the connection to make us wary of consuming too much cholesterol.

Nutritionists suggest limiting egg intake to three or four per week. If you don't eat beef (another prime source of cholesterol), you can probably up your egg count to five. That allows plenty of latitude in selecting between the soufflés, frittatas, and other egg dishes in this chapter. Each is so delicious that every egg indulgence will surely bring gustatory satisfaction.

About Fertilized Eggs

I would like to add a few thoughts here on fertilized eggs. As you probably know, most eggs purchased in the supermarkets are unfertilized, while health food stores generally carry eggs that have been fertilized. Many claim the latter are better for you because they contain a better balance of hormones and a sperm cell. However, every nutritionist I have ever spoken with on the subject states there is no significant difference in the food value of these two types of eggs.

The real issue is a moral one. Laying hens, like other animals kept by the food industry, simply are not treated very well. They do nothing but eat, lay eggs, and are slaughtered when they stop producing. If you commiserate, then you may very well wish to buy (at about double the price) the eggs of hens that are free to wander and peck and enjoy their lives as nature intended. But it is pointless to pay double for fertilized eggs in the hopes of eating a nutritionally superior food.

About Soufflés

The first recipe in this section is a soufflé, one of the most delightful egg dishes you can enjoy. Despite the relative ease of preparing a soufflé, many people hesitate to try. If you fall into that category, here are a few simple rules, which, if followed, will produce a perfect, light soufflé every time.

Basically, a soufflé consists of a flavored white sauce into which beaten egg whites are folded. A hot oven causes the air in the egg whites to expand, and thus the whole mixture puffs up splendidly.

To make the white sauce, butter is melted in a heavy saucepan. Flour is then stirred in and cooked a few moments to remove any raw flavor; this mixture should not be permitted to brown. Liquid, usually milk (but variations are possible), is then added and heated until it is smooth and thickened. It must be stirred vigorously during this time so that the bits of flour and butter become fully incorporated into the milk. A wire whisk is the best utensil for this purpose. When the mixture has reached the desirable consistency, egg yolks are beaten in, one at a time. And finally, flavorings (seasonings, cheese, vegetables, etc.) are added.

If the soufflé is to be completed immediately, just go on to follow the rest of the steps in the recipe. But if you wish to prepare the sauce in advance, dot the top with butter to prevent the formation of a skin, and refrigerate the mixture. Before folding in the egg whites, heat it to just lukewarm. A cold sauce will not properly expand in the oven, and too hot a sauce may curdle the egg yolks.

After preparing the sauce, the egg whites are beaten until stiff, either using an electric mixer or a hand wire whisk. The whites will reach a greater volume if at room temperature. Now you must fold the egg whites into the sauce, thoroughly but gently. First, stir about one-third of the egg whites into the sauce. This will lighten the sauce so that the rest of the whites may be folded in without becoming crushed. When folding in the remaining egg whites, a rubber spatula works best. Fold until they are incorporated; but you should still be able to see small bits of egg white throughout.

The soufflé mixture is now turned into a baking dish. A round casserole of the Pyrex type really works as well as a true soufflé dish. Place the soufflé in a preheated oven and do not open the door until you are ready to check whether or not it is done. The soufflé is done when it has risen, browned, and set. Serve it immediately, or it will begin to fall. When making a soufflé for guests, it's a good idea to have everyone assembled before placing it in the oven. This prevents panic if the soufflé is ready to be eaten and the guests are late.

CARROT SOUFFLÉ

If you carefully review the immediately preceding hints on easy soufflé-making, you will have no trouble producing this airy and elegant dish. To ward off guests' hunger pangs while it is baking to perfection, serve one of your favorite party soups as a first course.

PREPARATION TIMES: 30 minutes kitchen work
                   1 hour baking

YIELD: 4 main course servings

2 cups sliced carrots	1 cup pineapple juice
3 tablespoons butter or	1 teaspoon salt
unsaturated margarine	½ teaspoon nutmeg
3 tablespoons unbleached	4 eggs, separated
white flour	pinch salt

1. Place the carrots in a saucepan. Add water to the depth of 1 inch and cook, covered, over a high heat until they are tender, about 15 minutes. Drain and mash.

2. Meanwhile, in a heavy saucepan, melt the butter. Add the flour and cook, stirring, 1 minute. Add the pineapple juice, 1 teaspoon salt, and nutmeg, and cook, stirring with a wire whisk, until thickened and just at the boiling point. Remove from the heat and beat in the egg yolks, one at a time. Stir in the mashed carrots.

3. In a large bowl, beat the egg whites with a pinch of salt until stiff. Stir about one third of these into the carrot mixture to lighten it. Then fold in the rest of the whites gently.

4. Turn the soufflé mixture into a well-greased 2-quart casserole. Place in a shallow pan of hot water and bake in a 325-degree oven 1 hour. Serve immediately.

OMELETTE PIPERADE

Here's an unrolled omelette that is more like scrambled eggs. As the olive oil, basil, garlic, and tomatoes might suggest, the dish hails from the Provençal region of France. To serve, cut the omelette into wedges, like a pizza, and accompany with a full-bodied red wine, hot French bread, and a tossed salad.

PREPARATION TIME: 30 minutes

YIELD: 4 lunch or 3 dinner servings

1 large onion, thinly sliced (about 1 cup)
1 clove garlic, minced
2 green peppers, cut into narrow strips
3 tablespoons olive oil
2 cups peeled, seeded, and chopped tomatoes
1 teaspoon salt
¼ teaspoon pepper
½ teaspoon basil
1 tablespoon minced fresh parsley
6 eggs, beaten

1. Sauté the onion, garlic, and green pepper in olive oil in a large skillet until the onion is soft but not brown. Stir in the tomatoes and cook until most of the liquid has evaporated. Stir in the seasonings.

2. Add the eggs to the pan and cook them, stirring gently until the bottom is set and the top cooked through.

SFORMATO DI SPINACHI

An Italian spinach mold, this is made in a manner similar to a soufflé, except that it is covered when baked. The result is quite dense, yet still light. The recipe may be doubled to serve four, and baked in a 2-quart mold. Serve the dish with red or white wine, a tossed green salad, and pasta with tomato sauce.

PREPARATION TIMES: ½ hour kitchen work
1 hour baking

YIELD: 2 main course servings

2 tablespoons butter or unsaturated margarine
6 tablespoons minced onion
3 tablespoons unbleached flour
1 cup milk
½ teaspoon salt
⅛ teaspoon pepper
⅛ teaspoon nutmeg
3 eggs, separated
1 10-ounce package frozen chopped spinach, thawed and squeezed dry
¼ cup Parmesan cheese
2 tablespoons fine, dry, whole wheat bread crumbs

1. In a heavy saucepan, sauté the onions in the butter or margarine until softened. Stir in the flour very well. Add the milk, and cook, stirring with a wire whisk, until the mixture just comes to a boil and thickens. Remove from the heat. Stir in the spices, egg yolks, spinach, and Parmesan cheese.

2. In a bowl, beat the egg whites until stiff. Fold into the spinach mixture gently.

3. Butter a 1-quart round baking dish with a cover, and butter the cover, also. Sprinkle the bread crumbs over the bottom and sides of the dish. Pour in the spinach mixture and cover the dish. Place in a large, shallow pan containing 1 inch of boiling water. Bake in a 325-degree oven 1 hour.

FRITTATA

Frittata are Italian omelettes, and they're much easier to make than the classic rolled French ones. Frittata seem to come in as many varieties as the omelette, with fillings or toppings that include bacon, ricotta cheese, green beans, and even macaroni. This one features mushrooms and melted mozzarella cheese.

PREPARATION TIMES: 20 minutes kitchen work
                   5 minutes baking

YIELD: 4 lunch or 3 dinner servings

1 cup sliced mushrooms
3 tablespoons butter or
  unsaturated margarine,
  divided usage
6 eggs
3 tablespoons light cream or
  half and half
¾ teaspoon salt
¼ teaspoon pepper

⅛ teaspoon basil
1 tablespoon minced fresh
  parsley
2 tablespoons Parmesan
  cheese, divided usage
1 tablespoon olive oil
½ teaspoon lemon juice
4 ounces mozzarella cheese,
  shredded

1. In a large, ovenproof skillet, sauté the mushrooms in 1½ tablespoons butter or margarine. Remove the mushrooms from the skillet and set aside.

2. In a bowl, beat the eggs with the cream, seasonings, and 1 tablespoon Parmesan cheese.

3. Heat the remaining butter or margarine with the olive oil in the skillet. Pour in the egg mixture. Cook over a very low heat until cooked on the bottom but still soft on the top.

4. Sprinkle with the mushrooms, remaining Parmesan cheese, lemon juice, and the mozzarella cheese. Place in a 450-degree oven about 5 minutes or until the eggs are cooked through and the cheeses have melted.

TOMATO STRATA

Stratas are like a cross between a quiche and a bread pudding. To date, they have been slow to catch on, but once they do, I predict they'll be terrific new items in restaurants and at home. Like quiches, they contain cheese and custard and can be varied endlessly. *Strata* means layered, and that is exactly how it is put together—layers of bread cubes, sauce, and cheese, all topped with a custard mixture. It must sit for several hours prior to baking so that the bread can absorb all the flavors of the sauce and custard. Any bread may be used for the strata, so long as it is firm. Even stale bread is fine. I prefer the flavor and texture of a good, hearty whole wheat bread.

PREPARATION TIMES: 40 minutes kitchen work

at least 6 hours chilling (before baking)

1 hour 20 minutes simmering and baking

YIELD: 4 servings

1 onion, chopped

1 green pepper, chopped

1 clove garlic, minced

2 tablespoons vegetable oil

4 tomatoes, peeled, seeded, and chopped

¼ cup catsup

¾ teaspoon salt, divided usage

⅛ teaspoon plus a dash pepper

2 tablespoons minced fresh parsley

½ teaspoon oregano

1 4-ounce can diced green chili peppers, drained

3 thick slices firm bread, cubed

¾ cup shredded Cheddar cheese

¾ cup shredded Swiss cheese

2 eggs, beaten

1½ cups milk

1 teaspoon dry mustard

1. In a large skillet, sauté the onion, pepper, and garlic in oil until softened. Stir in the tomatoes, catsup, ½ teaspoon salt, ⅛ teaspoon pepper, parsley, oregano, and chili peppers. Simmer, uncovered, about 20 minutes, or until most of the liquid has evaporated. Stir occasionally during this time.

2. Grease a 2-quart round casserole. Place half the bread cubes in it. Cover with half the sauce and press down well so that no air pockets remain. Sprinkle with half the Cheddar and Swiss cheeses. Repeat these layers.

3. In a bowl, mix together the eggs, milk, mustard, ¼ teaspoon salt, and dash pepper. Pour over the ingredients in the casserole. Cover and refrigerate at least 6 hours or overnight.

4. Bake the strata in a 350-degree oven 1 hour, or until set, browned, and bubbly.

CURRIED EGG SALAD

Here is an egg salad with plenty of flavor and crunch. Serve it on a lettuce-lined plate, stuffed in a tomato, or as a filling for your favorite bread.

PREPARATION TIMES: 45 minutes, plus cooking the eggs and chilling the salad

YIELD: 2½ cups, or enough filling for 5 sandwiches

6 hard-cooked eggs, coarsely chopped	2 tablespoons chopped peanuts
¼ cup shredded carrots	¼ cup mayonnaise, or to taste
¼ cup minced celery	¼ teaspoon salt
2 tablespoons minced green pepper	⅛ teaspoon pepper
	¾ teaspoon curry powder

Mix all ingredients together and chill, covered, in the refrigerator.

CURRIED EGGS WITH ONIONS

I am not fond of store-bought curry powders, as they are too hot and lacking in character. It takes only 5 minutes to fix my own, and a jar lasts several months. The mixture here suits my taste. Follow it exactly or adjust the proportions of spices as you wish.

PREPARATION TIMES: 35 minutes kitchen work, plus cooking eggs
20 minutes baking

YIELD: 6 servings

Curry Powder:

2 tablespoons ground
  coriander
2 tablespoons ground
  turmeric
2 tablespoons ground black
  pepper
2 tablespoons fenugreek
  seeds
2½ tablespoons cumin seeds

1½ tablespoons poppy seeds
1½ tablespoons ground
  cardamom
1½ teaspoons mustard seeds
1½ teaspoons ground ginger
1 tablespoon cinnamon
½ teaspoon ground cloves
½ teaspoon nutmeg

Place all ingredients in the blender and blend until the seeds are mostly ground up. Store in a tightly covered jar. Makes about 1 cup. Incidentally, most curry powders contain dried chili peppers, which I find too hot. Add one or two if you wish.

3 cups sliced onions
¾ teaspoon salt
3 tablespoons butter or
  unsaturated margarine
3 tablespoons flour
1 tablespoon curry powder

1½ cups milk
½ cup light cream or half
  and half
10 hard-cooked eggs, shelled
  and sliced

1. Sauté the onions with the salt in the butter or margarine over low heat until they are tender. Add the flour and curry powder and cook, stirring, 1 minute. Add the milk and cook, stirring with a wire whisk, until thickened and just at boiling. Stir in the cream.

2. Spread half of the egg slices in a greased 8″ × 8″ pan. Cover with half the onion mixture. Repeat the layers.

3. Bake in a 375-degree oven 20 minutes.

22
Cured (or Aged) Cheeses

Whenever I enter a cheese shop, I am nonplussed by the dazzling array of cheeses on display. Besides the familiar standbys, I'm intrigued by many unknown varieties from all parts of the world. Making choices is nearly impossible.

If I am selecting cheeses for an appetizer or dessert course, I am quite spontaneous in my choices, generally picking out what catches my fancy of the moment. I'll take a cheese from each of several countries, varying from soft to hard in texture, perhaps including a cheese that's been flavored with wine or herbs.

Cooking with cheese, however, requires much more care. Generally, a particular texture and taste is necessary to insure that the dish being prepared comes out properly. Also, some flavors naturally seem to complement each other. But beyond these reasons, there is also the consideration of cost. When cooking, I try to buy inexpensive American-made cheeses of the most popular varieties. Cheddar and brick cheeses are native to this country, but it is now possible to purchase domestic Swiss, Gouda, Parmesan, and a host of others.

So, when eating just to savor the mellow taste of the cheese, buy whatever suits your fancy. But when following the cheese recipes here, it will be better to stick to the cheeses called for. Fancier cheeses are unnecessary and will greatly add to the cost.

Incidentally, all whole milk cheeses, are very similar nutritionally. A one-ounce serving of brick, Cheddar, Parmesan, or Swiss rings in at about 100 calories and supplies about 7 grams of protein and 7.5 grams of fat (most of which is saturated). It also is a good source of calcium, phosphorus, and vitamin A.

MEXICAN SPOON BREAD

A moist, custardy corn bread, filled with corn kernels, spicy chili peppers, and melted cheese, this is best eaten with a fork. While there's enough protein in the bread to use it as a main course, a large serving is perhaps a bit too heavy for some. I personally prefer to serve it as an accompaniment to a soup.

In case you are unfamiliar with Mexican chili peppers, the mild green ones add bite but not a great deal of hotness.

PREPARATION TIMES: 15 minutes kitchen work
45 minutes baking
YIELD: 6 generous servings

1 1-pound can cream-style corn	½ teaspoon baking soda
¾ cup milk	1 teaspoon salt
⅓ cup (5⅓ tablespoons) butter or margarine, melted	1 4-ounce can mild green chili peppers, seeded and chopped
2 eggs, beaten	1½ cups shredded Cheddar cheese
1 cup cornmeal	

1. In a large bowl, stir together the corn, milk, melted butter or margarine, and eggs.

2. In another bowl, stir together the cornmeal, baking soda, and salt. Add this mixture to the bowl of liquid ingredients, and stir just until the dry ingredients are moistened.

3. Turn half the batter into a well-greased 9″ × 9″ pan. Sprinkle with the chili peppers and half the cheese. Cover with the remaining batter and sprinkle with the rest of the cheese.

4. Bake in a 400-degree oven 45 minutes. Serve warm.

CAMEMBERT OR BRIE QUICHE

In case you are unfamiliar with quiches, they are French single crust pies served generally as an appetizer course or as a luncheon dish, preferably accompanied by a salad and white wine. The most common quiche served in this country is from the French province, Lorraine. In a quiche Lorraine, bits of bacon and melted cheese are imbedded in a rich custard.

A different quiche that doesn't puff up like the usual quiche Lorraine, this one is sinfully rich and dense. The mellow cheese lends an exotic flavor and wonderfully smooth creaminess. The quiche makes a sensational first course for any dinner party.

PREPARATION TIMES: about 1¼ hours making and chilling the dough
25 minutes kitchen work
35 minutes baking

YIELD: 6 servings

1 9-inch partially baked pastry shell
1 teaspoon spicy brown mustard
6 ounces Camembert or Brie cheese, rind removed
1 cup cottage cheese

4½ tablespoons light cream or half and half
3 eggs
½ teaspoon salt
¼ teaspoon pepper
1 tablespoon minced green onion

1. Brush the pastry shell with the mustard. This will give the pastry a good flavor and prevent it from becoming soggy.

2. Place the cheeses, cream, eggs, salt, and pepper in a blender or food processor and process until smooth. Stir in the green onion.

3. Turn the cheese filling into the pastry shell and bake in a 375-degree oven about 35 minutes, or until the filling is browned and set.

Note: If you have any leftover quiche, it will be delicious the next day if you just let it warm to room temperature.

Pastry Crust

You may have noticed that until now, no pie recipes have appeared in this book. The fact is that with a few exceptions (the preceding recipe being one), I am not particularly fond of sweet or savory pies. When I do make a pie, I prefer my own crust to packaged mixes or those found in the freezer case. And pie pastry is not difficult to make. Although there are many, many recipes for pastry dough, the same rules generally apply to all. Very cold butter (or other shortening) is cut into flour, using two knives, an electric mixer on low speed, a pastry blender, or your fingertips, until the mixture resembles coarse meal. Ice water is added, and the dough is mixed with a fork, just until it holds together. Overhandling of the dough produces a tough crust. To facilitate working with the dough, it is generally chilled before being rolled out. This also makes the dough less sticky, so that little flour need be used when rolling it.

For those with food processors, pastry dough may be made almost instantaneously. However, since a mere few extra seconds of processing can, like overworking the dough with your hands, produce a tough crust, I use the machine only to cut the butter into the flour. For the addition of the ice water, I use a fork.

The following recipe is a standard one that reliably produces a light, crisp crust. It makes a one-crust pie but may be doubled.

PREPARATION TIMES: 15 minutes, plus at least one hour to chill the dough

1 cup unbleached white flour	⅓ cup chilled butter or
½ teaspoon salt	unsaturated margarine
pinch sugar	2½ tablespoons ice water

1. In a bowl, stir together the flour, salt, and sugar. Using a pastry blender, two knives, an electric mixer, or your fingertips, cut in the butter or margarine until the mixture resembles coarse meal. Add the ice water and blend with a fork until the mixture holds together.

2. Wrap the dough in plastic wrap and chill at least 1 hour.

3. On a very lightly floured board, roll out the dough to 2 inches

larger than your pie plate. It should be about ⅛-inch thick. Transfer to the pie plate, and crimp the edges neatly.

4. Either fill as it, or bake (prick all over with a fork before baking) in a 425-degree oven until browned (about 12 to 15 minutes) for a baked pastry shell, or about 8 to 10 minutes for a partially baked shell.

PARMESAN SOUFFLÉ

Freshly grated Parmesan cheese tastes immeasurably better than the prepackaged, already grated cheese, so try to buy a chunk of it and grate just before using. Parmesan cheese lends a pleasantly sharp taste; so this soufflé has a more pronounced flavor than Swiss cheese gives the usual French souffles.

PREPARATION TIMES: 20 minutes kitchen work
40 minutes baking

YIELD: 4 servings

1 cup milk
3 tablespoons butter or unsaturated margarine
2 tablespoons minced green onion
3 tablespoons unbleached white flour
1 cup grated Parmesan cheese
½ teaspoon salt
¼ teaspoon pepper
5 eggs, separated
pinch salt

1. In a heavy saucepan, cook the green onions in the butter for two minutes. Add the flour and cook, stirring, another 2 minutes. Add the milk and cook, stirring with a wire whisk, until the sauce is thick and smooth and just at boiling. Stir in the Parmesan cheese, and remove the pan from the heat.
2. Stir in the salt and pepper and then beat in the egg yolks, one at a time.
3. In a large bowl, beat the egg whites with the pinch of salt until stiff. Stir one third of them into the cheese mixture, then pour the contents of the saucepan into the bowl with the egg whites, and gently fold the egg whites through the cheese mixture.
4. Grease very well a 2-quart soufflé or casserole, and turn the mixture into it. Bake in a 375-degree oven about 40 minutes. Serve immediately.

CHILIS RELLENOS CON QUESO

If you've sampled Chilis Rellenos in a Mexican restaurant, you'll surely be delighted by this version—the same luscious cheese-stuffed peppers, but instead of being deep-fried in oil, the peppers are baked in a light soufflé-like mixture. The result is less greasy and dramatically impressive.

PREPARATION TIMES: 40 minutes kitchen work
                   30 minutes simmering
                   20 minutes baking

YIELD: 6 servings

6 green bell peppers
6 pieces of Monterey Jack
  cheese, ½ × ½ × 2 inches
6 pieces of Cheddar cheese,
  ½ × ½ × 2 inches
6 egg yolks

8 egg whites
4 tablespoons butter or
  unsaturated margarine,
  melted
2 tablespoons flour
sauce, below

1. Slice the tops off the peppers and seed them. Place them in a large saucepan with enough boiling water to cover the peppers, and cook them 10 minutes, until softened. Drain well. Place one piece of each kind of cheese into each pepper.

2. Beat the egg yolks with a fork. Then beat the egg whites with a mixer until stiff. Stir the yolks gently into the whites, and stir in the melted butter or margarine.

3. Grease a deep casserole, just a little larger than the size required to hold the peppers. Pour ½-inch of batter into the dish. Arrange the peppers in the dish, and sprinkle them with flour. Pour the remaining batter over the peppers. Bake in a 375-degree oven 20 minutes, or until puffed, browned, and set. Serve with the following sauce.

Sauce: (prepare just before putting the peppers in to bake;
  then the sauce will simmer and the peppers bake at the same time)

1 onion, chopped
1 clove garlic, minced

1 tablespoon vegetable oil
6 tablespoons tomato paste

1 cup peeled, seeded, and
  chopped tomatoes
1⅓ cups water

½ teaspoon salt
1 teaspoon red wine vinegar

In a heavy saucepan, sauté the onion and garlic in oil until the onion is tender. Add all remaining ingredients and simmer 20 minutes.

PARMESAN GNOCCHI

This is similar to polenta except that farina is used in place of cornmeal. The cooked grain is heavily flavored with Parmesan cheese, chilled, sliced, and baked until golden. Serve the gnocchi as a side dish with soup or as a main course. Either way, the tasty squares are unusual and delightful.

PREPARATION TIMES: 30 minutes kitchen work
                 1 hour chilling
                 15 minutes baking
YIELD: 4 main course, or 6 side dish servings

3 cups milk, divided usage
1½ teaspoons salt
pinch nutmeg
⅛ teaspoon pepper
¾ cup farina

2 eggs, beaten
1 cup freshly grated
  Parmesan cheese, divided
  usage

1. In a large, heavy saucepan, bring 2¼ cups milk to a boil, along with the salt, nutmeg, and pepper. Meanwhile, stir the farina into the remaining ¾ cup cold milk. Add this to the boiling milk, stirring constantly to prevent lumps. Cook, stirring with a wooden spoon, until very thick, about 15 minutes. Remove from the heat and beat in the eggs and ¾ cup Parmesan cheese.

2. Spread the mixture in a lightly greased 9″ × 13″ baking pan. Chill until firm, about 1 hour.

3. Cut the farina mixture into approximately 2-inch squares and place on a greased baking sheet. Sprinkle with the remaining ¼ cup Parmesan cheese. Bake in a 400-degree oven 15 minutes, or until golden brown.

CHEESE SANDWICH SPREADS

I enjoy making my own cheese spreads. I am continually devising new combinations, but the four following are my favorites. These keep well, refrigerated in a screw-top jar for a week or two. They are delicious on whole wheat bread, plain or toasted. For each spread, just mix well all ingredients listed.

PREPARATION TIME: 10 to 20 minutes per recipe

Apple-Cheddar:
2 cups grated Cheddar
  cheese
2 cups coarsely chopped
  apples, peeled or unpeeled
  according to your
  preference
1 cup slivered almonds,
  toasted in an ungreased
  skillet
1 cup raisins
enough mayonnaise to hold
  all together (about ½ cup)

Makes about 4 cups.

Pimiento-Swiss:
2 cups grated Swiss cheese
½ cup slivered roasted
  pimientoes
enough mayonnaise to hold
  together (about 3
  tablespoons)

Makes about 2 cups.

Muenster-Olive:
2 cups grated Muenster
  cheese
½ cup sliced pimiento-stuffed
  olives
enough mayonnaise to hold
  together (about 3
  tablespoons)

Makes about 2 cups.

Caraway-Brick:
2 cups grated brick cheese
1 tablespoon caraway seeds
enough mayonnaise to hold
  together (about 2
  tablespoons)

Makes about 2 cups.

23
Yogurt

Yogurt is perhaps the fad food of the decade. The sale of those little half-pint cartons with their multitudinous flavors is constantly increasing as more and more people down a yogurt for breakfast, lunch, or snack. And why not? Advertising campaigns have touted yogurt as a highly nutritional, ready-to-eat food, as indeed it is. Yogurt is a milk product, and milk is certainly one of the most complete foods we can eat.

But is yogurt more nutritious than milk? The answer is a resounding *no*. In fact, milk and yogurt are quite similar. An 8-ounce glass of partially skimmed milk contains slightly more protein (8.5 grams versus 7.7) than 8 ounces of partially skimmed yogurt. The milk is also a somewhat better supplier of calcium, phosphorus, potassium, and vitamin A. Caloriewise, the milk contains 134, yogurt 114.

Another consideration is that most of the flavored yogurts contain a tremendous amount of sugar. While a cup of plain yogurt contains 114 calories, a cup of most fruited varieties comes in at about 250 (that's 136 calories from sugar-sweetened fruit preserves!). What is quite amazing is that few people would accept a lunch composed of several spoonfuls of preserves stirred into a glass of milk; but these same people will happily eat yogurt day after day, quite certain that what they are eating is good for them.

Despite these cautionary comments, yogurt is still a great food for a variety of reasons: it is nearly as nutritious as milk; it has a creamy texture and tart flavor that make it good for cooking and baking and just plain eating; it may be used in many recipes as a low-fat substitute for sour cream; it is often tolerated by those who are allergic to milk; and it can be of benefit to those taking antibiotics (such medications tend to kill off the beneficial stomach bacteria that normally live in the digestive tract, thereby producing diarrhea). Yogurt may help recolonize the intestines with beneficial bacteria, thus relieving the diarrhea.

I do not, however, believe in eating highly sweetened foods on a regular basis. So if you are fond of yogurt, I suggest you either make your own (considerably more economical) or purchase it plain, and sweeten it as little as possible with your own preserves, honey, or molasses. One teaspoon of honey contains only 21 calories, and that should be quite sufficient to flavor a carton of plain yogurt.

One of my favorite ways to eat yogurt is in what I call my "cantaloupe picnic." For two people, empty two 8-ounce cartons of plain yogurt into a large, screw-top jar or bowl with a cover. Stir in a ripe, sliced banana, ½ cup raisins, and ½ cup granola. Bring this to the picnic site, along with a nice, ripe cantaloupe. When ready to eat, cut the melon in half, scoop out the seeds, and use as a bowl for the yogurt mixture. Of course, my "cantaloupe picnic" is also great at home and with any number of different foods stirred into the yogurt. Try sliced peaches or strawberries, peanuts, wheat germ, chunky applesauce, or whatever suits your fancy.

The following recipes make use of plain yogurt in a variety of ways, and you will find several other such recipes throughout the book.

APPLE-YOGURT SOUP

There is, in Princeton, New Jersey, a wonderful health food store and restaurant, The Whole Earth Center. I sampled this cool, refreshing soup there one day and persuaded the cook to give me her recipe. Try it on a hot day for lunch or as a first course before dinner.

PREPARATION TIMES: 20 minutes, plus time to chill the soup.

YIELD: 6 servings

1 hard-cooked egg, chopped
½ cup raisins
3 cups yogurt
1 cup milk
1 cucumber, peeled and
  chopped
¼ cup finely chopped green
  onions
1 teaspoon salt
¼ teaspoon pepper

3 tablespoons curry powder
  (or, to taste)
5 green cooking apples,
  unpeeled, cored, and
  chopped
6 ice cubes
1 tablespoon minced fresh
  parsley
1 tablespoon minced fresh
  dill

1. Mix all ingredients except the parsley and dill in a large bowl. Chill until ready to serve.

2. Just before serving, garnish with the herbs.

SPINACH QUICHE

This recipe is different from the usual quiche because yogurt replaces the cream, making the pie less rich, with a more tart flavor. The mozzarella cheese gives it a chewy quality.

PREPARATION TIMES: 1¼ hours making and chilling the pastry
15 minutes kitchen work
45 minutes baking

YIELD: 4 appetizer or 3 luncheon servings

1 onion, minced
1 tablespoon butter or unsaturated margarine
1 cup shredded mozzarella cheese
1 partially baked 9-inch pastry shell
1 tablespoon unbleached white flour
2 eggs

1 cup yogurt
1 teaspoon salt
¼ teaspoon pepper
⅛ teaspoon nutmeg
1 cup chopped cooked and drained spinach (or use a 10-ounce package frozen chopped spinach, thawed and squeezed dry)

1. Sauté the onion in the butter until softened. Sprinkle it and the cheese on the bottom of the pastry shell.

2. Beat the flour into the eggs. Stir in the remaining ingredients. Pour over the onion and cheese.

3. Bake the pie in a 450-degree oven 15 minutes. Reduce the heat to 350 degrees and bake 30 minutes longer.

SUPER SUPPER SALAD I

The recipe here is actually for a hearty and nutritious salad dressing containing creamy yogurt and hard-cooked egg and spiced with herbs, garlic, and tomato. Serve it on a summer evening over a bowl of greens, sliced cucumbers, cherry tomatoes, green pepper slivers, parsley sprigs, cauliflower pieces, bean sprouts, Muenster cheese cubes, and anything else you wish to include. A hot bread would make a perfect accompaniment; Mexican Spoon Bread, for example.

PREPARATION TIMES: 5 minutes, plus preparation of the salad

YIELD: enough dressing for 2 generous portions of salad

1 cup yogurt
⅓ cup catsup
1 clove fresh garlic
1 hard-cooked egg,
    quartered
2 teaspoons chives

1 teaspoon spicy brown
    mustard
1 teaspoon paprika
2 teaspoons soy sauce
½ teaspoon salt

Place all ingredients in a blender and blend until smooth. Refrigerate until ready to serve. Pour over salad and toss well.

SUPER SUPPER SALAD II

Here's a mixed salad with the greens, vegetables, and dressing all tossed together. The result is a crunchy experience of a variety of tastes and textures. The salad, containing cottage and Cheddar cheeses, yogurt, nuts, and egg, supplies a goodly amount of protein. Hot corn muffins—Molasses Apple Muffins, for example—make a delightful accompaniment.

PREPARATION TIME: 20 minutes kitchen work

YIELD: 6 to 8 main course servings

2 cups chopped romaine
    lettuce
2 cups finely chopped
    cabbage
1 cucumber, sliced
1 zucchini, sliced
3 tomatoes, chopped
2 stalks celery, sliced
1 apple, unpared, cored, and
    diced
2 tablespoons raisins

1 green pepper, chopped
¼ cup almonds, slivered
¼ cup chopped walnuts
½ cup shredded Cheddar
    cheese
2 carrots, grated
2 hard-cooked eggs, diced
salt and pepper, to taste
1 cup cottage cheese
1 cup yogurt

In a large bowl, toss together all ingredients except the cottage cheese and yogurt. Mix these two together and then toss with the rest of the salad.

YOGURT–BLEU CHEESE DRESSING

This is an excellent dressing for a bowl of mixed greens to accompany dinner. While most bleu cheese dressings are very rich and calorie-laden, here's a version that's lighter and nearly fat-free. Yet it still has that marvelous bleu cheese flavor we all crave.

PREPARATION TIME: 10 minutes kitchen work

YIELD: 2¼ cups, or enough for about 6 portions of salad

¼ cup crumbled bleu cheese
1 tablespoon minced fresh
  parsley
1 clove garlic, crushed
1 teaspoon salt
¼ teaspoon pepper
2 cups plain yogurt

In a bowl, mix together the bleu cheese, parsley, garlic, salt, pepper, and ¼ cup yogurt. Gradually stir in the remaining yogurt. Chill until ready to serve.

WHOLEMEAL BREAD

This nonsweet quick bread has a wholesome whole wheat flavor similar to that found in the biscuits of the same name from England. It's a remarkably simple loaf to put together, since it doesn't even require the use of a mixer. Slice thinly and serve with tea.

PREPARATION TIMES: 20 minutes kitchen work
                   1 hour baking time

YIELD: 1 loaf

¾ cup farina cereal
1½ tablespoons vegetable oil
1½ cups yogurt
½ cup brown sugar
1 egg, beaten

1 cup whole wheat flour
1 cup unbleached white flour
2 teaspoons baking powder
¾ teaspoon baking soda
¾ teaspoon salt

1. In a large bowl, stir together the farina, vegetable oil, yogurt, brown sugar, and egg. Let sit 10 minutes.

2. In another bowl, stir together the remaining ingredients and stir into the yogurt mixture, mixing only until the dry ingredients are moistened.

3. Turn the batter into a greased and floured 9" × 5" loaf pan. Bake in a 350-degree oven 1 hour or until a toothpick inserted in the center comes out clean. Let cool before slicing.

Note: Using yogurt in baking tends to make lighter breads and cakes. It may be substituted cup for cup in recipes calling for buttermilk or sour cream, although for the latter, you must also add one tablespoon butter or margarine for each cup of yogurt used.

ORANGE-YOGURT FRUIT SALAD

This thick, not-too-sweet orange and yogurt mixture is great served over cottage cheese and fruits for a lunch salad, or just over fruits for an appetizer or dessert course. Choose a selection of seasonal fresh fruits, enough for 4 people.

PREPARATION TIME: 5 minutes kitchen work

YIELD: 1½ cups, or enough for 4 servings salad

1 cup yogurt
⅓ cup nonfat dry milk
powder
⅓ cup orange juice
1 tablespoon honey
1 teaspoon vanilla

Place all ingredients in the blender and blend until smooth. Refrigerate until ready to serve.

24
Cottage Cheese

There are few people who love food who don't have at least occasional battles with waistline bulges. And, as most of us are aware, cottage cheese is included in almost every weight loss diet that's ever been devised. Cottage cheese is indeed an excellent food for those who wish to reduce. A ½-cup serving of low-fat cottage cheese supplies about 30 percent of the recommended daily allowance of protein—and the protein here is nearly complete. What's more, cottage cheese contains few calories—only about 95 in that same serving.

However, plain cottage cheese can be *most* unappealing. In cafeterias and coffee shops, there it sits—already scooped out into small, pale, often rather warmish lumps. Because cottage cheese is often served so unappealingly, it may be rather difficult for anyone to regard it as anything other than a food for dieters.

Fortunately, however, for both dieters and those who wish to obtain good quality protein easily and inexpensively, ordinary cottage cheese becomes transformed into marvelous dishes when cooked. Blend in some eggs with a few seasonings, and creamy cottage cheese pancakes are ready in minutes. Or add any of a tremendous array of vegetables, and you have a highly flavored casserole that can be varied endlessly (again, eggs are added to solidify the cheese mixture). Following are a few ways to turn bland cottage cheese into delicious meals.

SPINACH-CHEESE CASSEROLE

I could eat this type of dish every day of the week—a well-seasoned cheese casserole, filled with a plentiful variety of vegetables and chewy mozzarella cheese. It goes well with hot Italian bread and sliced tomatoes.

PREPARATION TIMES: 30 minutes kitchen work
50 minutes baking

YIELD: 4 servings

¼ pound mushrooms, sliced
1 zucchini, sliced
1 green pepper, diced
3 tablespoons butter or
  unsaturated margarine
1 pound (2 cups) cottage
  cheese
1 cup shredded mozzarella
  cheese

3 eggs, beaten
1 10-ounce package frozen,
  chopped spinach, thawed
  and squeezed dry
½ teaspoon salt
¼ teaspoon pepper
⅛ teaspoon nutmeg

1. In a large skillet, sauté the mushrooms, zucchini, and green pepper in butter or margarine until softened. Let cool somewhat.

2. In a large bowl, mix together the remaining ingredients. Stir in the contents of the skillet.

3. Turn the mixture into a greased 2-quart casserole and bake in a 350-degree oven about 50 minutes, until set and browned on top.

SALAD CASSEROLE

Here is another delicious cottage cheese and vegetable melange. Alone, the radishes, scallions, watercress, and green pepper would make a crisp and flavorful salad. Here, they are held together by a spicy cottage cheese mixture. Bake a few potatoes along with this colorful casserole for a good accompaniment.

PREPARATION TIMES: 30 minutes kitchen work   1 hour baking
YIELD: 4 generous servings

10 scallions, sliced
2 tablespoons butter or
  unsaturated margarine
½ cup whole wheat flour
½ cup dry milk powder
1 teaspoon salt
¼ teaspoon pepper
1 teaspoon basil

2 cloves garlic, pressed
2 cups cottage cheese
4 cups chopped watercress
2 green peppers, chopped
16 radishes, sliced
4 eggs, beaten
4 tablespoons soy sauce

1. Sauté the scallions in butter or margarine until softened, about 3 minutes.

2. In a large bowl, combine the whole wheat flour, milk powder, seasonings, and cottage cheese. Stir in the watercress, green peppers, radishes, scallions, eggs, and soy sauce. Mix well.

3. Turn the mixture into a greased 2-quart casserole. Bake in a 340-degree oven 1 hour or until set.

COTTAGE CHEESE PANCAKES

These light, high-protein cakes can serve a variety of purposes—a good breakfast, light lunch, or nutritious dessert. For extra sweetness, top them with a bit of molasses, honey.

PREPARATION TIME: 20 minutes kitchen work
YIELD: 15 small pancakes, or 3 servings

1 cup cottage cheese
½ teaspoon salt
1 tablespoon cornstarch

2 eggs
2 teaspoons molasses

1. Place all ingredients in a blender and blend until smooth.

2. Oil a large skillet, and heat to 300 degrees (moderately hot). Drop the batter by tablespoonfuls. Cook on one side, turn, and cook the other side.

COTTAGE CHEESE FONDUE

Traditional cheese fondues containing Swiss cheese, wine, and kirsch are very rich—too rich, I think, for a whole meal. Here's a version that's as creamy as the traditional fondue but much lighter because cottage cheese substitutes for much of the Swiss cheese. Serve the fondue with a variety of dippers—French bread cubes, chunks of homemade whole wheat bread, steamed cauliflower and broccoli pieces, cherry tomatoes, red and green pepper cubes, and fried potato nuggets.

PREPARATION TIMES: 20 minutes kitchen work, plus preparation of the dippers

YIELD: 4 to 6 servings

2 tablespoons butter or
  unsaturated margarine
2 tablespoons unbleached
  white flour
1 clove garlic, pressed
1 teaspoon spicy brown
  mustard

1¼ cups milk
1 cup cottage cheese
8 ounces shredded Swiss
  cheese

1. Melt the butter or margarine in a saucepan. Add the flour and garlic. Cook, stirring for 2 minutes. Add the mustard and milk. Cook, stirring with a wire whisk, until the sauce comes to a boil and thickens.

2. Remove from the heat. Add the cottage cheese and beat until smooth with an electric mixer.

3. Return to the heat. Add the Swiss cheese, a small amount at a time, stirring until melted. Transfer to a fondue pot.

CHEESE AND PARSLEY SANDWICH SPREAD

Here's a sandwich spread that's full of crisp, crunchy vegetables. It's a far more nutritious filling than most. Made with low-fat cottage cheese, it's also fairly low in calories. It's best served very cold, so if you pack a lunch for work, keep it refrigerated if possible.

PREPARATION TIME: 10 minutes kitchen work

YIELD: 3¼ cups, or enough for 6 sandwiches

2 cups cottage cheese
¼ cup chunk-style peanut
  butter
¼ cup grated Parmesan
  cheese
1 teaspoon spicy brown
  mustard

2 stalks celery, finely diced
1 cup minced fresh parsley
1 small green pepper, finely
  diced
½ teaspoon paprika
⅛ teaspoon salt

Mix all ingredients together well in a bowl. Store, covered, in the refrigerator. The mixture keeps satisfactorily for a week or longer.

SPINACH-RICOTTA GNOCCHI

Although this chapter is devoted to cottage cheese recipes, I couldn't resist including just this one calling for ricotta cheese—that lovely, creamy Italian cheese that's quite similar to cottage cheese, but with a marvelous flavor all its own and also a higher fat content. This recipe for gnocchi, exceptionally light dumplings, is spectacularly good, quite unusual, and loved by all who have sampled them. Usually, I pull my husband into the kitchen to help me prepare the gnocchi. He taught me how to make them (he used to watch his mother when he was young), and he has far more patience than I when it comes to forming the dough into small ovals. But gnocchi are definitely worth the little extra work involved, for they make a fabulous appetizer course or lunch dish.

PREPARATION TIMES: 40 minutes kitchen work
              2 hours (or more if you wish) chilling the
              gnocchi   15 minutes cooking

YIELD: 6 servings as an appetizer, 4 servings as a lunch dish

1 10-ounce package fresh
   spinach, tough stems
   removed
1½ cups ricotta cheese
1 cup Italian style bread
   crumbs (these are the kind
   with seasonings added)
2 eggs, beaten
¼ cup grated Parmesan
   cheese

¼ cup finely minced green
   onion
1 teaspoon salt
1 teaspoon basil
½ teaspoon nutmeg
1 clove garlic, pressed
flour
Lemon-Butter Sauce
   (optional)

1. Place the spinach in a large pot with about 1 inch of boiling water. Cook, covered, until the leaves wilt, about 5 minutes. Drain and chop finely. You need 1 cup. Any leftover may be used in another dish. Dry the spinach very well.

2. Mix the spinach with all remaining ingredients except the flour and sauce. Form this mixture into cylinders about 2 inches long and ¾ inches wide. Roll each in flour and shake off any excess. Note: If you find the mixture too sticky to work with, you may refrigerate it for an hour before forming the cylinders.

3. Place the cylinders on a baking sheet and refrigerate at least 2 hours or longer.

4. In a wide saucepan, heat 2 inches of water with 1 teaspoon salt to boiling. Drop the gnocchi in, several at a time. The water should not stop boiling. They will sink to the bottom and rise to the surface when cooked. Remove with a slotted spoon and place on a baking sheet in a 200-degree oven while cooking the rest. Serve as soon as they are all cooked.

   I prefer the gnocchi plain, but those who dote on rich foods pour generous portions of Lemon-Butter Sauce over them and then eat as though in ecstasy. If you think you are apt to fall into that category, here is the recipe for this rich, rich sauce (which incidentally makes a delicious topping for any green vegetable, such as asparagus, broccoli, and so on).

Lemon-Butter Sauce

PREPARATION TIME: 15 minutes kitchen work
YIELD: 1 cup, or enough for 6 servings of gnocchi

½ cup fresh lemon juice
¼ teaspoon salt
pinch pepper

2 sticks (1 cup) butter, each
    cut into 8 pieces, softened
5 tablespoons hot water

1. In a small, heavy saucepan, boil down the lemon juice with the salt and pepper until it is reduced to about 2 tablespoonfuls. Beat in the butter, one piece at a time, not adding the next piece until the last has melted. This mixture may sit for 30 minutes to an hour over hot water if not yet ready to serve.

2. Just before serving, beat in hot water. Serve immediately.

BAMBOLI

This light and spicy Italian casserole is quite nutritious—very high in protein and low in fat. It goes well with pasta.

PREPARATION TIMES: 20 minutes kitchen work
                   50 minutes baking
YIELD: 4 to 6 servings

¾ cup chopped mushrooms
2 tablespoons vegetable oil
2 cups cottage cheese
4 teaspoons grated lemon rind
3 tablespoons milk
¾ teaspoon salt
1½ teaspoons paprika

4 egg whites
½ cup fine dry bread crumbs,
    preferably from Italian-
    type bread
2 cups plain yogurt
3 tablespoons slivered
    almonds

1. In a small skillet, sauté the mushrooms in oil until tender.

2. In a bowl, combine the contents of the skillet, cottage cheese, lemon rind, milk, salt, and paprika. Mix well.

3. Beat the egg whites until stiff and gently fold into the cheese mixture. Turn into a greased 1-quart casserole. Bake in a 350-degree oven 40 minutes.

4. Remove from the oven and gently spread the yogurt evenly over the top of the casserole. Sprinkle with the almonds. Return to the oven for 10 minutes longer. Serve immediately.

25
Dairy Desserts

When I was a child, I first began to make desserts primarily because I so much enjoyed eating what I had made. I adored chocolate cakes and tried nearly every recipe I came across—dark devil's food layer cakes, rich fudge loaves, milder chocolate spice cakes, and even some sinfully rich European tortes. My family, needless to say, was happy enough to consume the results of my endeavors. And my mother put me to use baking banana breads when the bananas were turning dark brown; meringues when she had extra egg whites to dispose of, and any number of fancy goodies when guests were expected.

But by the time I reached adulthood, I realized that if I wished to look good and remain healthy, my sweet tooth would have to be carefully channeled. And so I began to build up a repertoire of desserts that were good for me. These generally fell into two categories—the light fruit desserts so refreshing after a heavy meal (see recipes for Banana Sherbet or Pear Snow, for example) and the heavier, nutritious dairy desserts made with cottage or ricotta cheese, yogurt, or buttermilk.

Desserts made with these ingredients have several advantages. While they are not terribly low in calories, they do provide substantial nutrition for the calories consumed. They are also filling and so are appropriate after a light meal, such as a soup and salad. Finally, because their amino acid balance complements that of many foods, these dishes make a dinner composed primarily of vegetables and grains more nutritious.

This description of dairy desserts gives assurance of their health value but does not convey how truly delicious they are. Each of the recipes here gives the impression of being rich and sweet and is guaranteed to satisfy even the most demanding dessert lover.

HONEY-DATE KUCHEN

This rich coffee cake is flecked with dates and nuts in a luscious, honey-sweetened cottage cheese filling. It makes a fantastic sweet for brunch or a great dessert anytime. The dough rises in the refrigerator, taking 8 hours (overnight), and may remain chilled for up to 5 days.

PREPARATION TIMES: 50 minutes kitchen work, plus preparation of mashed potatoes
1½ hours rising
8 hours (or longer) chilling
50 minutes baking

YIELD: 12 generous servings

Refrigerator-Rising Dough:
½ package active dry yeast
¾ cup warm water
¾ teaspoon salt
⅓ cup sugar
⅓ cup butter or unsaturated margarine, melted and cooled

1 egg
½ cup lukewarm mashed potatoes
2 cups whole wheat flour
about 1½ cups unbleached white flour

Cottage Cheese Filling:
¾ cup cottage cheese
3 eggs
1 teaspoon vanilla
⅓ cup honey
1 teaspoon cinnamon

2 tablespoons unbleached
  white flour
½ cup chopped dates
½ cup chopped walnuts

1. The day before or up to 5 days before you plan to eat the Kuchen, make the dough: In a large mixing bowl, dissolve the yeast in the warm water. Add the salt, sugar, melted butter or margarine, egg, mashed potatoes, and 1 cup of whole wheat flour. Beat until smooth. Beat in the remaining 1 cup whole wheat flour. Turn the dough out onto a board heavily floured with the unbleached white flour and knead until smooth, elastic, and nonsticky, adding more flour as needed. Place the dough in a greased bowl. Turn once so the greased side faces up. Cover with plastic wrap and refrigerate 8 hours to 5 days.

2. Punch down the dough and stretch it to fit on the bottom and sides of a greased 9″ × 13″ pan. Cover and let rise until doubled in bulk, about 1½ hours.

3. Meanwhile, make the filling: Beat together the cottage cheese, eggs, vanilla, honey, cinnamon, and flour until smooth. Stir in the dates and nuts.

4. Pour the filling into the center of the dough, and spread it evenly. Bake in a 375-degree oven 15 minutes. Lower the oven to 325 degrees and bake 35 minutes longer. The dough should be crisp and browned and the filling set.

COTTAGE CHEESE PIE WITH WHEAT GERM SHELL

A great variety of fillings—fresh fruit, custard, chiffon—go well with this all-purpose wheat germ cookie crust. The cheese filling here has a taste similar to the center of a blintze. It's also very light since the egg whites cause it to puff up as it bakes.

PREPARATION TIMES: 15 minutes kitchen work
45 minutes baking

YIELD: 6 servings

Pie Shell:
½ cup wheat germ
¾ cup vanilla or macaroon
   cookie crumbs
⅓ cup vegetable oil
1 tablespoon honey

Filling:
1½ cups cottage cheese
⅓ cup sugar
¾ cup milk
1 teaspoon lemon rind
3 tablespoons lemon juice
3 eggs, separated
⅛ teaspoon salt

1. Prepare the pie shell: Just mix all ingredients and press evenly into a 9-inch pie plate.

2. To make the filling, place all the ingredients except the egg whites and salt in a blender, and blend until smooth.

3. In a large bowl, beat the egg whites with the salt until stiff. Gently fold in the cottage cheese mixture.

4. Pour the filling into the pie shell. Bake in a 450-degree oven 10 minutes. Lower the heat to 350 degrees and bake 35 minutes longer or until a knife inserted in the center comes out clean.

APPLE CUSTARD PIE

It may be un-American, but I don't happen to care for ordinary apple pies. But this one, I do love! It has a bottom layer of spiced, sweet apples and a top layer of thick and creamy, cheesy custard.

PREPARATION TIMES: preparation of pastry, about 1¼ hours
20 minutes kitchen work
1¼ hours baking
2 or more hours chilling the finished pie

YIELD: 6 servings

1 deep 9-inch unbaked pastry shell	2 eggs
2 cups peeled apple slices	½ cup granulated sugar
¼ cup brown sugar	¼ teaspoon salt
½ teaspoon cinnamon	1 cup milk
¼ teaspoon nutmeg	1 teaspoon vanilla
	1 cup cottage cheese

1. Stir together the apple slices, brown sugar, cinnamon, and nutmeg. Arrange in the pastry shell.

2. Put the remaining ingredients into a blender or food processor and process until smooth. Pour over the apple mixture.

3. Bake the pie in a 325-degree oven about 1¼ hours, or until set. Cool to room temperature on rack, then chill before serving.

BUTTERMILK LEMON PIE

Buttermilk pies are an American tradition—smooth and creamy, with a lightness from the beaten egg whites and a wonderful tart lemon and buttermilk flavor.

PREPARATION TIMES: preparation and chilling pastry, about 1¼ hours
20 minutes kitchen work
35 minutes baking
2 or more hours chilling finished pie

YIELD: 6 servings

3 eggs, separated	¼ cup lemon juice
¾ cup sugar, divided usage	grated rind from 1 lemon
3 tablespoons unbleached white flour	2 tablespoons butter or unsaturated margarine, melted and cooled
¼ teaspoon salt	1 9-inch pastry shell
1½ cups buttermilk	

1. In a bowl, beat the egg whites until stiff. Gradually beat in ¼ cup of sugar until the eggs are glossy.

2. In another bowl, stir together the flour, salt, and remaining ½ cup of sugar. Gradually stir in the buttermilk. Add the lemon juice and rind and the melted butter or margarine. Beat in the egg yolks well. Gently fold in the egg whites.

3. Pour the filling mixture into the pastry shell. Bake in a 425-degree oven 10 minutes. Reduce the heat to 350 degrees and bake until set, about 25 minutes longer. Cool to room temperature on a rack and then chill.

PEACH CHEESE PIE

This is just about the juiciest cheese pie you will ever encounter. It's well flavored with fresh peaches. Wheat germ, walnuts, honey, raisins, and orange all add their good tastes, too. The crust is firm and chewy, with a wholesome wheaty flavor.

PREPARATION TIMES: 1 hour kitchen work
1 hour chilling the crust
1 hour baking
2 or more hours chilling the finished pie

YIELD: 12 servings

Crust:
1 cup whole wheat flour
¼ cup wheat germ
¼ cup vegetable oil
2 tablespoons ground walnuts
1 egg, beaten
⅛ teaspoon salt

⅓ cup chopped walnuts
⅓ cup wheat germ
1 orange, diced, seeded, and ground in a blender

Cheese Filling:
2 cups cottage cheese
2 eggs
⅓ cup yogurt
¼ cup sugar
¼ cup apple juice
2 tablespoons honey
2 teaspoons sesame seeds
1 tablespoon whole wheat flour
1 teaspoon vanilla

Peach Filling:
½ cup honey
½ cup sugar
¼ cup apple juice
¼ teaspoon salt
4 large peaches, peeled and sliced (about 1½ cups)
½ cup raisins

1. With a fork, combine all the crust ingredients. Chill for 1 hour. On a lightly floured surface, roll out the dough to line the bottom and sides of an 8″ × 10″ baking pan. Prick all over with a fork. Bake in a 350-degree oven 25 minutes.

2. Meanwhile, make the peach filling: In a large saucepan, combine the honey, sugar, apple juice, and salt. Bring to a simmer. Add the peaches and cook, covered, 5 minutes, or until tender. Remove from the heat and stir in the remaining ingredients.

3. Make the cheese filling, also: Combine all ingredients for the filling in a blender, and blend until smooth.

4. Pour the peach filling into the baked crust. Pour the cheese filling over the peach filling. The two fillings will blend together somewhat.

5. Bake the pie in a 350-degree oven 1 hour, or until set and lightly browned. Let cool to room temperature on a rack and then chill well.

BERRY-BANANA FROZEN YOGURT

Commercially frozen yogurt has often been deservedly dubbed a "junk" health food. Usually it contains a variety of synthetic ingredients, preservatives, artificial colors and flavors, gum, dextrin, and modified food starch. In some, the yogurt has been heat-treated, so that the yogurt culture is no longer even alive. Most brands are too soft, too sweet, and too much like ice cream. But good frozen yogurt is another story indeed. The tartness of the yogurt and its low fat content make it an extremely refreshing dessert. So if you are tired of the junk health food version, try making your own. This recipe is tart, tangy, and has a lovely pink color.

PREPARATION TIMES: 5 minutes, plus freezing in an ice cream maker.

YIELD: 1 quart, or 4 to 6 servings

1 cup light cream or half and half
1 cup yogurt
½ cup sugar
few grains salt

½ cup frozen concentrated cranberry cocktail, thawed
1 teaspoon lemon juice
½ cup chopped banana

1. Stir together all ingredients except the banana in a bowl.

2. Freeze in an ice cream maker according to the manufacturer's directions. When the mixture begins to harden, add the bananas and continue freezing until firm.

3. Pack in a container and store in your freezer.

ITALIAN CHEESE DESSERTS

The Italians make marvelous ricotta cheese desserts. There's the crunchy cannoli shell, filled with sweetened cheese and pistachio nuts or chocolate bits, and the cassata, a torte rich with ricotta cheese and chocolate icing. The three recipes below are simple to make and are deliciously nutritious besides.

PREPARATION TIME: 10 minutes for each
YIELD: 6 servings for each

Mocha Cheese Dessert

1 pound ricotta cheese	2 tablespoons instant coffee
¼ cup confectioners' sugar	1 tablespoon cocoa
3 tablespoons rum	

1. Mix together the ricotta cheese, sugar, and rum. Divide among 6 sherbet glasses or other dessert dishes. Chill until ready to serve.

2. Just before serving, mix together the coffee and cocoa and sprinkle over the cheese. To eat, stir the mocha mixture into the cheese. Serve with plain cookies, if desired.

Brandied Ricotta Spread

1 pound ricotta cheese	3 tablespoons brandy
¼ cup confectioners' sugar	¼ teaspoon cinnamon

Mix together all ingredients, and mound in a serving dish. Surround with pear and apple slices, fresh strawberries, and plain cookies. A dessert wine would go well with this.

Banana Ricotta Dessert

2 cups mashed ripe bananas	1 cup ricotta cheese
1 teaspoon lemon juice	⅓ cup milk
½ cup confectioners' sugar	1½ teaspoons vanilla
3 tablespoons cocoa	

Beat all ingredients until smooth, either with a mixer or in a blender. Turn into individual serving dishes and chill.

part 6
Selected Fresh Vegetables

26
Eggplant

The eggplant is very much a victim of circumstances. With only 92 calories in an entire pound, raw, eggplant is still considered to be a fattening vegetable, simply because of the way in which it is usually cooked. The eggplant can absorb incredible quantities of oil; and at 100 calories per tablespoon, you can end up with a pretty rich dish if you are not careful.

A Middle East folktale points up eggplant's spongelike capacity. It seems there was a certain priest (or imam) who had a nearly insatiable appetite for an eggplant dish that his fiancee made. The recipe, since named Eggplant Imam Baaldi after the priest, called for great quantities of oil because, to make it, whole eggplants were treated to a long, slow simmering in oil. In order that he might enjoy this dish after his marriage, the imam requested that his fiancee's dowry be in oil. Accordingly, huge jars of oil were brought into their home, and on the first two nights after their marriage, the bride made the eggplant dish. But on the third night, she failed to do so. The priest asked why his favorite dish was missing, and his wife responded that the oil supply had been depleted, at which point the imam fainted.

This tale may be fiction, but it is a fact that eggplant will stick while it is being sautéed unless more and more oil is added to the skillet. When I wish to cook eggplant without its absorbing an excessive amount of oil, rather than sautéing the slices as the recipe suggests, I lay the slices on a greased baking sheet, brush them with oil, and bake them in a 375-degree oven for about 30 minutes. They will be browned, soft, and nongreasy.

TWO EGGPLANT DIPS

Either of these recipes may be used as a dip, spread, or to fill pockets of pita bread. I also serve them raw with vegetables, especially crisp green pepper strips, either before or with a meal. The first recipe is very rich because of the sesame paste. The second is considerably lower in calories.

For each of these dips, the eggplant is cooked whole. In the Middle East, where the recipes originated, the vegetable is cooked on an open flame over charcoal for about an hour, rotated frequently so it chars evenly. This procedure may be nearly duplicated by cooking the unpeeled eggplant directly on your gas burner. However, the simplest method, which requires much less surveillance, is to bake the eggplant on a baking sheet in a 375-degree oven for about an hour or until it has "collapsed." When the eggplant has cooled, peel and discard the skin and mash the pulp. Then let the eggplant sit in a colander for about an hour to drain off any excess moisture.

Baba Ghanouj

PREPARATION TIMES: 15 minutes kitchen work
1 hour baking
1 hour draining the eggplant

YIELD: 2 cups, or 8 servings

3 tablespoons tahini (sesame
  paste that is available in
  health food stores, Middle
  Eastern groceries, and
  many large supermarkets)
¼ cup water

2 tablespoons lemon juice
1 clove garlic, mashed
½ teaspoon salt
pulp from 1 eggplant,
  prepared by one of the
  preceding methods

In a small bowl, whisk together the tahini and water. Stir in the
lemon juice, garlic, and salt. Then add the eggplant pulp. Refrigerate until ready to serve.

Eggplant with Yogurt

PREPARATION TIMES: 15 minutes kitchen work
                        1 hour baking
                        1 hour draining the eggplant

YIELD: 1½ cups, or 6 servings

pulp from 1 eggplant,
  prepared by one of the
  preceding methods
1 clove garlic, mashed
1 teaspoon lemon juice
½ cup yogurt

½ teaspoon salt
¼ teaspoon pepper
3 tablespoons sesame seeds,
  toasted in an ungreased
  skillet until browned

Simply mix all ingredients together in a small bowl.

RATATOUILLE AND RATATOUILLE CASSEROLE

Ratatouille is a sort of vegetable stew from the Provençal area of France. Any number of vegetables may go into it—tomatoes, eggplant, pumpkin, zucchini, green peppers, celery, etc. It is delicious hot, cold, or reheated, and is generally served as a salad course.

When eggs and cheese are added and the ratatouille is baked, the result is a delicious casserole that makes a great main course. Because it is so solid, it may also be taken cold on a picnic. If you plan to serve it cold, omit the mozzarella cheese topping, as this becomes rather tough when chilled.

PREPARATION TIMES: for Ratatouille: 20 minutes kitchen work
20 minutes simmering

additional for casserole: 20 minutes kitchen work
30 minutes baking

YIELD: 4 servings

1 eggplant, peeled and cubed
2 zucchini, sliced
1 large onion, chopped
(about ¾ cup)
3 tablespoons olive oil
4 tomatoes, peeled, seeded, and chopped
3 eggs
¾ cup grated Parmesan cheese, divided usage

2 tablespoons minced fresh parsley
½ teaspoon basil
½ teaspoon oregano
1 teaspoon salt
¼ teaspoon pepper
4 ounces mozzarella cheese, thinly sliced

1. In a large skillet, sauté the eggplant, zucchini, and onion in the olive oil for about 10 minutes or until the vegetables are softened. Add the tomatoes and cook, covered, over a moderate heat for 10 minutes. If you wish to serve plain ratatouille, simply season with salt and pepper, and you have it.

2. If you wish to make the casserole, cook the mixture, uncovered, over a fairly high heat until most of the liquid has evaporated. Let cool slightly.

3. In a large bowl, beat the eggs with ¼ cup Parmesan cheese and the seasonings. Stir in the eggplant mixture.

4. Pour half of this mixture into a greased 8″ × 8″ pan. Sprinkle with ¼ cup Parmesan cheese. Repeat the layers. Top with the mozzarella cheese. Bake in a 400-degree oven about 30 minutes or until browned and set.

POLENTA WITH EGGPLANT SAUCE

Here is another variation of polenta (refer to part 4, Chapter 19 for the basic recipe), this one topped with a tomato sauce teaming with vegetables—eggplant, celery, mushrooms, and onions. The almonds add an unusual crunch to the sauce. As this is filling but does not supply complete protein, it would be appropriate to end your meal with one of the dishes in the chapter on Dairy Desserts; any of the ricotta cheese desserts would go especially well.

PREPARATION TIMES: 1 hour kitchen work
45 minutes simmering
30 minutes baking

YIELD: 4 servings

1 onion, chopped
1 clove garlic, minced
½ cup diced celery
½ pound sliced mushrooms
3 tablespoons vegetable oil
1 15-ounce can tomato puree
1½ cups tomato juice
1 large eggplant (about 1¼ pound), peeled and cubed

¼ cup dry sherry
¼ cup minced fresh parsley
¼ cup slivered almonds
½ teaspoon salt
¼ teaspoon pepper
½ teaspoon oregano
1 bay leaf
1 recipe Polenta
grated Parmesan cheese

1. In a large skillet, sauté the onion, garlic, celery, and mushrooms in oil until tender. Stir in the tomato puree, tomato juice, eggplant, sherry, parlsey, almonds, and seasonings. Simmer, covered, 45 minutes.

2. Meanwhile, prepare the polenta according to the recipe in Chapter 19 of part 4, and turn it into a greased 8″ × 10″ baking pan. Bake in a 375-degree oven 30 minutes.

3. Serve the polenta cut into squares, with plenty of eggplant sauce poured over it. Sprinkle with Parmesan cheese.

ITALIAN EGGPLANT LASAGNE

Similar to traditional lasagne, Italian Eggplant Lasagne has that great flavor and melting cheese but is without the fattening noodles. The tomato sauce recipe given here is a good, all-purpose sauce that may be made in quantity and frozen.

PREPARATION TIMES: Tomato Sauce: 10 minutes kitchen work
45 minutes simmering
Lasagne: 30 minutes kitchen work
1 hour baking

YIELD: 6 generous servings

Tomato Sauce:

1 onion, chopped
1 clove garlic, minced
2 tablespoons olive oil
1 6-ounce can tomato paste
¾ cup water
1 28-ounce can Italian plum tomatoes, undrained and

coarsely chopped
2 tablespoons dry sherry
½ teaspoon salt
¼ teaspoon pepper
½ teaspoon oregano
1 bay leaf

1. Brown the onion and garlic in olive oil in a heavy pot or large skillet.

2. Add the remaining ingredients. Bring to a boil. Then lower the heat, cover, and simmer 45 minutes.

Lasagne:

1 eggplant, peeled and sliced into ½-inch slices
2 medium zucchini, sliced
1 green pepper, chopped
2 onions, sliced
2 tablespoons olive oil

1 pound mozzarella cheese, sliced
½ teaspoon salt
2 tablespoons grated Parmesan cheese
tomato sauce, above

1. First, start the tomato sauce simmering.

2. Place the eggplant slices on a greased baking sheet, and bake in a 375-degree oven for 30 minutes.

3. Meanwhile, sauté the zucchini, green pepper, and onions in olive oil in a skillet.

4. In a 4-quart greased casserole or dutch oven, layer the egg-

plant, sautéed vegetables, mozzarella cheese, and tomato sauce, sprinkling salt on the vegetables as you go. End with a layer of sauce, and sprinkle the top with Parmesan cheese.

5. Bake in a 350-degree oven 30 minutes.

BAKED CHEESY EGGPLANT

This wonderfully rich and cheesy eggplant vegetable dish is definitely company fare. Use it to spark up a spaghetti dinner or as an unusual accompaniment to a thick minestrone.

PREPARATION TIMES: 45 minutes kitchen work
                   55 minutes baking

YIELD: 4 servings

2 medium eggplants (about 1 pound each)
salt
1 onion, chopped
4 tablespoons butter or unsaturated margarine
3 tablespoons unbleached white flour

¾ cup milk
¾ cup grated Parmesan cheese, divided usage
1 teaspoon spicy brown mustard
¼ teaspoon pepper
1 egg, beaten

1. Trim the top and bottom off the eggplants and cut them in half lengthwise. Make several deep slashes in the flesh. Sprinkle the flesh with salt. Place the eggplants on a baking sheet and bake in a 375-degree oven 35 minutes. When cool enough to handle, remove the pulp without damaging the skin, and dice it. Place the skins in a greased shallow baking dish.

2. Meanwhile, in a heavy saucepan, sauté the onion in butter or margarine until softened. Stir in the flour and cook 2 minutes. Add the milk, and cook, stirring, until the mixture comes to a boil and thickens. Remove from the heat and stir in the eggplant pulp, ¼ cup Parmesan cheese, 1 teaspoon salt, and the mustard, pepper, and beaten egg.

3. Spoon this mixture into the eggplant skins. Sprinkle the tops with the remaining ½ cup Parmesan cheese. Bake the dish in a 375-degree oven 20 minutes.

27
Corn

Of all American vegetables, corn on the cob must be one of the most popular. There is no denying that freshly picked ears, boiled, buttered, and salted, make for pretty good eating. But limiting yourself to corn prepared only in this manner is like always eating your rice boiled, your beans baked, or your yogurt from cardboard cups. A little variety can only make your dinners more enjoyable.

For many, the most common way of eating corn is to open a can and turn the contents into a creamed vegetable dish or add the corn to a stew or casserole. But canned corn lacks the fresh crispness of that from the garden. So, when in season, why not make such dishes when the best in corn is available? And if you have a plentiful supply, corn cut from the cob may be successfully frozen in plastic bags, ready for use year-round.

Some people think it difficult or tedious to scrape the kernels from an ear of corn. But in reality, when using a small, sharp knife, it is no harder than peeling a cucumber. Simply hold the corn at an angle, and run the knife down the length of the ear, cutting off the kernels. Turn the ear slightly to expose more kernels, and cut off those rows. Keep turning and cutting until all the corn has been removed.

In other countries of the world, where affluence has not permitted the vast meat consumption of America, corn is a basic source of protein. So these other cuisines have developed marvelous casseroles, stews, and breads utilizing this vegetable. Corn lacks tryptophan, isoleucine, and lysine. But when it is combined with soy or other beans, pumpkin, squash, or sunflower seeds, cashews, wheat products, rice, brussels sprouts, broccoli, cauliflower, okra, spinach or other greens, or dairy products (or meats), a complete protein food results.

Following are several international recipes calling for fresh (or defrosted frozen) corn kernels. If you're in a rut, always serving up corn on the cob, summer after summer, why not try one of these more unusual, highly flavored, and very nutritious recipes?

From the time I was a child, I have always been fascinated by the changes in texture that result in a final baked product when just one or two ingredients were just slightly manipulated. For this reason, the first two recipes following greatly interest me. The ingredients in each are almost identical. Yet the textures emerge as totally different. The corn bread is very dense and coarse, while the soufflé is light and airy. This is due to two basic differences in the recipes. One is a difference in proportions. The bread contains 1½ cups of cornmeal to ⅔ cup milk, while the soufflé has only ¼ cup of flour to 2 cups of milk. More grain produces a denser, heavier product.

The other difference is in the treatment of the eggs. They are added whole to the bread but separated for the soufflé, with the egg whites stiffly beaten. When the soufflé is baked, the air that has been incorporated into the whites expands with the heat, resulting in a puffing up of the whole dish. If you choose, you could make the bread lighter by separating the eggs and folding in the beaten whites just before turning the batter into the pan. And you could turn the soufflé into a pudding by stirring in the entire egg where the recipe calls for adding only the yolks.

CHEDDAR-CORN BREAD

A bread so hearty and full of protein, this could really be served as a main course, accompanied by just a big tossed salad and some refreshing beer. But many would find a dinner of large portions of bread just too heavy, in which case it makes an ideal "go-with" for all types of soups.

PREPARATION TIMES: 15 minutes kitchen work
30 minutes baking

YIELD: 6 to 8 servings as an accompaniment

3 eggs
¼ cup (½ stick) butter or
  unsaturated margarine
1½ cups (about 2 ears)
  freshly cut corn kernels
1 tablespoon minced onion

⅔ cup milk
1½ cups cornmeal
1 teaspoon salt
½ teaspoon baking powder
1½ cups grated Cheddar
  cheese

1. Place the eggs, butter or margarine, corn, onion, and milk in a blender, and blend until smooth.

2. In a large bowl, stir together the cornmeal, salt, and baking powder. Add the contents of the blender and stir just until the dry ingredients are moistened. Stir in the Cheddar cheese.

3. Turn the mixture into a well-greased 8″ × 8″ pan, and bake in a 375-degree oven about 30 minutes. Serve warm.

CORN SOUFFLÉ

This flavorful soufflé is filled with corn, green pepper, and onion. Serve it with a green vegetable, such as zucchini or green beans, and a good whole wheat bread.

PREPARATION TIMES: 30 minutes kitchen work
10 minutes simmering
45 minutes baking

YIELD: 4 servings

3 eggs, separated
pinch salt
½ stick (¼ cup) butter or
   unsaturated margarine
1½ cups (about 2 ears)
   freshly cut corn kernels
1 green pepper, chopped
1 onion, chopped

¼ cup unbleached white
   flour
2 cups milk
½ teaspoon salt
¼ teaspoon Tabasco
1 cup shredded Cheddar
   cheese

1. In a large bowl, beat the egg whites with the pinch of salt until stiff. Set aside.

2. Melt the butter or margarine in a large saucepan. Add the corn, green pepper, and onion. Cook 5 minutes, uncovered. Then cover and simmer another 5 minutes.

3. Stir in the flour and cook, stirring, for 2 minutes. Add the milk, salt, and Tabasco and cook, stirring with a wire whisk, until just at boiling and beginning to thicken. Add the cheese and cook over a low heat until melted.

4. Remove the pan from the heat and beat in the egg yolks one at a time. Gently fold in the egg whites.

5. Turn the mixture into a well-greased 1½- to 2-quart soufflé dish or casserole. Bake in a 375-degree oven 45 minutes. Serve immediately.

CHILI CORN SOUFFLÉ

This is absolutely the simplest soufflé I have ever made. All ingredients except the egg whites go into the blender. The soufflé rises high and light, with a wonderfully fresh corn flavor and a distinctly Mexican touch. Serve it with black beans, seasoned with garlic and oil-and-vinegar dressing.

PREPARATION TIMES: 20 minutes kitchen work
40 minutes baking

YIELD: 4 appetizer or 2 main course servings

4 eggs, separated
1 4-ounce can green chili
  peppers
kernels from 4 ears of corn
  (about 3 cups)

½ teaspoon salt
1 teaspoon chili powder

1. Place all ingredients except the egg whites in a blender and blend until nearly smooth.

2. Beat the egg whites until stiff in a large bowl and gently fold in the contents of the blender.

3. Turn the batter into a well-greased 2-quart soufflé dish or casserole. Bake in a 375-degree oven 35 to 40 minutes, or until it is puffed, browned, and set.

BOLIVIAN POTATO AND CORN CASSEROLE

Here is another recipe based on eggs, milk, Cheddar cheese, onion, and, of course, corn. But here, the eggs are hard-cooked and so remain distinct. Sliced potatoes deliciously absorb the corn-flavored liquid. Serve the casserole with a bowl of red or black beans and a plate of sliced tomatoes.

PREPARATION TIMES: 30 minutes kitchen work
15 minutes baking

YIELD: 6 servings

2 cups fresh corn kernels
(about 3 ears)
½ cup milk
1 onion, chopped finely
1 green pepper, diced
⅛ teaspoon nutmeg
1 teaspoon salt, divided usage

2 pounds (about 4) potatoes,
peeled and thinly sliced
¼ teaspoon pepper
¾ cup shredded Cheddar
cheese
4 hard-cooked eggs, sliced

1. Place the corn and milk in a blender and puree. Place this mixture in a saucepan and add the onion, green pepper, nutmeg, and ½ teaspoon salt. Simmer 5 minutes.

2. In a greased 2-quart casserole, make layers of potatoes, cheese, and eggs, sprinkling the layers with the pepper and the remaining ½ teaspoon salt. Pour the corn mixture over all.

3. Bake the casserole in a 400-degree oven 15 minutes.

FRENCH CORNCAKE

This is one of the few recipe contributions we have from France for corn dishes. Most French people regard corn as a food better left to barnyard animals; but with their customary ingenuity in the kitchen, they have, nevertheless, turned the vegetable into a light, lovely, baked pancake that makes excellent breakfast fare or a change-of-pace accompaniment to dinner.

PREPARATION TIMES: 25 minutes kitchen work
20 minutes baking
YIELD: 4 servings

2 cups corn kernels (about 3
ears corn)
⅓ cup unbleached white flour

3 eggs
½ teaspoon salt
⅛ teaspoon pepper

1. Simmer the corn kernels in boiling water 5 minutes. Drain well.

2. Place all ingredients in a blender and blend until smooth.

3. Turn the batter into a well-greased 9-inch pie plate. Bake in a 375-degree oven 20 minutes, or until the corncake is set and browned. Cut into wedges to serve.

CORN AND CHEDDAR SOUP

Here's a great soup to start out a light dinner, or to serve as a complete meal in itself, if accompanied by a substantial salad and hot bread. The milk makes the soup creamy, the Cheddar cheese lends richness, and the corn adds an incomparable freshness. The result is very much like an old-fashioned chowder.

PREPARATION TIMES: 30 minutes kitchen work
                   25 minutes simmering

YIELD: 8 servings

1 onion, chopped
1 clove garlic, minced
2 tablespoons butter or
  unsaturated margarine
2 tablespoons unbleached
  white flour
2 cups water
2 carrots, diced

4 cups fresh corn kernels
  (about 6 ears corn)
4 cups milk
1 teaspoon salt
1 teaspoon chili powder
¼ teaspoon black pepper
2 cups shredded Cheddar
  cheese

1. Sauté the onion and garlic in the butter or margarine in a large heavy saucepan until soft. Add the flour and cook, stirring, 1 minute. Add the water and cook, stirring, until the mixture comes to a boil and thickens slightly. Stir in the carrots and corn and simmer 20 minutes.

2. Stir in the milk and seasonings. Heat to nearly boiling. Add the Cheddar cheese and heat until nearly melted. Do not let it boil.

28
Zucchini

Zucchini is my favorite vegetable, and one that is delicious in a great variety of vegetarian preparations. So, in the following pages, I present an 8-course zucchini banquet. Of course, I cannot imagine that anyone would actually make or even eat an entire meal based on zucchini (although for five successive nights, I tried out these recipes without tiring of the vegetable). It is given here just to show how wonderfully versatile this squash can be. Zucchini has a distinctive flavor, yet is subtle enough to blend with many other ingredients. The taste and texture change depending on whether it is sliced, grated, or blended; whether it is raw or cooked.

GREEK VEGETABLE STEW

This dish is very similar to the French ratatouille, with the main difference being that in ratatouille the vegetables are sautéed and then simmered only until barely tender, whereas the stew is simpler; the sautéing has been eliminated and the vegetables simmer a good long time. The stew has little liquid, yet the vegetables remain in distinct, nice-sized chunks. It is delicious mopped up with pieces of hot bread. Besides being a soup course, it may be served as a lunch dish, accompanied by feta cheese and a dish of black olives.

PREPARATION TIMES: 30 minutes kitchen work
                   1 hour simmering

YIELD: 6 servings

1 large onion, chopped
  (about 1¼ cups)
3 tablespoons vegetable oil
3 eggplants, peeled and
  cubed
6 zucchini, sliced

4 tomatoes, peeled and diced
½ cup chopped fresh parsley
2 cloves garlic, pressed
2 teaspoons salt
½ teaspoon pepper

In a large, heavy saucepan, sauté the onion in oil until beginning to brown. Add the eggplant and cook 2 minutes longer. Add all remaining ingredients and simmer, covered, 1 hour.

ZUCCHINI-CHEDDAR QUICHE

This is a sumptuously rich quiche because of the large propor-tion of cheese to custard. Besides qualifying as an appetizer, it can also make a delicious lunch or light dinner.

PREPARATION TIMES: 1¼ hours making and chilling the pastry
20 minutes kitchen work
25 minutes baking

YIELD: 4 appetizer, or 2 to 3 lunch or light dinner servings

1 9-inch pie shell, unbaked
1 tablespoon butter or
  unsaturated margarine,
  divided usage
¾ cup coarsely grated
  zucchini
3 eggs, beaten

¾ cup light cream
¼ teaspoon salt
few grinds black pepper
pinch nutmeg
1½ cups grated Cheddar
  cheese

1. Prick the pie pastry all over with a fork and bake it in a 400-degree oven 8 to 10 minutes, until it just begins to brown but is not fully baked. When the crust has cooled, smear it with half the butter or margarine. This will protect it from becoming soggy.

2. In a small skillet, sauté the zucchini in the remaining butter or margarine for about 3 minutes.

3. In a small bowl, combine the eggs, light cream, and season-ings. Stir in the zucchini.

4. Sprinkle the Cheddar cheese over the bottom of the pie shell. Pour the zucchini filling over this. Bake in a 375-degree oven about 25 minutes or until brown and set.

MEXICAN ZUCCHINI TORTE

This is a wonderfully rich main course, with layers of puffy egg, melted cheese, tender zucchini rounds, and spicy tomato sauce. Serve the casserole with rice and beans or corn bread, a tossed salad, and plenty of cold beer.

PREPARATION TIMES: 45 minutes kitchen work
30 minutes baking

YIELD: 4 servings

2 good-sized zucchini (about 8 inches long), sliced ¼-inch thick
1 onion, chopped
1 tablespoon vegetable oil
3 tomatoes, peeled, seeded, and chopped

1 4-ounce can mild green chilies, chopped
½ teaspoon salt
3 eggs, separated
pinch salt
4 ounces Monterey Jack cheese, thinly sliced

1. Cook the zucchini in boiling water to cover until just tender. Drain.

2. Sauté the onion in oil until softened. Add the tomatoes and chilies. Cook until the liquid is nearly evaporated, about 10 minutes. Stir in the ½ teaspoon salt.

3. Beat the egg whites until stiff with a pinch of salt. Then beat in the egg yolks, one at a time.

4. Grease a 2-quart casserole. Place one-third of the zucchini on the bottom. Cover with half the tomato mixture, then one-third of the cheese, and one-third of the eggs. Repeat these layers. Finish with the rest of the zucchini, then eggs, then cheese.

5. Bake the dish in a 350-degree oven 25 to 30 minutes or until golden brown on top. Serve immediately.

ZUCCHINI RAITA

This cool Indian side dish is generally served with hot, curried foods. Most commonly made with cucumber, raita may also include spinach, pumpkin, tomatoes, potatoes (or zucchini).

PREPARATION TIME: 15 minutes kitchen work

YIELD: 6 to 8 servings

1 good-sized zucchini (about 8 inches long), grated
3 cups yogurt
1 teaspoon salt
1 teaspoon cumin seeds
2 tablespoons raisins (optional)

In a bowl, stir together the zucchini, yogurt, and salt. Toast the cumin seeds in an ungreased skillet until they begin to jump. Crush them slightly with the back of a spoon and add them to the zucchini mixture along with the raisins, if desired (the raisins will make a slightly sweeter relish).

RAW ZUCCHINI AND APPLE SALAD

Very crunchy and refreshing, this salad goes well with both egg and rice dishes. If you happen to like raw onions, a few thin slices from a red onion would make an appropriate addition.

PREPARATION TIME: 15 minutes kitchen work

YIELD: 4 servings

1 pound (2 medium) zucchini, thinly sliced
1 apple (preferably Red Delicious), unpeeled, cored, and chopped
2 green peppers, chopped
⅓ cup salad oil
¼ cup red wine vinegar
2 tablespoons lemon juice
1 teaspoon sugar
½ teaspoon salt

Mix all vegetables in a bowl. In a screw-top jar, mix the remaining ingredients. Pour over the vegetables and toss well.

ITALIAN BAKED ZUCCHINI

The olive oil, garlic, and Parmesan cheese lend a distinctly Italian savor to this dish.

PREPARATION TIMES: 25 minutes kitchen work
20 minutes baking

YIELD: 4 to 6 servings

2 tablespoons olive oil
2 stalks celery, diced
1 green pepper, diced
1 onion, chopped
1 clove garlic, minced
2 pounds (4 medium) zucchini, sliced

1 teaspoon salt
¼ teaspoon pepper
½ teaspoon basil
½ cup fresh bread crumbs
⅓ cup grated Parmesan cheese

1. In an ovenproof skillet, sauté the celery, green pepper, onion, and garlic in olive oil until the onion is tender. Add the zucchini and spices. Cover and simmer over a medium heat 10 minutes.

2. Sprinkle the zucchini mixture with the bread crumbs and cheese. Bake, uncovered, in a 375-degree oven 20 minutes.

ZUCCHINI MUFFINS

Zucchini breads, once thought strange, are now becoming commonplace. Zucchini muffins have the same texture and flavor as the breads but have the added advantage of being crisp all over and requiring no slicing. As the muffins are rather sweet, they are best not served with a meal unless the main course is quite plain. They do, however, make great between meal snacks.

Vegetable breads, such as this one and carrot or pumpkin

bread, are generally made with oil, which can leave a greasy taste and texture. Substituting melted butter or margarine eliminates this.

Just a note on preparing zucchini for baking: The zucchini should be fresh, firm, and of a medium size. Do not use the huge, overgrown squash as they are watery and lack flavor. Grate the unpeeled zucchini on the coarse edge of your grater and wrap it in a paper towel to absorb any excess moisture, but do *not* squeeze—the liquid in the zucchini is what keeps these foods moist.

PREPARATION TIMES: 20 minutes kitchen work
25 minutes baking

YIELD: 9 large muffins

¾ cup whole wheat flour
⅓ cup unbleached white
flour
½ teaspoon baking powder
½ teaspoon baking soda
½ teaspoon salt
½ teaspoon nutmeg
2 eggs

¾ cup brown sugar
½ stick (4 tablespoons) butter
or unsaturated margarine,
melted
1½ cups shredded zucchini
½ cup raisins
⅓ cup chopped walnuts

1. In a bowl, stir together the flours, baking powder, baking soda, salt, and nutmeg.

2. In a large bowl, beat the eggs. Gradually beat in the brown sugar. When done, the mixture should be thick. Beat in the melted butter or margarine. Add the dry ingredients and zucchini. Stir just until well mixed. Fold in the raisins and walnuts

3. Pour the batter into greased muffin tins until nearly full. Bake in a 375-degree oven 20 to 25 minutes, or until the muffins test done with a toothpick.

CHOCOLATE ZUCCHINI CAKE

Of all the hundreds of recipes printed in my newspaper column, the following received the most attention. I was inundated with letters of praise for the cake from my readers, for not only does the cake offer all that one would wish from a chocolate cake (being moist, chewy, and very flavorful), but it makes a great conversation piece. What guest can resist: "Try a slice of my Chocolate Zucchini Cake." You'll always get a response!

PREPARATION TIMES: 30 minutes kitchen work
                              1 hour baking

YIELD: 1 large tube cake, or about 12 to 16 servings

1 stick plus 1 tablespoon (9
   tablespoons altogether)
   butter or unsaturated
   margarine
2 cups sugar
3 eggs
3 1-ounce squares
   unsweetened chocolate,
   melted
2 teaspoons vanilla

2 teaspoons grated orange
   rind
½ cup milk
2 cups grated zucchini
2½ cups unbleached white
   flour
2½ teaspoons baking powder
1½ teaspoons baking soda
1 teaspoon salt
1 teaspoon cinnamon

1. In a large bowl, cream together the butter or margarine and sugar. Beat in the eggs, then the chocolate, vanilla, orange rind, and milk. Stir in the zucchini.

2. In another bowl, stir together the remaining ingredients. Beat these into the zucchini mixture.

3. Turn the batter into a greased and floured tube pan. Bake in a 350-degree oven about 1 hour or until a toothpick comes out clean. Cool on a rack before removing from the pan.

ZUCCHINI ROCKS

I felt compelled to include this recipe as my husband insists these are the best cookies he's ever eaten. Rocks, unlike the name, are not particularly hard. Rather, they are large, irregularly shaped drop spice cookies, containing dried fruits and nuts. Because of their size and shape, they resemble miniature boulders. These rocks are especially moist and chewy because of the addition of the shredded zucchini.

PREPARATION TIMES: 30 minutes kitchen work
15 minutes baking

YIELD: 24 large cookies

1 stick (½ cup) butter or
  unsaturated margarine,
  softened
1 cup brown sugar
1 egg
1 teaspoon vanilla
1 cup shredded zucchini
1 cup whole wheat flour

1 cup unbleached white flour
1 teaspoon baking soda
1 teaspoon cinnamon
½ teaspoon cloves
½ teaspoon salt
⅔ cup coarsely chopped
  walnuts
⅔ cup snipped dates

1. In a large bowl, cream together the butter or margarine and brown sugar. Beat in the egg, then the vanilla and zucchini.

2. In another bowl, stir together the flours, baking soda, spices, and salt. Beat into the zucchini mixture until moistened. Stir in the walnuts and dates.

3. Grease two 11″ × 16″ baking sheets, and drop the batter by tablespoonfuls about 1 inch apart. Bake in a 375-degree oven about 15 minutes, or until the cookies are just beginning to brown on the edges. Remove to a rack to cool.

29
Carrots

E at your carrots; they're good for your eyes" is a phrase said at one time or another by nearly all mothers. This is quite true because the vitamin A in carrots is indeed essential for night vision. In daylight, the cones, one type of visual receptor, function to give us color vision. But at dusk and in the near-darkness, the more sensitive rods take over. The rods contain a pigment, rhodopsin (also called visual purple), which is bleached when they respond to light (it is this bleaching that allows us to see an object at night). Rhodopsin, when bleached, becomes opsin, which cannot respond to light. Thus, opsin must return to rhodopsin or else when each rod has been bleached, we would then have night blindness. It is vitamin A that makes the conversion from opsin back to rhodopsin so that we may see objects over and over again in the darkness.

Cooking or processing reduces the vitamin A in foods. Dehydration, on the other hand, intensifies the vitamin A content.

Of all the yellow vegetables, carrots rank highest in levels of vitamin A. They are also delicious and can form the basis of many delightful dishes.

You will note that many of the recipes here call for *grated* carrots. If you do not have a food processor, the easiest way to grate carrots is in a blender. Place about 1 cup of ½-inch carrot slices in the blender and cover with plenty of water. Blend until the carrots are finely chopped and immediately pour into a colander to drain.

JOYCE'S VEGETABLE SOUP

When I lived in Los Angeles, I had a friend, Joyce, who was a fantastic cook. She put this soup together one day, and I've made it many times since. Most leek and potato soups are rather bland; but here's a very tasty version with the added pronounced flavors of broccoli and carrot, plus the tangyness of watercress.

PREPARATION TIMES: 25 minutes kitchen work
                   50 minutes simmering

YIELD: 6 servings

6 carrots, peeled and sliced
1 stalk broccoli, coarsely
   chopped
2 large or 4 small leeks,
   sliced (about 2½ cups)
3 potatoes, peeled and diced

6 cups water
2 teaspoons salt
1 bunch watercress, coarsely
   chopped
½ cup cream

1. Place all ingredients except the watercress and cream in a large pot. Bring to a boil. Reduce the heat, cover, and simmer 45 minutes. Add the watercress and cook 5 minutes longer.

2. Drain the vegetables, reserving 2¼ cups of cooking liquid. Place the vegetables and liquid in a blender, and blend until smooth (this may require 2 blender loads).

3. Return the soup to the pot. Stir in the cream and heat through.

CURRIED CARROT AND RAISIN SOUFFLÉ

This rather sweet soufflé makes a good lunch dish served with hot rolls. The Cheddar cheese melts deliciously into the egg mixture, and the carrots and raisins lend crunchy and chewy textures.

PREPARATION TIMES: 40 minutes kitchen work
50 minutes baking

YIELD: 4 servings

3 tablespoons butter or
  unsaturated margarine
3 tablespoons unbleached
  white flour
1½ cups milk
¾ teaspoon curry powder

¾ teaspoon salt
¾ cup shredded Cheddar
  cheese
3 eggs, separated
⅓ cup raisins
3 cups grated carrots

1. In a heavy saucepan, melt the butter or margarine. Stir in the flour and cook, stirring, 2 minutes. Add the milk and cook, stirring with a wire whisk, until thick and smooth. Add the curry powder, salt, and Cheddar cheese, and cook over a low heat until the cheese melts. Remove from the heat and beat in the egg yolks, one at a time. Stir in the raisins and carrots.

2. In a large bowl, beat the egg whites until stiff with a pinch of salt. Stir one-third of them into the carrot mixture and then fold in the rest gently.

3. Turn the soufflé mixture into a well-greased 2-quart soufflé dish or casserole. Bake in a 325-degree oven about 50 minutes.

CARROT SANDWICH SPREAD I

Carrots and raisins are a well-loved combination. Here's a spread that is highly nutritious and tastes great in whole wheat sandwiches (especially when toasted) or stuffed into pita bread.

PREPARATION TIMES: 15 minutes kitchen work
                    30 minutes or more chilling

YIELD: enough for 3 sandwiches

½ cup raisins   1 tablespoon mayonnaise
½ cup grated carrots   ⅛ teaspoon salt
½ cup cottage cheese

Mix all ingredients together and chill at least 30 minutes to soften the raisins.

CARROT SANDWICH SPREAD II

Anyone fond of peanut butter is certain to love this creamy, crunchy spread. One of my friends, responsible for bringing a morning snack to a group of nursery school tots, regularly serves this spread, and the children love it.

PREPARATION TIME: 15 minutes kitchen work

YIELD: enough for 4 sandwiches

½ cup peanut butter,   ¼ cup yogurt
   preferably crunch-style   2 tablespoons honey
⅔ cup grated carrots

Mix all ingredients together and store, covered, in the refrigerator.

CARROT BREAD

If carrot breads are among your passions, try this exceedingly simple version. All the work, including the grating of the carrots, is done by the blender.

PREPARATION TIMES: 15 minutes kitchen work
1 hour baking

YIELD: 1 loaf

¾ cup unbleached white flour
¾ cup whole wheat flour
1½ teaspoons baking soda
1½ teaspoons cinnamon
½ teaspoon salt
2 eggs
¾ cup sugar

1 stick (½ cup) butter or margarine, melted
1 teaspoon vanilla
1½ cups carrot slices, in ½-inch pieces
1 cup chopped cashews or other nuts

1. In a large bowl, stir together the flours, baking soda, cinnamon, and salt.

2. Place the eggs, sugar, melted butter or margarine, and vanilla in a blender, and blend until smooth. Add the carrot pieces, and blend just until the carrots are grated coarsely.

3. Pour the contents of the blender over the dry ingredients, and stir just until moistened. Stir in the cashew nuts.

4. Turn the batter into a greased and floured 9″ × 5″ loaf pan. Bake in a 350-degree oven about 1 hour. Let cool on a rack before slicing. Serve plain with tea or with cream cheese or other mild cheese in sandwiches.

CARROT-MUSHROOM CUSTARD PIE

An excellent lunch or supper dish, this is very delicately flavored, tasting mostly of mushroom. The carrots add crunch to the creamy smooth custard.

PREPARATION TIMES: 30 minutes kitchen work
1¼ hours making and chilling the pastry
45 minutes baking

YIELD: 4 servings

1 onion, chopped
½ pound mushrooms, sliced
3 tablespoons butter or
  unsaturated margarine
2 eggs
1 cup light cream or half and
  half

½ teaspoon salt
⅛ teaspoon pepper
⅛ teaspoon nutmeg
2 tablespoons minced fresh
  parsley
1 cup grated carrot
1 9-inch unbaked pastry shell

1. In a medium skillet, sauté the onion and mushrooms in butter or margarine until the onion is softened.

2. In a large bowl, beat the eggs. Stir in the cream, seasonings, carrot, and contents of the skillet.

3. Pour this mixture into the pastry shell. Bake the pie in a 350-degree oven 45 minutes, or until a knife inserted in the center comes out clean.

CARROT COFFEE CAKE RING

Here's an unusual recipe with a carrot-flavored yeast dough wrapped around a filling of grated carrots and dried fruits. The result is exceptionally attractive, moist, crunchy, nutritious, and tasty.

PREPARATION TIMES: 60 minutes kitchen work
2¼ hours rising
30 minutes baking

YIELD: 1 ring cake, or 10 servings

Cake Dough:
2 tablespoons butter or
  unsaturated margarine
¼ cup sugar
1 egg
½ cup milk, scalded
½ teaspoon salt
1 cup grated carrots
½ teaspoon lemon rind
1 package active dry yeast
2 tablespoons warm water
1 cup whole wheat flour

about 1½ cups unbleached
  white or bread flour

*Filling: (Mix all ingredients
  together)*
½ cup chopped prunes
½ cup raisins
1 cup grated carrots
1 tablespoon lemon juice
2 tablespoons honey

1. In a large bowl, cream the butter or margarine with the sugar. Beat in the egg, then the scalded milk, salt, carrots, and lemon rind. Dissolve the yeast in the warm water and beat in. Stir in the whole wheat flour and then enough white flour to make a stiff dough.

2. Turn the dough out onto a surface coated with white flour. Knead the dough until it is smooth, elastic, and no longer sticky, adding more flour as needed. Place the dough in a greased bowl, and turn once so the greased side faces up. Cover the bowl with plastic wrap, and let the dough rise in a warm, draft-free spot until it has doubled in bulk, about 1½ hours.

3. Knead the dough a few minutes longer. Roll out to an 11″ × 16″ rectangle. Spread with the filling evenly. Roll up jelly roll

style, beginning with a long edge. Join the ends to make a ring, and pinch the edges together. Transfer to a greased baking sheet, with the open edge facing down. Let rise, covered, until nearly doubled in bulk, about 45 minutes.

4. Bake the ring in a 375-degree oven 30 minutes. Transfer to a rack. Serve warm or at room temperature.

CARROT-BEET CAKE

This is a very moist cake, as are most that include grated vegetables. In baking, the beets turn a warm brown, which, with the orange carrot pieces, give an unusually attractive look to the cake. As the cake is so moist, it is best stored in the refrigerator.

PREPARATION TIMES: 35 minutes kitchen work
40 minutes baking

YIELD: 1 9″ × 13″ cake, or 16 servings

4 eggs
1½ cups sugar
½ cup vegetable oil
2 teaspoons vanilla
1 cup whole wheat flour
1 cup unbleached white flour
2 teaspoons baking soda

2 teaspoons baking powder
½ teaspoon salt
1 teaspoon cinnamon
2 cups grated carrots
1 cup grated raw beets
½ cup chopped walnuts

1. In a large bowl, beat the eggs. Gradually beat in the sugar. The mixture should be thick and pale yellow. Beat in the oil and vanilla.

2. In another bowl, stir together the flours, baking soda, baking powder, salt, and cinnamon. Beat into the egg mixture until moistened. Stir in the carrots, beets, and walnuts.

3. Turn the batter into a greased and floured 9″ × 13″ baking pan. Bake in a 350-degree oven 40 minutes, or until the cake tests done with a toothpick. Let cool on a rack.

CARROT HALVA

I once belonged to a group of professional women that met monthly for lunch with different members preparing foods from a different country each time. The Indian lunch was unsurpassed, and the dessert, a creamy rich carrot pudding, was sensational. Note: The Halva must be made with whole milk. The butterfat is necessary to give the pudding proper flavor and consistency.

This dessert should not be confused with *halvah* or *halavah,* a Middle Eastern confection made of ground sesame seeds and honey that is now widely sold in this country.

PREPARATION TIMES: 20 minutes kitchen work
                   2 hours simmering
                   several hours chilling

YIELD: 8 generous servings

2 quarts whole milk
1½ pounds carrots, grated
1 tablespoon cornstarch
2 tablespoons honey
1/16 teaspoon saffron
½ teaspoon cinnamon
½ teaspoon cardamom
1½ cups sugar
1 teaspoon salt
¼ cup raisins
5 tablespoons butter or
    unsaturated margarine,
    divided usage

1. Place the milk in a large skillet. Bring just to boiling and stir in the carrots. Boil 15 minutes.

2. Dissolve the cornstarch in the honey. Add to the skillet along with all remaining ingredients, except 1 tablespoon of the butter or margarine. Reduce the heat and simmer the mixture until only a small amount of liquid is left, about 1½ hours.

3. Stir in the remaining 1 tablespoon butter or margarine and cook, stirring occasionally, 10 minutes longer, or until all the liquid has evaporated.

4. Turn the pudding into a serving dish and chill several hours.

30
Squash

I am referring in this chapter to the winter squash, *Cucurbita maxima* or *C. moschata;* my favorite summer squash, *Cucurbita pepo*, was discussed in the Zucchini chapter. As you know, the assortment of winter squash varieties is tremendous. It includes the banana, acorn, hubbard, turban, and pumpkin, to name but a few.

Although the sizes of squash may vary considerably, they are virtually interchangeable in recipes, unless you wish to stuff them. For small stuffed squash, use the acorn or dumpling, allowing one half per person. Or for an elaborate presentation of a stew or casserole, fill a large hubbard or turban squash or a pumpkin and bake or stew it until tender. It really makes a spectacular sight when brought to the table!

There are basically three methods of cooking squash. One is to cut it in half, remove the seeds and fibers, and bake it in a shallow pan with ½-inch of water in a moderate oven until it is tender (the time varies with the size of the squash). The filling is then scooped out and mashed, often stuffed back into the skins, which are browned and delicious from the oven baking. A second method, somewhat simpler, particularly if you are only interested in the mashed pulp, is to steam the whole squash, either in a steamer or in a large pot with two inches of boiling water. When tender, the squash is peeled and seeded and the pulp mashed. Or, you may peel and cube the raw, seeded squash and simmer in a small amount of boiling water (or steam it) until tender.

As one might expect, the various types of winter squashes have similar nutritional profiles. All types contain large amounts of vitamin A (about 1,250 International Units in a 3½-ounce serving of acorn, 6,000 IU in butternut, and 4,450 IU in hubbard). Strangely enough, the vitamin A content of squash *increases* during periods of storage, the amount of the increase depending on the conditions of the storage. These values apply to freshly harvested squash. The vegetable is also high in potassium, with a moderate calorie count.

CREAMED BROCCOLI AND EGGS IN SQUASH

This is a very simple casserole—just crisp broccoli and hard-cooked eggs folded into a seasoned white sauce. Serving it in a cooked squash is what makes it so special.

PREPARATION TIMES: 30 minutes kitchen work
1 hour simmering, plus cooking the eggs
30 minutes baking

YIELD: 4 servings

1 2- to 3-pound round winter squash
1 bunch broccoli, chopped coarsely
1 onion, chopped
2 tablespoons butter or unsaturated margarine
2 tablespoons unbleached white flour
1½ cups milk

½ teaspoon salt
⅛ teaspoon pepper
⅛ teaspoon nutmeg
1 tablespoon minced fresh parsley
4 hard-cooked eggs, shelled and sliced
½ cup chopped walnuts
¼ cup whole wheat bread crumbs

1. Place the squash in a large pot. Add 2 to 3 inches of water. Cover the pot, and boil the squash until tender when pierced with a fork, about 50 minutes. Drain. When cool enough to handle, cut a hole in the top and scoop out the seeds. Wash the squash. Place on a baking sheet.

2. Meanwhile, place the broccoli in a saucepan. Add 1 inch of water. Cook covered, until tender, about 5 minutes. Drain.

3. Sauté the onion in butter until tender. Add the flour and cook 1 minute. Add the milk and cook, stirring with a wire whisk, until it comes to a boil and thickens. Stir in the spices, eggs, walnuts, and broccoli.

4. Turn the creamed mixture into the squash. Top with the bread crumbs. Bake in a 350-degree oven about 30 minutes.

ORANGE-BAKED STUFFED SQUASH

Here is a simple-to-prepare vegetable dish that seems to be loved by all. It adds a sweet touch to any meal and should be served with a fairly plain main course.

PREPARATION TIMES: 15 minutes kitchen work
                     1½ hours baking

YIELD: 4 servings

2 acorn squash, halved and seeded	½ teaspoon cinnamon
2 tablespoons butter or unsaturated margarine	¼ cup orange juice
	1 teaspoon grated orange rind
½ teaspoon salt	⅓ cup brown sugar

1. Place the squash, cut side down, in a large, shallow baking pan. Add ½ inch of water and bake in a 325-degree oven 1 hour, or until tender.

2. Scoop out the squash pulp, reserving the shells, and place it in a bowl. Add the remaining ingredients and beat well with a spoon or a fork. Spoon the squash mixture back into the shells. Bake 30 minutes longer.

BANANA-STUFFED ACORN SQUASH

Here's another stuffed squash recipe, this one with the flavors of honey and bananas. It is delicious.

PREPARATION TIMES: 15 minutes kitchen work
1½ hours baking
YIELD: 4 servings

2 acorn squash, halved and seeded	2 tablespoons honey
	1 teaspoon lemon juice
1 banana, mashed	¼ teaspoon nutmeg
2 tablespoons butter or unsaturated margarine	

1. Place the squash, cut side down, in a large, shallow baking pan. Add ½ inch of water and bake in a 325-degree oven 1 hour, or until tender.

2. Scoop out the squash pulp, reserving the shells, and place it in a bowl. Add the remaining ingredients and beat well with a spoon or a fork. Spoon the squash mixture back into the shells. Bake 30 minutes longer.

The next two recipes may start you wondering. They both call for squash, apples, brown sugar, lemon juice, cinnamon, and butter. Yet one is a vegetable and one a dessert. Why should this be? Part of it has to do with proportions. The dessert contains more butter and sugar, so is richer and sweeter. The other reason has to do with expectations. The vegetable dish is boiled; and while it might seem soggy as a dessert, we expect vegetables often to be rather soft or mashed. The dessert, on the other hand, has a sweet, crumbly-crisp, baked-on topping which would seem odd to eat with a meal. At any rate, here are the recipes. Try them both, and see if you can determine exactly why one belongs *with* the meal and one *after* it.

SQUASH AND APPLES (A VEGETABLE)

PREPARATION TIME: 30 minutes kitchen work
YIELD: 4 servings

about 1 pound any winter
squash, peeled, seeded, and
cut into ½-inch cubes
1 large apple (about 1¼
cups), peeled, cored, and
cubed
2 tablespoons butter or
unsaturated margarine

¼ cup water
2 teaspoons lemon juice
¼ teaspoon cinnamon
⅛ teaspoon nutmeg
¼ teaspoon salt
2 tablespoons brown sugar

Place all ingredients in a large skillet. Cover and cook over medium high heat, about 5 minutes, until squash is tender.

SQUASH AND APPLES (A DESSERT CRISP)

PREPARATION TIMES: 30 minutes kitchen work
                   15 minutes simmering
                   45 minutes baking
YIELD: 6 servings

1 butternut squash, about 1
pound
3 cups apple slices (peeled or
unpeeled, as desired)
⅓ cup brown sugar
2 tablespoons lemon juice
1 teaspoon cinnamon
½ teaspoon salt

Topping:
½ cup unbleached white
flour
½ cup rolled oats
¼ cup brown sugar
6 tablespoons butter or
unsaturated margarine

1. Place the whole squash in a saucepan. Add 1 inch of water. Cook, covered, over a fairly high heat until tender, about 15 minutes. When cool enough to handle, peel and seed it, and slice into pieces about equal in size to your apple slices. Mix with the remaining ingredients, except for the topping, and turn the mixture into a greased 9″ × 9″ pan.

2. In a bowl, beat together the topping ingredients until the mixture forms little coarse bits. Sprinkle over the squash-apple mixture.

3. Bake in a 375-degree oven about 45 minutes. This is best served warm, either plain or with whipped or ice cream.

PUMPKIN BREAD

A moist, spicy quick bread that makes great cream cheese sandwiches, this is also an ideal between-meals treat with a cup of tea. For the pumpkin, either steam or bake it until tender (see the first page of this chapter), and mash the pulp. If you have a great deal of extra pulp, freeze it in small plastic containers to use in other recipes.

PREPARATION TIMES: 30 minutes kitchen work, plus time to prepare the pumpkin pulp
1 hour baking

YIELD: 1 loaf

⅓ cup hot water
⅓ cup raisins
⅓ cup butter or unsaturated margarine, softened
1 cup sugar
⅓ cup molasses
2 eggs
1 cup mashed, cooked pumpkin pulp
¾ cup unbleached white flour

¾ cup whole wheat flour
½ teaspoon cinnamon
¼ teaspoon cloves
¼ teaspoon nutmeg
½ teaspoon baking soda
¼ teaspoon baking powder
1 teaspoon salt
⅓ cup chopped walnuts

1. Pour the hot water over the raisins and let them soak while preparing the batter.

2. In a large bowl, cream the butter or margarine with the sugar. Beat in the molasses and eggs and then the pumpkin pulp.

3. In another bowl, stir together the dry ingredients. Beat these into the pumpkin mixture until moistened. Stir in the raisins, any extra soaking liquid, and the walnuts.

4. Turn the batter into a greased and floured 9″ × 5″ loaf pan. Bake in a 350-degree oven about 1 hour, or until the bread tests done with a toothpick. Let cool on a rack before removing from the pan and slicing.

PUMPKIN-OATMEAL COOKIES

Oatmeal, in cookies, has the effect of making them chewy, while pumpkin adds flavor and moistness. The result, combined with spices, whole wheat flour, raisins, and nuts, is a great-tasting morsel for snacking. The pumpkin, too, produces an attractive orange cookie.

PREPARATION TIMES: 20 minutes kitchen work plus preparation
of the cooked pumpkin
15 minutes baking

YIELD: 30 large cookies

1 stick (½ cup) butter or
unsaturated margarine,
softened
¾ cup brown sugar
1 egg
¼ cup molasses
1½ cups cooked pumpkin
puree (or use squash
puree)

1¾ cups whole wheat flour
½ teaspoon salt
1 teaspoon baking soda
1 teaspoon cinnamon
½ teaspoon cloves
½ teaspoon nutmeg
1 cup rolled oats
½ cup chopped walnuts
½ cup raisins

1. In a large bowl, cream the butter or margarine with the brown sugar. Beat in the egg, then the molasses and pumpkin.

2. In another bowl, stir together the flour, salt, baking soda, spices, and oats. Beat into the pumpkin mixture until fully moistened. Stir in the nuts and raisins.

3. Drop the batter by heaping tablespoonfuls onto greased baking sheets. Bake the cookies in a 375-degree oven about 15 minutes, or until they are lightly browned. Let cool on a rack.

part 7
Selected
Fresh Fruits

INTRODUCTION

With many of the fruit recipes in the chapters in this section being for desserts, it seems an appropriate place to consider the subject of sugar. I am well aware that this book contains more recipes calling for sugar than do most other nutritional cookbooks, which generally call more frequently for honey or molasses.

Sugar has come into disrepute because it contains "empty calories," that is, food energy with little or no additional nutritive value. Yet, honey has little more to offer in the way of vitamins or minerals. You would have to consume an entire pound of honey to receive very small amounts of protein and minerals. Brown sugar, in most instances, actually has more nutritive value than does honey. On the other hand, molasses, and particularly black strap molasses 3,100 milligrams. They also contain 4,800 milli- of medium molasses supplies 1,300 milligrams of calcium, black strap molasses 3,100 milligrams. They also contains 4,800 milligrams and 13,300 milligrams of potassium respectively.

Molasses does taste marvelous in some dishes, particularly baked into certain breads and cakes. But the flavor is so overpowering and the consistency so thick that it simply cannot be used as an all-purpose sweetener. The delicate Pear Snow in the first chapter following, for example, would be ruined with molasses.

Honey, although as intractable in consistency as molasses, does have a more subtle flavor. Although it offers little in food value, health food followers prefer it because it is "natural," not refined. However, this is more a philosophical issue than a nutritional one. According to most nutritionists, natural sweeteners are no better for our bodies than processed ones. Honey acts the same way in the body as sugar acts. What's more, it usually sells for about five times the price!

Unless you have diabetes, neither honey nor sugar is harmful to you, *taken in moderation*. It is unfortunate that the American cuisine, particularly in its commercial aspects, has evolved to the point where sugar seems to be everywhere. Not only are donut stands, ice cream vendors, and candy stores ever-present, but the usual cakes are covered with gooey frostings, pies are filled with gelatinously sweet fillings, and sugar is "hidden" in a phenomenally large proportion of the prepared foods we buy—catsup, baby foods, soups, pancake and biscuit mixes, salad dressings, etc. It requires a real and conscious effort to avoid consuming an incredible number of calories per day in sugar alone.

But there are times when you want a sweet treat. A piece of raw fruit simply will not satisfy the craving. And there are times, when entertaining, that beg for serving a real dessert. The recipes in this book for the fruit or cheese desserts and the sweet breads, whether containing sugar, honey, or molasses, are meant for just such occasions. They are delicious ways to indulge, and many, because of other ingredients in the recipe, do contain substantial nutritive value.

So I suggest that you pause for a moment before smearing your bread with honey and that you think, too, about your reasons for banning sugar from the kitchen (if indeed you have). And then you may wish to make some of the recipes in this and other sections.

31
Pears

Of all fruits, perhaps none arouses our sense of elegance so much as the pear. Think, for example, of the perfection of a single buttery ripe pear, accompanied by a slice of melting brie or a wedge of aromatic Roquefort. You'd be hard-put to find a more fitting end to a fine meal.

Pears are so elegant in themselves that next to nothing need be done to turn them into a spectacular dessert. Just poach the fruit in a wine syrup—and there you have it. Or coat cooked pears with a bath of zabaglione, crème anglaise, or strawberry puree, and the result is an impressive finale. Another classic dessert simply tops the pears with a scoop of vanilla ice cream and a ladleful of hot fudge sauce; a garnish of crystallized violets adds an exotic touch. The delicate texture and subtle flavor of pears also make them ideal for such baked desserts as open-faced tarts and homey fruit crisps.

We tend to think of pears as a single type of fruit. But there are actually more than 3,000 varieties grown in this country (although only about twelve are commercially important). This staggering variety was for the most part developed in the mid-

1800s by the French landed gentry in contests to see who could produce the finest species of pear.

A happy result of these many varieties was that when pears were first grown in America, it was relatively easy to adapt the fruit to the various climatic conditions on this continent. Because of this, pears have thrived particularly well. And throughout the fall and winter months, when many other fruits are scarce, pears are generally one of the better buys at the produce counter.

In the recipes that follow, any of the commonly found varieties of pear may be used. For eating out of hand, a fully ripe pear is the most inviting. But for cooking and baking, rather firm fruits are easiest to handle.

PEAR CRISP

This is absolutely delectable when made with crumbs from soft macaroon cookies, which should be baked in a slow oven (about 275 degrees) until crisp and then crumbled. Lacking these, a topping of coconut or vanilla wafers or even a crunchy granola still makes a great dessert.

PREPARATION TIMES: 25 minutes kitchen work
20 minutes baking (plus 30 minutes toasting macaroon crumbs, optional)

YIELD: 6 servings

2 pounds pears, peeled, cored, and cut into slices
¼ cup rum
¼ cup sieved apricot preserves

¾ cup macaroon or other crumbs
2 tablespoons butter or unsaturated margarine

1. Place the pear slices in a shallow, buttered baking dish or pie plate. Mix together the rum and preserves and pour over the pears. Sprinkle with the macaroon crumbs and dot with butter.

2. Bake in a 400-degree oven about 20 minutes or until the pears are tender and the top browned. Serve warm or cold.

PEAR SNOW

A dessert called "snow" generally means that it contains beaten egg whites with grated raw fruit folded in (although occasionally cooked fruit puree is used). The result is a light, fluffy treat.

PREPARATION TIME: 15 minutes kitchen work

YIELD: 6 to 8 servings

2 cups grated peeled pears (about 3 medium)	6 tablespoons sugar, divided usage
¼ cup fresh lemon juice	2 egg whites
⅛ teaspoon salt	

1. Mix the pears with lemon juice immediately after grating to prevent darkening. Stir in salt and 2 tablespoons sugar.

2. Beat the egg whites until stiff. Gradually beat in the remaining 4 tablespoons sugar. Fold in the pear mixture gently.

3. Spoon the pear mixture into dessert dishes and either chill or serve immediately.

PEARS IN RED WINE

The pears here are poached in fragrant red wine, which turns them a lovely pink color as they absorb the potent wine flavor. The dessert is very easy, and elegant. Serve in glass bowls.

PREPARATION TIMES: 30 minutes kitchen work
40 minutes simmering
2 or more hours chilling

YIELD: 6 servings

1 teaspoon lemon juice	6 whole pears, peeled and cored
1 cup dry red wine	
½ cup sugar	

Place all ingredients except the pears in a large saucepan. Add 3 pears and cook, covered, until just tender, about 15 to 20 minutes. Remove to a serving dish and cook the other 3 pears. Pour the wine mixture over the pears and chill well.

CRANBERRY-PEAR TART

This is a great fall or holiday dessert. The cranberries and pears complement each other, both in sweetness and in color. It is also an especially easy tart to make because the filling requires no baking.

PREPARATION TIMES: 20 minutes kitchen work
1½ hours making, chilling, and baking the pastry crust
25 minutes simmering

YIELD: 1 pie, or about 6 servings

3 pears, peeled, cored, and cubed
½ cup water
4 cups cranberries
2 cups sugar

⅛ teaspoon salt
1 teaspoon vanilla
1 tablespoon lemon juice
¼ cup cornstarch
1 9-inch baked pastry crust

1. In a large saucepan, bring the pears and water to a boil. Reduce heat and simmer 15 minutes. Add the cranberries, sugar, salt, vanilla, and lemon juice. Cook until the cranberries pop, about 10 minutes longer.

2. Remove 1 cup of the fruit mixture and stir in the cornstarch very well. Return the mixture to the saucepan. Bring to a boil, stirring constantly, and boil for 1 minute.

3. Turn the cranberry-pear filling into the pastry shell. Cool and then chill, if desired. Serve plain or with ice cream or whipped cream.

PEAR PRESERVES

Preserves can be delicious when homemade. They also are ideal holiday gifts. These preserves are unusual; and their equivalent is not, to my knowledge, obtainable in the store. The preserves taste very much like apple butter, but somewhat sweeter and coarser in texture. They are perfect on toast or English muffins.

PREPARATION TIMES: 15 minutes kitchen work
                  30 minutes simmering

YIELD: about 1¾ cups

1 pound pears, chopped (cored, but not peeled)	1 slice orange, quartered
1½ cups sugar	¼ teaspoon ginger
1 slice lemon, quartered	pinch salt
	½ cup golden raisins

1. Put all ingredients except the raisins in a saucepan, being sure to include any juice from cutting the pears. Bring to a boil slowly and simmer 10 minutes.

2. Transfer to a blender and blend until fairly smooth. This may require 2 batches.

3. Return to the saucepan, add the raisins, and simmer until thick, about 20 minutes.

4. Ladle the preserves into clean jars, cover, and chill.

Note: To store unchilled, ladle into sterilized jars and seal with parafin.

32
Apples

As American as apple pie" goes the saying. But before the middle 1800s, apples and apple pie were quite a rarity in this country. We've all learned in elementary school that we have Johnny Appleseed to thank for the sprouting up everywhere of apple orchards.

But some accounts make John Chapman (his real name) appear too capricious, simply scattering apple seeds as he roamed. Chapman was an ecologist who gave up a prosperous farm in order to satisfy a strong drive to make apples available to all. He traveled around the eastern United States, planting trees and then coming back to care for them year after year. Also, to people traveling west on the Oregon Trail, he gave apple seeds and growing instructions. John Chapman was regarded as rather eccentric, but so are many who live with a vision.

For a number of years, apple trees were regarded as supplying "pie timber," because apples have gone into dozens of varieties of pies from the flaky two-crust types to crumb-topped deep-dish pies. The pies may be topped with ice cream, cheese, or heavy cream. But beyond apple pies, a great number of other very

American apple desserts have been developed over the years. There is the apple rolly polly (the fruit is rolled up in a biscuit-like dough), the apple grunt (with dumplings poached on top), the apple pandowdy (like a deep-dish pie), the apple fritter (dipped in batter and deep-fried), the apple dumpling (coated with dough and poached), the apple crisp (covered with buttered bread crumbs), and, of course, applesauce.

The majority of people, if asked, would probably guess that Americans eat more fresh fruit today than they did in 1910. After all, even in mid-winter, supermarkets display a plentiful supply of apples, pears, and citrus fruits, many of these shipped from thousands of miles away. Seventy years ago, people had to make do with what was locally available.

Yet according to a fascinating booklet, *The Changing American Diet* by Lettia Brewster and Michael F. Jacobson, that compares the current American diet to that of 1910, today's Americans eat far less fresh fruit than did their forebears. From about 125 pounds per person per year in 1910, we now consume only about 80 pounds per person. And these figures represent only purchased fruits; in 1910, undoubtedly a great deal of fresh fruit eaten was home-grown, resulting in the consumption of even more fresh fruit than the figures indicate. (The book is published by the nonprofit organization, Center for Science in the Public Interest, 1755 S Street NW, Washington, DC 20009.)

What has substantially increased, particularly since World War II, is the purchase of processed fruits. In 1952, Americans drank 44 times more frozen citrus juice than just five years previously. Canned and frozen fruits have also become more popular.

One of the largest declines in fresh consumption is that of the apple. In 1920, Americans ate 63 pounds each per year. Today, we consume a mere 16 pounds each. Canned applesauce stocks shelves in the supermarket, but it will never taste as delicious as your own. Canned apple pie filling is a favorite convenience food, but the apples in the can are often far too sweet and gummy. Whatever happened to the fresh snap derived from biting into a crisp, firm fall apple?

Apples are truly my favorite fruit. Summer and winter, I crave the crunch of one a day. And recipes using fresh apples are extraordinarily good and bountiful. Over the years, I have collected and experimented with perhaps a hundred or so delicious apple recipes. So choosing only a few for this book has been extremely difficult. These are a few of my favorites.

SOUFFLÉED APPLE OMELETTE

This is far simpler to put together than an ordinary soufflé, yet it is very light and fluffy. I enjoy serving it for breakfast or lunch, but those who like eggy-tasting desserts will also appreciate it sprinkled with powdered sugar following a meal.

PREPARATION TIMES: 20 minutes kitchen work
                   25 minutes baking

YIELD: 4 dessert, or 2 breakfast or lunch servings

2 apples, peeled, cored, and
  sliced
2 tablespoons water
½ tablespoon butter or
  unsaturated margarine

2½ teaspoons sugar
⅛ teaspoon nutmeg
4 eggs, separated
pinch salt

1. Place the apples and water in a small saucepan. Cover and cook until the apples are tender, about 5 minutes. Mash the apples, and transfer them to a bowl. Beat in the sugar, butter, nutmeg, and egg yolks.

2. In a clean bowl, beat the egg whites with a pinch of salt until they are stiff. Fold the egg whites into the apple mixture gently.

3. Turn into a greased 9- or 10-inch pie plate. Bake in a 350-degree oven about 20 to 25 minutes, until puffed, browned, and set.

APPLE-ALMOND SOUFFLÉED CAKE

Really a cake, this is called a soufflé because the egg whites are beaten separately and give the almost flourless cake a light, spongy texture. The cake is baked in a large, shallow pan, so it rises very little and therefore is not at all tricky to make. Also, unlike true soufflés, it need not be served immediately and, in fact, is best chilled before serving.

PREPARATION TIMES: 45 minutes kitchen work
45 minutes baking
2 or more hours chilling, optional

YIELD: 8 servings

Cake:

4 cups apples, peeled, cored, and sliced
3 tablespoons butter or unsaturated margarine
⅓ cup sour cream
juice and grated rind of 1 small lemon
½ cup sugar
1½ tablespoons unbleached white flour
5 eggs, separated

¼ cup slivered almonds
pinch salt

Topping:

2 tablespoons sugar
1 tablespoon cinnamon
2 tablespoons dry bread crumbs
2 tablespoons slivered almonds

1. In a large skillet, cook the apples in the butter or margarine until they are tender but not browned.

2. Stir together the sour cream, lemon juice, lemon rind, sugar, flour, egg yolks, and almonds. Add this to the apples, and cook over a low heat until the mixture thickens. Set aside to cool slightly.

3. Beat the egg whites with a pinch of salt until stiff. Fold into the apple mixture gently. Spread the batter into a greased 9″ × 13″ pan.

4. Mix together the topping ingredients and sprinkle over the cake. Bake in a 325-degree oven 45 minutes or until set and browned. Let cool to room temperature. Then cover and chill. Serve plain or with whipped cream or ice cream.

APPLE–CREAM CHEESE COFFEE CAKE

This delightful cake tastes like a cross between a cinnamony apple muffin and a rich cheese cake. Serve it hot from the oven or at room temperature for a fantastic breakfast treat or brunch dish. Other fruits, by the way, may be substituted for the apples. Try blueberries, sour cherries, or peaches.

PREPARATION TIMES: 45 minutes kitchen work
                   30 minutes baking

YIELD: 12 servings

Cake:
⅓ cup butter or unsaturated
    margarine, softened
⅓ cup sugar
2 eggs
¾ cup milk
¾ cup whole wheat flour
¾ cup unbleached white
    flour
1 tablespoon baking powder
½ teaspoon salt
½ teaspoon cinnamon
2 cups apples (peeled or not,
    as you prefer), finely
    chopped, divided usage

Filling:
1 3-ounce package cream
    cheese, softened
2 tablespoons sugar
1 tablespoon lemon juice

Topping:
½ cup whole wheat flour
½ cup unbleached white
    flour
¼ cup sugar
½ stick (¼ cup) butter or
    unsaturated margarine
¼ teaspoon cinnamon

1. Cream the butter or margarine with the sugar in a large bowl. Beat in the eggs, then the milk.

2. In another bowl, stir together the flours, baking powder, salt, and cinnamon. Beat this into the butter mixture. Stir in 1 cup of apples.

3. Spread the batter evenly in a greased and floured 9″ × 9″ baking pan. Top with the second cup of apples.

4. Beat together the filling ingredients and drop by tiny spoonfuls to cover the apples.

5. Mix together the topping ingredients until crumbly, and sprinkle over the cake.

6. Bake in a 375-degree oven 30 minutes. Serve warm or at room temperature.

FRESH APPLE CAKE

Simple yet delightful with a firm, chewy texture, this fruit-filled cake is not overly sweet and may be served as a coffee cake. It is also great warm, à la mode.

PREPARATION TIMES: 25 minutes kitchen work
                            50 minutes baking

YIELD: 1 8″ × 8″ cake, or 9 servings

1 cup unbleached white flour
2 teaspoons baking powder
1 teaspoon baking soda
¼ teaspoon salt
1 teaspoon cinnamon
½ cup raisins
2 cups finely chopped, peeled apples, packed down to measure

½ stick (4 tablespoons) butter or unsaturated margarine, softened
1 cup sugar
1 egg
¼ cup sugar, mixed with 1 teaspoon cinnamon

1. In a bowl, stir together the dry ingredients. Stir in the raisins and apples.

2. In another bowl, cream together the butter or margarine and sugar. Beat in the egg. With a heavy wooden spoon, stir in the dry ingredients. This will be difficult at first, but the juice from the apples will moisten the batter and make it less stiff.

3. Spread the batter in a greased and floured 8″ × 8″ baking pan. Sprinkle with the sugar and cinnamon mixture. Bake in a 350-degree oven 40 to 50 minutes, or until a toothpick inserted in the center comes out clean. Transfer to a rack to cool.

APPLE-TOPPED SPICE CAKE

Here's a not-too-sweet spice cake with a crisp, honey-coated apple topping. The cake is good warm or cold and supplies plenty of necessary vitamins. Serve it plain as a snack food or topped with ice cream or hard sauce as an after-dinner treat.

PREPARATION TIMES: 30 minutes kitchen work
                  30 minutes baking

YIELD: 1 8″ × 10″ cake, or 12 servings

¾ cup All-bran cereal
¾ cup molasses
¾ stick (6 tablespoons) butter or unsaturated margarine, softened
⅓ cup boiling water
2 eggs
1 cup unbleached white flour
½ cup whole wheat flour
¾ teaspoon baking soda

¾ teaspoon baking powder
¾ teaspoon ginger
¾ teaspoon cloves
½ teaspoon salt
4 cups peeled apple slices
½ stick (4 tablespoons) butter or unsaturated margarine, melted
⅓ cup honey

1. In a large bowl, stir together the bran, molasses, butter or margarine, and boiling water until the butter melts. Beat in the eggs and let sit 5 minutes.

2. In another bowl, stir together the flours, baking soda, baking powder, spices, and salt. Add to the bran mixture, stirring only until the dry ingredients are moistened.

3. Turn the batter into a greased and floured 8″ × 10″ baking pan. Bake in a 350-degree oven 20 minutes.

4. Arrange the apple slices neatly over the cake. Mix together the melted butter and honey, and brush over the apples. Bake the cake 10 minutes longer, or until it tests done with a toothpick. Let cool on a rack.

APPLE-CRANBERRY SAUCE

A snap to fix and infinitely better than any canned cranberry sauce, this goes exceptionally well with dishes made with corn or cornmeal. Try it, for example, with Souffléed Spoon Bread. The apples are sweet; so less sugar than usual is needed to offset the tartness of the berries.

PREPARATION TIMES: 10 minutes kitchen work
                   10 minutes simmering
                   2 or more hours chilling

YIELD: 6 servings

2 cups cranberries
1 cup water
2 apples, peeled, cored, and
  cut into chunks
½ cup sugar

Place all the ingredients in a saucepan and simmer until the cranberries pop and the apples are tender, about 10 minutes. Chill until very cold.

33
Bananas

It rarely occurs to me, when I see the multitude of big yellow bunches of bananas in the produce section of the supermarket, that this fruit isn't grown in this country. Bananas just seem so American, but they have always been imported. One might expect that recipes from their native lands, such as the warm Indonesian banana and coconut milk compotes or the Philippine chicken and banana stews, would have traveled along with this popular fruit.

But either the recipes never reached the North American housewives, or they preferred to try the new fruit in more familiar guises. Even today, nearly all the banana dishes consumed in this country are of American origin. These include the spectacular banana split and banana breads, cakes, cream pies, and shakes. Bananas are sliced into cereal bowls (first suggested by Mrs. J. H. Kellogg, wife of the cereal pioneer, at the end of the nineteenth century, as a way of making breakfasts more nutritious), are mixed with cottage cheese in a fruit salad, and are often one of a baby's first foods.

Perhaps the only real change in our eating habits regarding bananas has come from the Polynesian influence via Hawaii.

Thus, we now have sweet potato casseroles layered with pineapples and bananas, baked banana desserts, and fabulous banana-rum drinks.

One of the most wonderful aspects of bananas is that they almost seem to have been designed for cooking. While other fruits have tightly bound skins and hard-to-extract seeds, the banana is freed of all inedible materials within seconds. Furthermore, bananas may be mashed, which means that their sweet, strong flavor can easily permeate every bit of a dish to which they are added.

BANANA FRENCH TOAST

If you like French toast, the version here will certainly be a delight. Mashed bananas are added to the dipping batter and give the bread a delicious, fruity flavor.

PREPARATION TIME: 20 minutes kitchen work

YIELD: 4 servings (2 slices each)

2 ripe bananas, sliced
¼ cup milk
3 eggs
1 tablespoon honey

pinch salt
8 slices firm whole wheat
    bread

1. Place all ingredients except the bread in a blender and blend until smooth. Pour into a large shallow bowl.

2. Dip the bread slices into the banana mixture, coating each side well.

3. Brown the bread on both sides in a large, fairly hot, well buttered skillet.

Note: Banana pancakes are also very good, with a flavor similar to the above dish. Simply prepare your favorite pancake batter. For each pancake, slice 3 banana pieces into a well-buttered skillet, pour the batter over the slices, and cook on both sides.

HAWAIIAN SWEET POTATO AND BANANA CASSEROLE

Here is a luscious combination of the flavors we associate with Hawaiian cooking—pineapple, bananas, sweet potatoes, and rum. It is the sort of sweet, festive casserole that bedecks many party tables at Thanksgiving and Christmastime. The dish is so fruity, though, that it could easily serve as a dessert.

PREPARATION TIMES: 40 minutes kitchen work
        30 minutes simmering
        30 minutes baking

YIELD: 6 to 8 servings

6 sweet potatoes
3 tablespoons butter or
 unsaturated margarine
½ teaspoon salt
6 bananas, sliced
1 cup crushed pineapple
 (fresh or canned in juice)

3 tablespoons brown sugar
2½ tablespoons lemon juice
½ cup orange juice
2 tablespoons dark rum

1. Place the potatoes in a large saucepan. Cover with water. Cook, covered, over a high heat until the potatoes are tender, about 30 minutes. Drain. When cool enough to handle, peel the potatoes and cut into ½-inch slices.

2. In a large, greased casserole, place a layer of sweet potatoes. Dot with butter or margarine and sprinkle with salt. Then place a layer of bananas and pineapple. Sprinkle with brown sugar and lemon juice. Continue making layers until all the potatoes, bananas, and pineapple are used. Dot the top with butter.

3. Mix together the orange juice and rum. Pour over the casserole. Bake in a 350-degree oven about 30 minutes.

CHOCOLATE-BANANA CAKE

An extremely moist and flavorful cake, this combines two favorite taste sensations—chocolate and banana. It is absolutely great "as is" and needs no frosting.

PREPARATION TIMES: 25 minutes kitchen work
35 minutes baking

YIELD: 1 9″ × 9″ cake, or 9 servings

1 stick plus 1 tablespoon (9 tablespoons) butter or unsaturated margarine
1¼ cups sugar
2 eggs
½ cup yogurt

1 cup mashed ripe bananas
1 cup unbleached white flour
½ cup cocoa
½ teaspoon salt
1 teaspoon baking soda

1. In a large bowl, cream the butter or margarine and sugar. Beat in the eggs, then the yogurt and bananas.

2. In another bowl, stir together the remaining ingredients. Beat into the banana mixture.

3. Turn the batter into a greased and floured 9″ × 9″ pan. Bake in a 350-degree oven about 35 minutes or until a toothpick inserted in the center comes out clean. Serve warm or at room temperature.

HUMMINGBIRD CAKE

Why this cake should have so odd a name, I don't know; perhaps because it's as flavorful as the nectar of flowers. The batter makes a large, beautiful tube cake that stays moist for days and freezes perfectly. The cake needs no icing, but for a special treat, you might wish to top each serving with a dollop of whipped cream.

PREPARATION TIMES: 20 minutes kitchen work
                       1¼ hours baking

YIELD: 1 tube cake, or 16 servings

2 sticks (1 cup) butter or unsaturated margarine, softened
2 cups sugar
3 eggs
½ cup milk
1 8-ounce can crushed pineapple (juice-packed), undrained

3 cups unbleached white flour
1 teaspoon baking soda
1 teaspoon salt
1 teaspoon cinnamon
2 large ripe bananas, diced

1. In a large bowl, cream the butter or margarine with the sugar. Beat in the eggs, then the milk and pineapple.

2. In another bowl, stir together the dry ingredients. Beat into the creamed mixture just until moistened. Stir in the bananas.

3. Turn the batter into a greased and floured tube pan. Bake the cake in a 350-degree oven 1 hour 10 minutes, or until it tests done with a toothpick. Cool the cake on a rack before removing from the pan.

HONEYED BANANA CAKE

If you have a craving for a good, wholesome slice of banana cake, this recipe produces one of the best. The cake is exceptionally moist, with the hearty flavor of whole wheat and the sweet tastes of honey and bananas. It is great warm from the oven or at room temperature.

PREPARATION TIMES: 25 minutes kitchen work
　　　　　　　　　　　35 minutes baking

YIELD: 1 8″ × 8″ cake, or 9 servings

1 cup whole wheat flour
⅔ cup unbleached white
　flour
¾ teaspoon baking powder
½ teaspoon baking soda
1 teaspoon cinnamon
½ teaspoon nutmeg
½ teaspoon salt
½ stick (4 tablespoons) butter
　or unsaturated margarine,
　melted

1 egg, beaten
½ cup honey
1 cup mashed ripe bananas
¾ teaspoon lemon juice plus
　enough milk to equal ¼ cup
　liquid
½ cup chopped walnuts
　(optional)

1. In a large bowl, stir together the flours, baking powder, baking soda, spices, and salt.

2. In another bowl, mix together well the melted butter or margarine, beaten egg, honey, mashed bananas, and lemon-milk mixture. Add to the dry ingredients and stir until they are moistened. Stir in the walnuts, if desired.

3. Turn the batter into a greased and floured 8″ × 8″ baking pan. Bake in a 350-degree oven 35 minutes, or until the cake tests done with a toothpick. Transfer to a rack to cool.

BAKED BANANAS WITH RUM SAUCE

This sort of dessert goes well after a variety of dinners, particularly those with Polynesian, Hawaiian, Caribbean, or Chinese accents. It's a good dish to have in your repertoire because it's not so rich and heavy as a cake or pastry; yet it is more substantial than most fruit desserts.

PREPARATION TIMES: 20 minutes kitchen work
20 minutes baking

YIELD: 6 servings

6 bananas, peeled and halved lengthwise
1 tablespoon melted butter or unsaturated margarine
¾ cup brown sugar, divided usage
⅛ teaspoon ground cloves

⅓ cup orange juice
2 cups water
½ cup granulated sugar
2 slices lemon, halved
4 slices orange, halved
¼ cup rum

1. Place the bananas in a single layer in a shallow, greased baking dish. Brush with the melted butter or margarine and sprinkle with ¼ cup brown sugar, the cloves, and the orange juice. Bake in a 350-degree oven 20 minutes.

2. Meanwhile, in a saucepan, cook together the remaining ½ cup brown sugar, water, granulated sugar, and fruits until a thin syrup is formed. Just before serving, stir in the rum.

3. To serve, place 2 banana halves on each plate and spoon rum sauce over them.

PRUNE-BANANA WHIP

Here's an easily made, soft swirl-type pudding. Because both prunes and bananas contain so much natural sugar, very little extra sweetener need be added.

PREPARATION TIMES: 10 minutes kitchen work
10 minutes simmering and cooling
1 or more hours chilling

YIELD: 4 servings

10 pitted prunes
½ cup water
2 tablespoons lemon juice
2 ripe bananas, sliced

⅓ cup evaporated milk
2 tablespoons dark brown
   sugar

1. Place the prunes, water, and lemon juice in a saucepan. Bring to a boil. Lower the heat and simmer 5 minutes. Remove from the heat and cool 5 minutes.

2. Place the prunes and any cooking liquid in a blender. Add the remaining ingredients and blend until smooth. Pour into individual dessert dishes and chill until cold, at least 1 hour.

BANANA-PUMPKIN PIE

This wonderful pie has the dense texture of traditional pumpkin pie, plus an appealing fruity flavor of mashed bananas.

PREPARATION TIMES: 20 minutes kitchen work, plus preparation
                    of pumpkin
                    1¼ hours making and chilling the pastry
                    40 minutes baking

YIELD: 6 to 8 servings

⅓ cup brown sugar
1 tablespoon unbleached
   white flour
½ teaspoon salt
1 teaspoon cinnamon
½ teaspoon ginger
¼ teaspoon nutmeg
⅛ teaspoon ground cloves

1 cup mashed cooked
   pumpkin (refer to Chapter
   30, part 6 for directions),
   or use canned pumpkin
1 cup mashed ripe bananas
3 eggs, beaten
1 cup evaporated milk
1 9-inch unbaked pastry shell

1. In a large bowl, stir together the brown sugar, flour, salt, and spices. Stir in the pumpkin, banana, eggs, and evaporated milk.

2. Pour the filling into the pastry shell. Bake the pie in a 400-degree oven about 40 minutes, or until set and a knife inserted in the center comes out clean. Transfer to a rack to cool.

34
Peaches

$\mathbf{A}$ few summers ago, my husband and I drove cross-country. If you have ever experienced such a trip, you will know how maddening it can be—a few spots of interest connected by miles and miles of highway to be traversed, a car that breaks down and overheats when crossing the Rockies, and most especially, the hot sticky feeling that comes from sitting for hours, rather bored, on a damp plastic car seat.

So when, beyond the mountains in Colorado, we saw the sign reading "Fresh Peaches for Sale" at the entrance to a farm, we enthusiastically turned into the driveway. A search through several of the farm buildings finally led us to the owner. "Sorry, I've sold all my good peaches," he said. Seeing our disappointment, he added that he had some peaches too ripe to sell that he'd willingly give us. Gratefully, we accepted his offer.

Too ripe to sell? Why, anyone would gladly pay a fortune for such peaches! Each was enormous, not less than four or five inches across, and simply bursting with juice. We devoured one sun-warmed peach after another, and the box of them sustained us for a whole day of tedious driving.

Never before or since have I tasted such peaches. But all others that I do eat remind me of that day and those fruits. The peach recipes following also convey some of that feeling.

BRANDIED PEACH CLAFOUTIS

A *clafoutis* is a French pancake that is baked rather than cooked in a skillet. Generally, it is sweet and filled with fruits—apples, cherries, and pears being common. Because the batter is made in a blender, it is a cinch to prepare. It is best served slightly warm, about 30 minutes after it comes from the oven. It may be topped with whipped cream or ice cream.

PREPARATION TIMES: 20 minutes kitchen work
                      1 hour soaking the peaches
                      45 minutes baking

YIELD: 4 servings

2 cups peeled, sliced peaches	⅔ cup light cream
¼ cup brandy	2 eggs
3 tablespoons sugar, divided usage	3 tablespoons unbleached white flour
⅔ cup liquid (brandy drained from peaches plus milk)	pinch salt
	1 teaspoon vanilla

1. Mix the brandy with the peach slices and let stand at least 1 hour. Before preparing the batter, drain the peach slices, reserving the brandy.

2. Butter well a 10-inch pie plate, and sprinkle it with 1 tablespoon of the sugar. Arrange the peach slices in the plate.

3. Place the remaining 2 tablespoons of sugar and the remaining ingredients in a blender and blend until very smooth.

4. Pour the batter over the peaches. Bake in a 375-degree oven about 45 minutes.

FRESH PEACH CAKE

This is a cross between a cake and a tart, with the biscuit-like dough topped with rows of fresh, juicy peaches. Serve this not-too-sweet dessert warm or at room temperature, plain or with whipped cream or ice cream.

PREPARATION TIMES: 35 minutes kitchen work
25 minutes baking

YIELD: 8 servings

1½ cups unbleached white
   flour
1½ teaspoon baking powder
½ teaspoon salt
3 tablespoons sugar
3 tablespoons butter or
   unsaturated margarine
1 large or 2 medium-size
   eggs
1 teaspoon vanilla

about ½ cup milk
6 cups ripe peach slices
   (peeled)

Topping:
2 tablespoons butter or
   unsaturated margarine
½ cup sugar
1½ teaspoons cinnamon

1. In a large bowl, stir together the flour, baking powder, salt, and sugar. Cut in the butter or margarine using two knives, a pastry cutter, or a mixer on low speed.

2. In a measuring cup, beat the egg(s). Add the vanilla and enough milk to make ¾ cup altogether. Add this to the flour mixture, stirring it in well.

3. Spread the batter evenly in a 9″ × 13″ baking pan. Arrange the peach slices over the batter.

4. Mix together the ingredients for the topping and sprinkle this over the fruit.

5. Bake the cake in a 425-degree oven about 25 minutes. The crust should be browned and the fruit bubbly.

SPICED PEACH BUTTER

This is similar to apple butter but with a distinctly different and more delicate flavor. The texture is velvety smooth and the taste spicy and exotic. Be forewarned, though, that making the butter involves quite a lot of work, what with the peeling, mashing, and stirring of the peaches. But if you have a rainy afternoon on your hands and plenty of ripe peaches, it is certainly worth the effort.

PREPARATION TIMES: 45 minutes kitchen work
2¾ hours simmering and stirring

YIELD: 4 1-cup jars

4 pounds (about 22 small) very ripe peaches
3 cups sugar
2 teaspoons cinnamon
1 teaspoon ground cloves
½ teaspoon nutmeg
juice and grated rind of 1 lemon
paraffin as needed

1. Bring a large pot of water to boiling. Immerse the peaches, 3 or 4 at a time, into it for 15 seconds. When cool enough to handle, slip the skins off. Halve and stone the peaches, and mash them with a potato masher.

2. Place the peaches in a pot and cook over a very low heat 45 minutes. Push them through a sieve or potato ricer.

3. Return the peach pulp to the pot, and add the remaining ingredients. Cook, stirring frequently, over a low heat until thick (to test, put a spoonful on a plate; no liquid should form around the edge of the butter), about 2 hours.

4. Place 4 1-cup jars and their lids in a pot of water and bring to a boil. Boil for 5 minutes. Remove with tongs, and place upside down on a towel to drain. Turn upright and fill with the hot peach butter (the spoon you use to ladle in the butter should also be sterilized). Immediately pour a thin film of paraffin over the top. Cover with the lids.

BANANA-PEACH FROZEN SOUR CREAM

Similar to a very fruity, rich frozen yogurt, this makes a thoroughly delightful and extremely refreshing way in which to polish off some perfectly ripe peaches and bananas.

PREPARATION TIMES: 15 minutes kitchen work
overnight soaking of fruit
1 hour chilling
45 minutes in ice cream maker

YIELD: 2 quarts, or 12 servings

6 peaches, peeled and diced
½ cup sugar
3 bananas, peeled and
quartered

2 cups sour cream
⅓ cup honey
¼ cup lemon juice

1. Mix the peaches with the sugar. Let sit, covered, in the refrigerator overnight.

2. The next day, puree the peaches, bananas, and syrup from the peaches in a blender until smooth (this may require 2 batches). Mix with the remaining ingredients and chill 1 hour.

3. Freeze the mixture in an ice cream freezer according to the manufacturer's directions.

PEACHY BREAD PUDDING

For this light bread pudding absolutely filled with juicy peaches, the riper the peaches, the better the pudding. It may be served warm or chilled, plain or with whipped cream or ice cream. Although bread pudding is not usually regarded as a summer dessert, the version here is definitely an exception.

PREPARATION TIMES: 15 minutes kitchen work
45 minutes baking

YIELD: 6 servings

1½ cups milk
2 tablespoons butter or
unsaturated margarine
2 cups rather stale whole
wheat bread cubes
2 eggs, beaten

¼ cup honey
½ cup sugar
1 teaspoon vanilla
1 teaspoon grated lemon rind
2 cups diced, peeled peaches

1. Melt the butter or margarine in a saucepan. Pour this over the bread cubes in a large bowl, and let stand 10 minutes. Stir in all remaining ingredients gently but well.

2. Turn the mixture into a greased 8″ × 8″ baking pan. Bake in a 350-degree oven 45 minutes, or until set and browned on top. Transfer to a rack to cool. To serve, cut into squares.

35
Orange Peel

The other chapters of this book give you information and recipes for foods customarily eaten. This chapter is on a substance we normally discard—the orange peel. Actually small amounts of orange peel are used frequently in cooking. A yellow cake becomes an orange one with a few gratings of peel; so, too, are plain cookies and icings transformed. The French often add the subtlety of orange peel to their dishes; a fresh tomato sauce, for instance, is made memorable by the addition of a few slivers of this peel.

Orange peel is more than just a flavoring; it is a veritable foodstuff. Three and a half ounces contain 93 calories, 1.5 grams protein, 161 milligrams calcium, 210 milligrams potassium, 420 IU vitamin A, and 136 milligrams vitamin C (about 2½ times the amount found in an equal quantity of fresh fruit of the orange!).

So the next time you eat an orange, pause a moment before discarding the peel.

One further note: If you use oranges infrequently and wish to save the peels until you have enough to make a recipe, store them in an airtight container in the refrigerator. If, on the other hand, you wish to make one of these recipes without consuming all the necessary oranges, wrap the fruit well in plastic wrap and return it to the refrigerator. Both the peels and the fruit will keep well for several days.

ORANGE PEEL BREAD

Certainly one of the most economical breads possible, this loaf has a bittersweet flavor, with strips of orange peel accenting the good whole wheat taste. The batter may be baked in 3 well-greased 1-pound cans (the kind vegetables, not coffee, come in), as well as in a loaf shape. Then, when sliced and spread with cream cheese, the bread makes perfect-looking tea sandwiches.

PREPARATION TIMES: 35 minutes kitchen work
40 minutes simmering
70 minutes baking

YIELD: 1 9″ × 5″ loaf, or 3 small round loaves

rind of 3 oranges (in its entirety, not just the outer zest)	1 egg
	1 cup milk
water	1½ cups unbleached white flour
1½ cups sugar, divided usage	1½ cups whole wheat flour
3 tablespoons butter or unsaturated margarine	1 tablespoon baking powder
	½ teaspoon salt

1. Boil the orange rinds in water to cover for 30 minutes, adding additional boiling water if too much evaporates. Drain and cut into ¼-inch strips. Return the rind to the saucepan and add 1 cup water and ½ cup sugar. Cook until nearly all the liquid has evaporated, stirring occasionally.
2. Meanwhile, in a large bowl, cream the butter or margarine with the remaining 1 cup sugar. Beat in the egg, then the milk.
3. In another bowl, stir together the dry ingredients. Stir into the butter mixture, mixing only until the dry ingredients are moistened. Stir in the orange peels.
4. Turn the batter into a greased and floured 9″ × 5″ loaf pan. Bake in a 350-degree oven 1 hour 10 minutes (1 hour if baked in cans). Cool thoroughly before slicing.

BLENDER ORANGE-HONEY BREAD

Blender breads appeal to me because they take only a few minutes to prepare for the oven. Here's a loaf with a pronounced honey flavor. It's a chance to show off the taste of the best honey you have. Because of the high honey content, the bread stays moist for at least several days.

PREPARATION TIMES: 15 minutes kitchen work
1¼ hours baking

YIELD: 1 loaf

2 tablespoons butter or
  unsaturated margarine
1 cup honey
1 egg
rind from 1 orange, removed
  with a vegetable peeler
¾ cup orange juice

1¼ cups unbleached white
  flour
1¼ cups whole wheat flour
2½ teaspoons baking powder
½ teaspoon baking soda
½ teaspoon salt

1. Place the butter or margarine, honey, egg, orange rind, and orange juice in a blender and blend until the rind is finely chopped.

2. In a large bowl, stir together the remaining ingredients. Add the contents of the blender and stir just until the dry ingredients are moistened.

3. Turn the batter into a greased and floured 9″ × 5″ loaf pan. Bake in a 325-degree oven about 1¼ hours. Cool on a rack before slicing.

SESAME CANDIED ORANGE PEELS

This confection is a cross between the sesame-coated jellies served in Chinese restaurants and the chocolate-covered orange peels available in candy shops. It's a delicate, not-too-sweet snack.

PREPARATION TIMES: 20 minutes kitchen work
1¼ hours simmering
YIELD: 3 dozen candies

entire rind from 3 oranges, cut into ¼-inch strips	1 teaspoon salt
water	¾ cup sugar
	sesame seeds

1. Place the orange rinds in a saucepan. Cover with water and add the salt. Boil, uncovered, 30 minutes, adding more water as needed.

2. Drain the rinds and cover with fresh water. Boil another 30 minutes.

3. Drain again. Add ⅓ cup fresh water and the sugar. Cook, stirring occasionally, until the liquid is absorbed. Roll the rinds in sesame seeds. Spread out on a tray and let sit until dry (several hours) before storing in a tightly covered container.

FOOD PROCESSOR UNCOOKED ORANGE MARMALADE

A recipe with many advantages, this takes only a few minutes to prepare. None of the nutrients in the orange peel are destroyed by cooking, and the marmalade has a remarkably fresh flavor. Serve it on whole wheat toast or English muffins, in peanut butter or cream cheese sandwiches, or use the marmalade in the ginger-bread recipe that follows. The marmalade keeps in the refrigerator for about a month and may also be frozen.

PREPARATION TIMES: 5 minutes, plus time for the marmalade to gel

YIELD: 2 cups

1 large, thick-skinned orange, quartered and seeded	1 cup sugar
	½ 6-ounce bottle Certo liquid pectin
¼ lemon, seeded	

Place all ingredients in the food processor fitted with the steel blade. Process several seconds, or until the peel is as fine as you would like. Pour into a large, clean glass jar and chill several hours or overnight, until firm. Stir before using.

VICTORIAN ORANGE PEEL LOAF

I could not resist including so delicious a cake here, because it is absolutely marvelous with a buttery, orange flavor that's perked up by bits of orange peel. I make it from a homemade orange marmalade, thus putting many rinds to a good cause. If you wish, you may use an imported, excellent quality marmalade.

The recipe has been adapted by me from a Victorian original. I enjoy serving it as the British do, with afternoon tea or with a glasss of Madeira wine following dinner.

PREPARATION TIMES: 30 minutes kitchen work
1 hour baking

YIELD: 2 small loaves (if you wish, freeze one for a later time)

1¾ sticks (14 tablespoons) butter
¾ cup confectioners' sugar
4 eggs
2½ tablespoons orange juice
2 tablespoons dark rum
1 teaspoon vanilla
⅓ cup milk

1¾ cups orange marmalade
grated rind from 1 orange and 1 lemon (just the outer rind)
3½ cups unbleached white flour
4 teaspoons baking powder
½ cup chopped walnuts

1. In a large bowl, cream the butter and confectioners' sugar. Add the eggs, beating them in well. Then beat in the orange juice, rum, vanilla, and milk. Finally, add the marmalade and rinds.

2. In another bowl, stir together the flour and baking powder. Beat into the orange mixture. Stir in the nuts.

3. Turn the batter into two 8″ × 4½″ greased and floured loaf pans and bake in a 350-degree oven 1 hour or until a toothpick inserted in the center comes out clean. Cool thoroughly before slicing.

ORANGE MARMALADE GINGERBREAD

In this snappy gingerbread the fresh orange rind lends a delightful fragrance. The cake is very moist and quite unusual. For a real treat, try it warm from the oven. The recipe makes a large cake which, incidentally, freezes perfectly.

PREPARATION TIMES: 20 minutes kitchen work
5 minutes to make marmalade
40 minutes baking

YIELD: 1 9″ × 13″ cake, or 20 servings

3⅓ cups whole wheat flour
1½ teaspoons baking powder
½ teaspoon baking soda
2 teaspoons ginger
2 teaspoons cinnamon
1 teaspoon salt
1 stick (½ cup) butter or unsaturated margarine, melted

2 eggs, beaten
1 cup molasses
2 cups Food Processor Uncooked Orange Marmalade (recipe on page 287)
½ cup boiling water

1. In a large bowl, stir together the flour, baking powder, baking soda, spices, and salt.

2. In another bowl, mix together well the melted butter or margarine, eggs, molasses, and marmalade. Add to the dry ingredients, mixing only until well moistened. Stir in the boiling water.

3. Turn the batter into a greased and floured 9″ × 13″ baking pan. Bake in a 350-degree oven 35 to 40 minutes, or until the cake tests done with a toothpick. Transfer to a rack to cool.

Index

M

MAIN DISHES
Baked Layered Polenta, 158
Bamboli, 202
Bolivian Corn and Potato
Casserole, 224
California Rice Casserole,
41
Carrot Cashew Patties, 92
Carrot-Mushroom Custard
Pie, 241
Carrot Soufflé, 174
Cashew and Egg Stuffed
Eggplant, 92
Casserole with a Crunch,
104
Chili Corn Soufflé, 224
Chilis Rellenos con Queso,
186
Corn and Bean Pie, 12
Corn Soufflé, 223
Cottage Cheese Fondue, 199
Cottage Cheese-Lentil
Casserole, 18
Creamed Broccoli and Eggs
in Squash, 246
Curried Carrot and Raisin
Soufflé, 238
Curried Eggs with Onions,
180
Frittata, 177
Italian Eggplant Lasagne,
218
Italian Stuffed Eggplant, 32
Lentil Loaf, 16
Mexican Zucchini Torte,
232
Millet Casserole, 50
Mushroom, Egg, and Barley
Casserole, 62
Omelette Piperade, 175
Parmesan Soufflé, 185
Pilaf-Stuffed Eggplant, 39
Polenta with Eggplant
Sauce, 217
Puffed Soy Casserole, 152
Ratatouille Casserole, 216
Rice and Squash Pie, 42
Salad Casserole, 198
Sformato di Spinachi, 176
Souffléed Spoon Bread, 159
Soy and Carrot Casserole,
34
Soy and Vegetable Stew, 33
Soy Granule Loaf, 31
Soy Granule Soufflé, 30
Spinach Cheese Casserole,
197
Spinach Quiche, 192
Spinach-Ricotta Gnocchi,
200
Split Pea Loaf, 21
Stuffed Pizza, 134
Summertime Vegetable
Casserole, 84
Super Supper Salad, I, 191
Super Supper Salad, II, 192
Sweet-and-Sour Stuffed
Cabbage, 40
Tomato Strata, 178
Vegetable Morsels, 111
Zippy Bean, Rice, and
Cheese Casserole, 10
Mexican Spoon Bread, 182
Mexican Zucchini Torte, 232
MILLET
Basic Cooked, 48
Casserole, 50
Pudding, 49
Stew, Berry, Bran, and, 53
with Mixed Vegetables, 48
Mincemeat Tea Loaf, 140
Mocha Cheese Dessert, 210
Modified Cornell Bread, 148
Molasses Apple Muffins, 160
Molasses Oatmeal Bread, 72
Muenster-Olive Sandwich
Spread, 188
MUFFINS
Bran, 141
Molasses Apple, 160
Oatmeal Raisin, 74
Peanut Butter Corn, 97
Sunflower-Oatmeal, 107
Wholewheat Berry Raisin, 55